Patterns for Performance and Operability

Building and Testing Enterprise Software

Patterns for Performance and Operability

Building and Testing Enterprise Software

Chris Ford

Ido Gileadi

Sanjiv Purba

Mike Moerman

Auerbach Publications
Taylor & Francis Group
Boca Raton   New York

Auerbach Publications is an imprint of the
Taylor & Francis Group, an **informa** business

Auerbach Publications
Taylor & Francis Group
6000 Broken Sound Parkway NW, Suite 300
Boca Raton, FL 33487-2742

International Standard Book Number-13: 978-1-4200-5334-0 (Hardcover)

Library of Congress Cataloging-in-Publication Data

Patterns for performance and operability : building and testing enterprise
    software / by Chris Ford ... [et al.].
        p. cm.
    Includes bibliographical references and index.
    ISBN 978-1-4200-5334-0 (alk. paper)
    1. Computer software--Development. 2. Computer
    software--Specifications. 3. Debugging in computer science. I. Ford, Chris
(Christopher B.)

    QA76.76.D47P3768 2008
    005.1--dc22   2007030244

Visit the Taylor & Francis Web site at
http://www.taylorandfrancis.com

and the Auerbach Web site at
http://www.auerbach-publications.com

Dedications

To my wonderful mother Susan; and my equally wonderful wife Emily
—Chris Ford

To my two bright daughters, Madelaine and Nicole; and to my father Eliezer,
who inspired me to write, and my mother Lucy, who inspired my creativity
—Ido Gileadi

To my wife Kulwinder, my son Naveen, my son Neil, and my daughter Nikhita
—Sanjiv Purba

To my daughter Aderyn and my wife Avideh
—Michael Moerman

Contents

The Purpose of This Book

Considerations for application performance and operability, two key non-functional requirements, are frequently neglected and postponed to the later phases of the development lifecycle on systems projects that produce enterprisewide software. High-quality software must meet business needs for performance, operability, and other non-functional requirements that typically also include the following: availability, maintainability, expandability, and throughput.

This book is designed to provide a practical approach to readers for addressing non-functional requirements—specifically, performance and operability—on systems projects. Our focus is on design, testing, and certification of applications for their target production environments. The key to successful system implementation is to specify the non-functional requirements early in a system development lifecycle and give them as much attention as functional requirements traditionally experience.

Delivering a highly available software solution means incorporating performance and operability considerations into every phase of the software lifecycle. This book is structured to follow the software lifecycle, providing advice and examples-based instruction at each phase. You can read this book from start to finish, or you may want to go directly to those chapters that interest you most. Whatever approach you choose, you will learn:

- The importance of early consideration and planning for performance and operability in the early phases of the project development lifecycle
- How to define and document comprehensive non-functional requirements for any software system
- How to incorporate performance and operability activities into each phase of the project development lifecycle
- How to execute non-functional tests and report results clearly and effectively
- Patterns for defensive software design in common software scenarios and patterns for software design that support high performance and scalability

- How to implement tracking mechanisms in the operations phase to ensure high system availability and rapid response for managing and troubleshooting during a production crisis
- Strategies for resisting pressures from the functional requirements stream that typically distract from the non-functional stream of activities

Functional and non-functional requirements, such as performance and operability, must all be met for any real-world application to be successful. This book provides the tools and techniques for making this happen.

Intended Audience

This book is intended for anyone who has a lead architectural, design, or business role on a systems project, including those working on the projects, the project sponsors, or those directly benefiting from the results. It also encompasses a wide range of roles and responsibilities, including project sponsors, executives, directors, project managers, program managers, project leaders, architects, designers, lead developers, business users, consultants, leads and testers, and other resources on a project team.

This book can be read and applied by beginners or experts alike. However, we do assume that the reader has some knowledge of the basic project development lifecycles and concepts of both functional and non-functional requirements.

Organization of the Book

This book contains 12 chapters that describe the incorporation of performance, operability, and other non-functional requirements into a project development lifecycle. The sequence of the chapters mirrors the phases in the standard development lifecycle (SDLC).

Chapters 1 through 8 focus on planning through deployment phases. Chapter 9 examines pressures experienced on most projects that cause teams to deviate from the advice presented in this book. Chapters 10 and 11 look at the project monitoring and rapid response to non-functional problems typically experienced when an application is placed into a production environment. Chapter 12 concludes with an examination of impediments to good design that can limit performance, operability, and other non-functional requirements.

Acknowledgments

This book represents the authors' accumulated experience and knowledge as technology professionals. Tackling difficult problems is thoroughly enjoyable when it is in the company of passionate and talented colleagues. Accordingly, we acknowledge the following individuals who have unknowingly contributed to this book: Andrew Adams, Daniil Andryeyev, Poorna Bhimavarapu, Neil Bisset, Lucy Boetto, Debi Brown, Dave Bruyea, Ryan Carlsen, Steve Carlson, Cono D'Elia, Olivie De Wolf, David Dinsmore, Bruno DuBreiul, Marc Elbirt, James Fehrenbach, Peter Ferrante, Oleg Fonarev, Kenny Fung, Michael Gardhouse, Wayne Gramlich, Frank Haels, Michael Han, Mark Harris, John Hetherington, Eric Hiernaux, Steve Hill, David Howard, Steve Hu, Hiram Hsu, Anand Jaggi, Tommy Kan, John Krasnay, Andre Lambart, Marcus Leef, Robert Lei, Clement Ma, Richard Manicom, Ronnie Mitra, Odette Moraru, Shankara Narayanan, Nader Nayfeh, David Nielsen, Rich O'Hanley, Kevin Paget, Alex Papanastassiou, Ray Paty, Cris Perdue, Neil Phasey, Betty Reid, Adam Scherer, Sean Shelby, Dan Sherwood, Manjit Sidhu, Greg Smiarowski, David A. Smith, Gilbert Swinkes, Chris Tran, Brent Walker, Mark Williamson, John Wyzalek, Bo Yang, Eric Yip, and George Zhou. We also acknowledge the talents of Richard Lowenburg in Toronto, Ontario for his contribution to the illustrations in this book.

About the Authors

Based in Toronto, Ontario, **Chris Ford** has extensive experience providing hands-on technical and strategy consulting services to large organizations throughout the United States and Canada. Chris is currently a managing principal with Capital Markets Company (Capco) (http://www.capco.com/), specializing in highly available software systems for the financial services industry. He is a graduate of the University of Waterloo's Systems Design Engineering program.

Based in Toronto, Ontario, **Ido Gileadi** is an experienced information technology executive with specialization in delivery of large technology implementations for the financial services and manufacturing sectors. Currently a senior partner and executive vice president for global delivery at Capital Markets Company (Capco) (http://www.capco.com/), Ido has delivered key strategic implementations at large financial institutions and high-tech manufacturing firms. Prior to working with Capco, Ido was the chief information officer at BCE Emergis and a senior manager at Deloitte Consulting.

Sanjiv Purba is a partner with Infomaxium, Inc., a Toronto-based information technology management consulting firm (www.infomaxium.com). He has more than 20 years of industry and consulting experience with organizations such as Blast Radius, Cognos, Deloitte Consulting, Goldman Sachs, IBM, Microsoft, and TD Waterhouse. He has managed projects that range from small six-person teams to those that include hundreds of employees, dozens of vendors, and hundreds of consultants. He has written more than 15 books and hundreds of articles for such newspapers as the *Globe and Mail* and the *Toronto Star*.

Michael Moerman is a managing principal with Capital Markets Company (Capco) (http://www.capco.com/). He specializes in designing the architecture, building, and delivering large-scale projects for financial institutions. Over the past ten years he has delivered large, complex solutions across Asia, Europe, and North America. Prior to joining Capco, Michael was chief technology officer (CTO) of eGlutek Ltd.

Chapter 1

Introduction

Performance and operability are two prominent categories of non-functional requirements. Application implementations can rarely be considered a success if either performance or operability is not satisfying some minimal metrics. Surprisingly, these and other non-functional requirements are still very much an afterthought on most information technology (IT) projects, while attention is focused on addressing functional requirements.

Non-functional requirements typically address the system needs dealing with availability and performance—e.g. operations. In addition to performance (e.g., response time) and operability, other non-functional requirements include areas such as: extensibility, flexibility, scalability, availability, maintainability, reliability, usability, and robustness. Quality and cost can also be considered non-functional requirements.

Production Systems in the Real World

Performance and operability considerations are often overshadowed by the focus that business and application development teams place on richness of functionality. Yet, significant challenges faced by production applications are due to non-functional aspects of the systems. Rich functionality is of little value to end users if system performance or availability is so poor that users cannot access the application. We illustrate this statement with two case studies drawn from the real world in the following section.

Case 1—The Case of the Puzzlingly Poor Performance

A major banking application carefully designed for rich functionality was launched for approximately 5,000 branch and back-office users. The application platform consisted of leading edge J2EE technology. During the two-month application rollout, users were gradually introduced to the new platform on a branch-by-branch basis. Application performance was satisfactory in the first few weeks following rollout.

Several weeks after the rollout, users started complaining about intermittent incidences of highly degraded performance. Business operations that were previously taking 2–5 seconds were now being reported to take 20–30 seconds. This inconsistency in performance led the technology team to identify the specific functions and data being used to execute the problematic operations. Unfortunately, the technology team was unable to correlate any common functional denominator.

In a technology management meeting, the vice president (VP) of technology asked, "Did we successfully complete performance testing prior to deployment? Did our testing simulate a business load equivalent to 5,000 end users?" The technology team assured the VP that they had indeed conducted these tests successfully.

As the application rollout continued, the performance became unbearable. Many business operations were consistently taking 30 seconds to complete. An intermittent problem had become a sustained and severe problem. Users were becoming increasingly frustrated in their efforts to use the application.

With growing pressure on the technology team, the VP of technology did what seemed very natural to her after many years of technology delivery: she shifted the focus to infrastructure issues. She suggested that this must be a network or system capacity issue. "This is the only reasonable explanation for why performance was fine when we first rolled out the application," she said, clearly believing that this could not be an application issue.

The infrastructure team had considerable experience as the focus for technology issues that were later shown to be application related. As a result of this experience, they had developed a set of discrete tests, capable of exercising each element of the infrastructure to establish its status. The infrastructure organization promptly ran these tests and was pleased to report the results to management. A bounty of evidence indicated no capacity or health issues could be identified affecting the infrastructure, including network, CPU (central processing unit), storage, clustering, memory, or I/O (input/output). Everything looked very normal from an infrastructure standpoint.

It was time to escalate the issue and bring in the expert team. Someone had to take the heat, and the VP of technology was starting to feel uncomfortably warm. The team was brought in to solve the problem with a mandate to resolve the issue as quickly as possible. Due to the criticality of the problem, all of the assets of the organization were to be made available to the expert SWAT team.

Soon after being engaged, the consulting team made the following observations:

- Based on performance test results, the application code itself was capable of supporting the expected performance assuming the required systems resources were available.
- Performance degradation was continuing over time. However, there was no indication as to whether the degradation was correlated to time itself or to the rollout to additional bank branches.
- Performance degradation was sporadic at first but had become more and more consistent over time.
- At the start of the day, performance appeared to be generally within the required range, but quickly worsened over the course of the day.
- Based on the infrastructure test results, the organization was correct in concluding that the infrastructure itself did not appear to be at fault.

Based on the preliminary assessment, the team decided to profile the J2EE application container for key application resources including memory, threads, connection pools and other internal resources. In doing so, the following observations were quickly captured:

- The application container (in this case, a Java virtual machine) was executing full garbage collections at a much higher than expected frequency. A garbage collection is a memory management service that is performed by the application container.
- Each time a full garbage collection was executed, all application threads were put on hold. In other words, all business processing was paused until the completion of the memory management task.
- Garbage collection operations were taking an average of 20 seconds to complete.

Based on this new information, the team was confident that they had identified the culprit. In collaboration with the development team, the expert team was able to do some fine-tuning of memory parameters and peace was restored to the organization.

Everyone thanked the technology team for their heroic efforts, late nights, and congratulated them for solving the problem. Only a few questions loomed; foremost amongst them, could this incident have been avoided? What was missing in the test-case coverage that did not identify this issue in advance of production deployment? How does the root cause explain the chronology of events observed in production?

In answering these questions, we begin to see the need for a structured approach to non-functional design and implementation.

1. How does one explain the events that were observed in production?

Table 1.1   Case Study Observations and Explanations

Event Observed in Production	Explanation
System resources were not strained. More specifically, the problem was memory exhaustion yet there was abundant memory on the server.	Application containers allocate a certain amount of system resources including memory, threads, and connection pools. Applications running within a container cannot use more resources than have been allocated. Ample system memory is of no use to an application running inside an application container that imposes limits.
Performance was initially good or at acceptable levels.	The memory usage profile changed dramatically with the introduction of more users to the system. More specifically, as time elapsed, objects were accumulating in memory with a life span of many days. This problem intensified with the introduction of additional users.
Performance testing with 5,000 simulated users did not show any performance degradation.	This is due to the fact that while conducting short term tests, even with a large number of simulated users, the state of the memory is fairly clean. When the system is used over a long period of time without restart, the memory saturates and there is a need for frequent full garbage collection (assuming the memory heap size was not set appropriately to begin with).
Performance was not consistent.	In the production architecture, there were several server load balancing user requests. If one of the servers was restarted, response time would return to normal for a short period until full garbage collections would resume at a high frequency.

2. What was missing in the test coverage that would have allowed us to see this problem in advance of production deployment?

Despite good performance test coverage, the project team did not fully simulate production conditions. In this case, the impact of long system uptime under heavy user operation was not factored into the test plan. Later in this book, we will formally introduce the concept of sustainability testing, which is designed exactly to avoid this type of incident. Sustainability tests simulate long periods of system operation under various loads to observe the effect on internal application resource and performance over a period of time.

3. Could this condition have been averted? The answer is a resounding YES. As noted above, a test can be designed such that the resource usage over time can be monitored under load and resource management issues can be surfaced at testing. In fact it is highly recommended that a sustainability test be designed for every system to closely simulate production behavior.

It is worth mentioning that an accurate simulation of production conditions is usually difficult to achieve because of the large number of permutations in usage patterns and data. Accordingly, avoiding an outage in production should not rely entirely on testing the systems in advance. A good set of monitoring tools and health checks can provide the technology operation team with forewarning of systemic issues that are brewing in the system.

In this case, assuming that the appropriate level of monitoring of memory management inside the container existed, the technology operation team would have detected frequent garbage collections well in advance of the rollout to additional branches. This would have allowed the project team to resolve the problem well before it had escalated to the level of consistent 20- to 30-second response time.

The case above clearly demonstrates the need for sound planning and appropriate test coverage as part of the delivery of any mission critical software system. It is interesting to note that this example did not include any fundamental design flaw in the deployed application.

Case 2—The Case of the Disappearing Database

A large financial institution deployed an application that relied heavily on database technology to maintain its process state and data. The application was deployed to production after extensive performance, sustainability, and functional testing.

The application was designed to take advantage of multiple failover technologies with clustering at the application server, database server, and Web server layers as well as load balancing between servers to take full advantage of the computing potential of all servers available. The institution had decided to host the application internally, and for that purpose had built an internal infrastructure and technology operation organization to service the applications.

As with any new organization, the newly created infrastructure team was having some challenges hiring and training skilled engineers, establishing robust processes and controls, and instilling the right level of operational discipline across the organization. Good progress had been made but there was still a long way to go.

Shortly after the application was deployed to production, the primary database server failed completely for hardware reasons. Failover did not succeed as expected and the secondary server did not automatically service the application. The application was faced with a catastrophic event whereby it had no access to its database to record the state of its processes or retain its data. The infrastructure team worked diligently to correct the issue and was able to restore service on the secondary database server in less than 4 hours.

During the 4-hour outage, users were frantically trying to assess the state of their transactions. In doing so, in some cases they had manually posted transactions through to the book of records system outside of the normal application-driven process.

Once the application had been restored, it became clear that many of the transactions that were initiated prior to the outage were now in an indeterminate or broken state. In other words, business users were unable to continue processing in-flight transactions. The business operations team was forced into the unenviable position of having to investigate each transaction individually. In many cases, a labor-intensive manual process was required to complete the transaction outside of the application. The full recovery became a very slow and painful exercise for both business and technology operations as technology was required to produce a variety of ad-hoc reports.

In the next four weeks, the database server infrastructure failed an additional 4–5 times due to a combination of human error and system configuration issues. Not surprisingly, business operations demanded that the technology team develop applications that were resilient. *Resilient applications* were defined as applications that can recover from a major infrastructure failure in a consistent way, mostly automated (a few manual exceptions were allowed).

The development team was faced with a challenging new requirement for which they had no prior experience. They had always assumed that the infrastructure would be there to support the application, based on the extensive investment that had been made in the highly available, fault-tolerant infrastructure. Ultimately the team met the challenge in two ways. First, they developed a set of recovery procedures and tools that would improve the efficiency and accuracy of any business recovery in the event of an application outage. Second, they enhanced the application design such that transactions would reliably transition to a state from which they could be recovered by the previously mentioned recovery procedure and tools.

The combination of these two efforts resulted in a system that was resilient to most types of failures, meaning that recovery would be automated and transparent to business users in most cases. The development approach leveraged the following technologies and approaches:

- Review and correction of transaction boundaries for all asynchronous messaging operations.
- Introduction of a dedicated "frozen" state for transactions that are impacted by a failure. Transactions that transition to this frozen state must be able to successfully resume processing if they are "unfrozen."

- Introduction of transaction-level error reporting accessible by both business and technology.
- Additional scripts for monitoring application failure conditions and exposing these conditions to an operator console.
- Automated retry and rehandling capability for many transaction types.
- Introduction of an extensive application health-check capability that allows operations to quickly verify critical application and system dependencies.
- Enhancements to the business workflow such that manual application tasks are automatically initiated when an automated task cannot resolve a failure.
- Implied timeout conditions that raise manual tasks or alerts.

This concerted effort yielded an application that was resilient to infrastructure as well as application components failures.

The case above demonstrates that there was a deficiency in the definition of non-functional requirements. It also demonstrates that when designing an application to run in a production environment the only assumption that project teams should make is that things will eventually go wrong. Mission-critical applications must be designed with failover, operability, and recovery requirements in mind.

Why Should I Read This Book?

Having read the above two real-life cases, it is likely that you were reminded of times in your experience where lack of specification, planning, design, testing, and monitoring for performance and operability have caused you grief. Unfortunately, such experiences are all too common. Non-functional issues frequently result in major outages and challenges for technology executives, managers, architects, and developers.

This book provides a comprehensive guideline, complete with examples and actionable templates for specifying, planning, designing, testing, and monitoring systems and applications for their non-functional characteristics. It provides a broad discussion on topics regarding a variety of non-functional aspects of application development, including the definition and the rationale for consideration of these topics.

The authors of this book are themselves IT practitioners with considerable cumulative experience. The content of this book is an aggregation of over 60 years of practical experience. Consequently, we hope that you will find this book very practical. We have tried to provide a balanced and pragmatic view of planning, design, and testing coverage that can provide maximum value with reasonable investment. As IT practitioners, we understand and frequently reference the constraints and limitations faced by most projects.

In the remaining chapters of this book, we share proven strategies and practices for avoiding the following serious pitfalls:

- Infrastructure that cannot scale
- Applications that cannot scale
- Limited ability to diagnose problems in real-time
- Unexpected production behavior patterns
- Applications that exhaust available hardware capacity
- Failure of the automated failover systems that result in outages
- Sudden degradation of applicaiton performance
- Low availability—reduced service
- Complex operation—software systems that can only be operated by a large and highly skilled team of specialized resources

This book is designed with the software development lifecycle in mind. Our hope is that you will be able to use it throughout your implementation as a reference and guide for achieving highly available systems.

The Non-Functional Systems Challenge

Production environments are very different from the typical functional test environments. These differences are due to the following occurrences in production:

- Unexpected user behavior
- Unexpected user inputs
- Unexpected volumes
- Unexpected usage over time (i.e., spikes) that is seasonal and/or related to the time of day
- For enterprise systems, functional environments that are usually not on the same scale as the production environment
- Functional test environments often omit or compromise on certain infrastructure components for reasons of cost
- Unexpected system performance issues due to network, database, and other non application-specific factors, particularly in a shared services environment
- Unlike test systems, production systems are subjected to use over a long period of time

It is common practice in most systems-delivery projects to include a User Acceptance Test (UAT) phase, which allows representatives of the target user community to verify and sign off on the functionality of the application. Yet when the application is placed in production we often find that performance, outages, memory leaks, and other non-functional issues become a serious impediment to the usage of the application.

Let us examine the shortcomings of the UAT as it pertains to testing the non-functional aspects of the system. User acceptance tests do not address the following:

■ **Load testing**—The test is usually conducted by a small number of users with a small subset of transactions, far from simulating the usage model in production

■ **Failover testing**—The test is conducted in a controlled environment with little interruption; very often component failure conditions do not occur, and if they do the system is restarted and the test continues at that point

■ **System capacity**—The technical infrastructure used for the UAT environment is in many cases very different than the target production environment, and as such, capacity cannot be predicted based on the usage during the UAT

■ **Production configuration**—The target production environment configuration is sufficiently different, which does not allow verification of the final configuration

In summary, while the UAT is well designed to verify and accept the functional aspect of an application, it is not designed to test and verify any of the key non-functional aspects of the application. This translates into the need for a set of dedicated environments for the sole purpose of testing for non-functional requirements and certification. At a minimum the requirements would be to have a project non-functional test environment and a non-functional certification environment. We will discuss the characteristics of these environments in more details in the chapters ahead.

The key challenges when designing and executing non-functional tests are:

■ The tests are executed in an environment that is not the final target environment and as such needs to predict the behavior of the target environment.

■ Some of the tests are designed to test for unforeseen conditions in production. These need to be simulated to the best of our ability.

■ The scope and characteristics of the tests are based on a predicted business utilization model that may or may not accurately predict the real usage of the application.

What Is Covered by Non-Functional Testing

Given unlimited time and budget, one can continuously increase the scope of non-functional testing. While more testing is always desired, unlimited budget and time is not a reality. Frequently, you will need to make judgment calls on the level of risk and the return on investment that is gained by minimizing that risk through non-functional testing.

When determining the scope of non-functional testing we will observe that some tests are fundamental and must be included within scope of the activities. Such categories of testing are as follows:

- Performance tests for online and offline key activities (such activities to be defined).
- Capacity test, to allow for a reasonable capacity plan.

Other tests are optional; their inclusion in scope is determined by examining specific requirements and then weighing the estimated level of risk against the cost of testing. These will include but are not limited to the following:

- Component failover tests
- Sustainability tests (to observe application behavior over time)
- Operability tests (this covers a wide range of what-if scenarios that may be encountered in a production context)

In the following chapters we will cover the requirements, planning, execution, and implementation of systems for best non-functional performance and operation. Table 1.2 includes an inventory of non-functional tests that are candidates for execution in any enterprise software system delivery project.

Planning for the Unexpected

Even if we execute all of the tests described in this book, we should still expect that unforeseen events may occur in production for which we have not tested the system and for which the application behavior is unexpected. In this book we introduce three primary strategies to minimize the business impact of this challenge, as follows:

1. Establish a comprehensive non-functional test suite to minimize the set of unexpected system conditions (i.e., the set of conditions for which application behavior is not known based on test results).
2. Enhance the application design to gracefully handle unexpected events.
3. Create a set of diagnostic tools to monitor and alert when an application is encountering exception conditions so that intervention and resolution can be swift and efficient.

Patterns for Operability in Application Design

Application design should always consider the environment in which the application will be deployed and operated. The design should provide for the key design patterns that would support operability in such environments. Designing for operability means observing the following key design principles:

- Data and transactions must never be lost or corrupted.
- Exception conditions (expected or unexpected) must be captured and reported in a consistent fashion.
- The application must recover in an automated fashion once the exception condition is removed.
- Applications must provide visibility into the availability and health of their various components, with hooks to monitor the health of the application as well as quickly detect and correct any issues.

Examples of some more detailed design patterns that draw on the above principles are listed below. This topic will be covered in further detail in Chapter 4, "Designing for Operability."

Ensuring Data and Transaction Integrity

Given the potential failure points in most applications, it is crucial to ensure data and transaction integrity. Here are several activities that should be followed to accomplish this:

- Understand and employ database transaction management, rollback and integrity services.
- Ensure that the backup and recovery system is robust and tested.
- Utilize two phase commit and distributed transaction management to ensure transaction integrity when multiple resources are involved in a transaction.
- Build the necessary compensating transactions to allow for a scenario where external systems have to be partially updated.
- Clearly define transaction boundaries to make sure the transactions rollback to a clean state from which the system can cleanly recover.

Capturing and Reporting Exception Conditions in a Consistent Fashion

Exception condition reporting is relevant for debugging and fixing problems as they occur. Here are some suggested approaches

Table 1.2 Non-Functional Test Inventory

Test Type	Description	Expected Outcome	Comments
User Online Performance	Testing of online response time as observed by a user of the application.	For each test case we would measure the average, maximum, minimum, and 90th percentile response times.	Typically measured as the time it takes the application to render the next page of the application.
System Online Performance	Testing of online system-to-system response time (i.e., the time it takes one system to respond to a request by another system).	For each test case we would measure the average, maximum, minimum, and 90th percentile response times.	The request can be synchronous or asynchronous; in both cases the time for the complete response to arrive will be measured.
Offline Performance	Testing of an offline activity, which could be a bulk operation that happens during the availability window or a batch operation that takes place outside of the availability window.	Average time to complete the full operation (bulk or batch) and a profile of the performance of each component of the offline operation.	In most cases, the batch operation would be broken into sub components profiling each component for potential improvements.
Component Failover	Testing of the system recoverability when critical components are failed over to the redundant component.	For each component we expect to see the system recover with no data or transaction lost. We observe and measure the time to recover, number of errors reported, and any loss of data or transaction.	All critical redundant components should be tested. Some examples are message broker, database server, application server, and disk volume.

—continued

Table 1.2   Non-Functional Test Inventory

Test Type	Description	Expected Outcome	Comments
Capacity	Testing of the system capacity requirements at peak volumes with transaction and user volumes that are based on the business-utilization model as stated in the non-functional requirements.	While the application is running at peak volumes for a period of at least an hour (for stabilization) we measure the system resource utilization such as memory, CPU, disk, and network bandwidth on all application tiers.	The requirements should include a projection for a period of at least one year to allow for all volumes anticipated a year in advance. This test is greatly facilitated by monitoring tools such as HP OpenView or Mercury to capture and record resource usage during the execution of the test.
Sustainability	Testing of application resource management behavior over time.	Monitor trending of resource availability and application server behavior over time. For example, we would monitor the following database connect pool/threads/MQ connection factory; full and minor garbage collection frequency and duration; memory recovery over time; and so on.	This test would allow us to observe behavior that would occur in production when the system is not recycled for a lengthy period of time. We can observe memory leaks, connection leaks, memory tuning requirements, connection, and thread pools configuration (high-water marks).
Operability	This is a broad category of testing that measures the system behavior under a variety of miscellaneous conditions. A typical example is boundary-condition testing in which the system is subjected to highly unexpected inputs outside the functional range to ensure that availability is not compromised.	For each defined test case we observe the application for errors being reported, potential data and transaction loss, and recoverability once the component is available again.	The challenge with this type of testing is to identify the critical elements that should be tested. The number of permutation of test cases that can be created is typically very large, and careful scoping and rationale must be applied.

- Centralize and standardize error logging.
- Classify exceptions for the purpose of monitoring, alerts, and reporting.
- Actively push exceptions to operations and application users teams with defined set of actions.
- Provide for application generated exceptions that are based on specific events as well as catch all scanners that would identify system exception conditions that are not associated with a specific trigger event.

Automated Recovery from Exception Conditions

The following list offers several suggestions for enabling automated recovery following the occurrence of exceptions:

- Automatically recover when exception conditions no longer exist
- Audit all stages of the automated recovery
- Create additional exception alerts if automated recovery fails
- Provide tools for manually triggered systemic recovery
- Provide clear documentation for manual recovery

Application Availability and Health

The list below provides some suggestions for monitoring and checking on the health of the application:

- Define and provide an availability service for all major components.
- Design a comprehensive health check with the capability to provide an overall health status as well as drill down to all components.
- A health check should be extensible to allow for additional plug-in probes for new application components.

Summary

While the functional-requirements side of software engineering has evolved and improved over the years, non-functional requirements are still very much an afterthought on most IT projects. In many cases it would seem that the scope of non-functional requirements and testing is limited to performance and load testing, excluding critical elements of non-functional requirements such as capacity planning, operability, monitoring, system health checks, failover, memory management, and sustainability, among others.

More than ever, technology executives, managers, and professionals are aware of the gap in the definition, design, testing, and implementation of systems' non-functional requirements. Such a gap has consistently been the cause for significant system outages and loss of credibility for IT organizations.

User and business communities have become better at defining their functional requirements, but are clearly not able to articulate the non-functional characteristics of the system in more than broad terms. It is up to the technology community to build the tools, templates, and methodologies needed to extract the correct level of detailed requirements, challenge the business as to their real requirements, design applications with operability in mind, ensure sufficient non-functional test coverage, and implement ongoing monitoring tools that will guarantee high availability.

This book addresses the development of scope, requirements, design patterns, test strategies, and coverage and deployment strategies for system non-functional characteristics. It can also be used to provide a detailed implementation guide for technologists at all levels. The book can also serve as a conceptual guide for the business and user communities in order to better develop and educate those communities on the importance of a system's non-functional requirements and design activities.

The detailed material provided in the chapters ahead is based on years of experience in designing, building, tuning, and operating large complex systems within demanding mission-critical environments. This book is filled with practical examples and advice that can be leveraged immediately to assist your current projects.

Chapter 2

Planning and Project Initiation

The Business Case for Non-Functional Testing

What Should Be Tested

Non-functional testing is a wide-ranging topic that covers many different aspects of systems behavior. Some of the most common non-functional tests that are routinely identified and conducted are performance, failover, and capacity tests, yet many projects neglect to test additional non-functional characteristics of the systems they implement, such as sustainability/soak test, operability and recovery, to name a few.

The range of non-functional behavior exhibited by an application and system combination is vast and further complicated by the unexpected nature of events taking place in the target production environment. In an ideal world we would have a complete set of non-functional requirements that identifies all elements of application behavior in a given environment and systems combination under a variety of usage patterns. The reality is that, at best, project teams are faced with a bare minimum set of requirements that identify the expected response time for a set of critical online functions, a batch processing window, and high-level availability requirements. Clearly an approach different than the traditional functional requirements gathering and specification is required to compile a list of non-functional requirements. Chapter 3 of this book suggests an approach to address this difficult task in detail. For the moment let us just say that a different approach, based on observation and prediction of usage patterns as well as a decomposition of all system components for availability analysis will be required to identify the scope of testing.

At a minimum, projects teams should perform the following non-functional tests:

Online Performance

- Test and report all critical functions identified in the requirement documentation
- Test for online response anomalies (responses that are well above an acceptable range)
- Test response time for the above tests under simulated load

Batch Performance

- Test and report the overall batch processing time as well as each individual component of the batch process
- Test the recovery time for failure during the batch processing window

Capacity Test

- Run the application/systems for a minimum period of one hour with full simulation of one- to two-year projected utilization at peak usage
- Observe system resource utilization during the test (including central processing unit [CPU], memory, execution threads, database [DB] connections, etc.)
- Overlay resource utilization results on top of a current production baseline and report overall system resource capacity requirements
- Determine any additional resource requirements based on the results of this test

Failover Test

- Analyze all key failure points in the system
- Initiate failover condition under load, based on a predicted utilization model to generate representative range of in-flight transactions during the test
- Fail component by component, and observe failover functionality and number of transactions impacted
- Confirm that all in-flight transactions are recovered on the failover system

In addition to the minimum set of tests above, there are many additional tests that are critical to understanding and verifying the non-functional behavior of your application and system. These are discussed extensively throughout this book and are highly recommended. However, it is expected that projects will have different areas of focus and criticality of functions, which will dictate the necessity for certain additional tests.

How Far Should the System Be Tested?

Non-functional testing is not limited to a pass-or-fail test case, as is the case in functional testing. There are always additional test conditions that can be executed. Consider for a moment that you are testing for the response time to a database query. You could compile a test that would demonstrate the time it takes to execute the query with no load on the system. You might then add load on the system and test again to verify that performance is still acceptable. That in itself would be a good test; however, consider the following factors that may impact your test results and therefore should be considered in your test cases:

- Data set being used for the queries
- Number of users running inquiries on the same data objects
- Other DB activity, such as bulk operations
- Response time during batch processing (if required)

It is clearly not feasible to test every condition and permutation. It is also not feasible to test all possible data combinations. We therefore are presented with the question, "How far should we test?"

The answer to this question is governed by the following parameters and the amount of flexibility or degree of freedom you can exercise on each:

- Delivery schedule (i.e., time available for testing)
- Risk associated with not testing certain conditions
- Potential mitigations if associated risk does materialize
- Funding and resources (people and systems) required to conduct additional tests
- Ability to create data sets and loads that would accurately simulate real life

For instance, if there is a very unique type of data set that is very difficult to create and has the risk of not performing as well as required, one may opt to mitigate that risk by observing the very low occurrence of this data set in production and by monitoring production performance to implement any additional fine-tuning as needed. This may save considerable time and money for a large implementation effort.

Another common question is, "How much load should be put on the system during testing?" One can argue that adding increasing load to the point of system failure may be interesting to graph, such that management is aware of the load under which the system will break. While this could be a useful test, the value it adds is marginal as it would typically be sufficient to test the system under peak anticipated projected load and two times that load for the event of a failover condition. Again, testing the extreme condition—while satisfying some need to know on the part of management—may be a costly exercise in getting information that might never be proven useful.

In summary, the extent to which one should conduct non-functional testing should be entirely driven by the level of risk assumed by not testing a given test scenario and the cost to execute such a test. You may find that management, faced with the cost of executing a certain test and the real risk of it actually happening in production, may be less inclined to invest the funds.

Justifying the Investment

Project teams and sponsors intuitively understand the need for performance testing as part of normal systems delivery. Unfortunately, this understanding is not always afforded to the other type of non-functional testing. The challenge the technology team is faced with is to educate and convince sponsors and management of the need for a multitude of test environments, some of which can be very expensive due to their production-like nature.

The investment in resource, environments, and time and effort can be justified based on the following arguments:

- Multifunctional use of the environments (e.g., a production-like certification environment that can be used for disaster recovery [DR] as well as certification)
- By relating specific types of error conditions (memory leak, resource overconsumption, etc.) to specific outages that have occurred in the past or may occur in the future, a dollar value can be associated with the prevention of such outages
- Once the system is implemented there would be a regular need to upgrade the underlying infrastructure, systems software, and application with a variety of patches and updates. The certification environment would be critical to verifying these update patches and ensuring that they do not create production outages
- Some components of the non-functional test environments can be shared across multiple projects to reduce cost
- Performance and automation test tools can be shared with other projects and are required for ongoing maintenance of the environment
- Investment in automation scripts and simulators can provide an immediate return on reduction of manual functional regression testing

Overall, it is important to recognize that non-functional test environments require a different set of characteristics than functional test environments. These environments require failover software and appropriate clustering/secondary systems to be installed. They require production-like configuration to test the interaction between application and systems, and for some of the tests they require production-size servers to confirm performance and capacity targets.

Non-functional test environments should be isolated from functional test environments to allow for:

■ Accurate measurement
■ Reduction in functional test interruption
■ Production simulation (size, capacity, performance, operability)
■ Certification with exact production-like configuration
■ Flexible scheduling of tests in parallel with other testing activities

Successful completion and ongoing operation of systems-delivery projects is highly dependent on making the investment in the appropriate set of environments and tools up front to allow for on-time delivery and solid production-ready systems.

Negative Reasoning

In the event that all the reasoning and business casing for non-functional test investment falls on deaf ears, it is useful to document all the risks to which the business will be subjected due to lack of investment in non-functional testing. This can be used to achieve the following goals:

■ Clearly communicate the risk and potential issues that have a high probability to occur in production
■ Create a sense of accountability with management for any future potential issues
■ Potentially reverse the decision not to invest based on the two previous points
■ Ensure that the technology team had done all in its power to alert management of the risks the project is about to undertake

Clearly communicating the risks and documenting these risks for management, business, and sponsors has, more often than not, influenced the decision to invest in non-functional testing.

Scoping and Estimating

Determining the Scope of Non-Functional Testing

The scope of the non-functional testing is determined using the following artifacts and methods:

The Non-Functional (or in Some Cases, Functional) Requirements Document

This document may contain useful information regarding the following:

- Response time for critical functions
- Definition of the application critical functions
- Expected availability
- Implied service level with internal and external clients
- Batch processing windows
- Expected recovery time
- Data retention requirements and archive specifications

The Business Utilization Model (BUM) Document

This document may not exist for your project. If it does not, it is highly recommended that the business analysis team sit down with the business users and create this document. The information contained in this document should include the following:

- Number of users that would use the application
- Number of users that would use each key function concurrently
- Peak usage times and estimated usage at peak times
- Expected growth in users and volume of transactions over the next 2–3 years
- Sequence of functionality usage
- Other applications that are used by the same user community
- Methods of access (i.e., network, branch, browser type, etc.)
- Bulk operations usage patterns
- Batch process volumes and projected growth

The Service Level Agreement (SLA) Document

This document may already exist, particularly where a service is being offered to an external customer. This document can be a very useful tool for the technology team to help derive a set of availability, operability, and performance requirements. One would expect to find the following information in an SLA:

- Response time for key functions and in some cases a broad statement regarding online response time
- Expected delivery time for reports, files, or other periodic artifacts that are routinely generated by the application
- Expected system availability time (i.e., system uptime)
- Acceptable maintenance windows
- DR and BCP (business continuity plan) requirements
- Key reporting metrics on which the service level is measured
- Penalties associated with not meeting certain service levels

Using the above documents, the technology team can provide a statement of non-functional testing scope that will describe the following.

Performance Testing

- Key functions to be tested and reported for response time, including expected response time ranges
- List of bulk and batch processes and the expected time to execute each
- Transaction volumes average and peak
- User volumes average and peak
- Transaction and user volumes at peak and peak × 2 under which the system will be tested

Capacity Testing

- "Transactions-per-minute" requirement for each transaction type to be executed
- Number of users logged on to the system
- Number of concurrent users executing a variety of key functions
- Duration of the test
- System resources to be monitored
- Approach to measurement of baseline

Failover Testing

- List of all components to be tested
- Expected failover results (automated versus manual, number of retried transactions)
- Criticality of automated failover per component

Operability Testing

- List of critical system functions to be tested
- Operability conditions to be tested against each system function
- Expected results and system alerts, report and recovery
- Automated versus manual recovery
- Expected time for recovery
- Expected transactions state for each test

Sustainability Testing

- Duration of test
- Volume of users and transactions to be run during the test
- Data setup requirements
- Key metrics to track and report on (i.e., memory profile, threads, connections)

Certification Testing

- Which tests are included in certification
- Scope of configuration management (i.e., application only or including system configuration)
- Code drop to be used for final certification
- Certification criteria—gating criteria for production deployment

Scoping and planning for appropriate non-functional test coverage is essential to ensure proper, expected system behavior in production. However, the nature of non-functional issues or defects that are identified through non-functional testing are often complex—and in some cases require code or systems redesign. Being faced with the need to redesign a component of the system or application at a late stage of the project would have far-reaching implications for delivery timelines and costs to the project.

Clearly one must employ an approach to identifying critical non-functional issues at the early stages of the project lifecycle. The following is a list of example actions and approaches that can be used to allow for early detection.

Architectural and Design "Hotspots"

Identify non-functional "hotspots" during the architectural and design review of the application and system. These hotspots are identified as the areas most likely to create performance, operability, or failover challenges. During the development of the system conduct initial tests and proof of concepts to verify that the non-functional behavior around these "hotspots" is as expected.

Unit Testing of Application Non-Functional Behavior

The development team should design unit tests that will simulate volume through to the specific components they are developing. There are several open-source tools in the market used by developers to achieve this such as Jmeter, Jprobe, and others. These tools allow the developer with minimum effort, to generate throughput to their component of work and observe the system and application behavior. They will also allow detection of potential performance bottlenecks and issues with transaction management and recovery. This is one of the most effective ways of achieving early detection of non-functional issues—in particular when coupled with a specific focus around the "hotspots."

Investment in Simulators and Injectors

While the development teams are busy developing and unit testing their applications, the non-functional test team should be developing the necessary simulators and injectors that will assist in simulating load, as well as any external systems interfaces. These simulators and injectors can be used early on to test the non-functional behavior of the system in advance of it being fully functional and ready to be formally tested.

Code and Data Review

Code design and implementation, as well as structured query language (SQL) statements and data model designs, should all be reviewed with performance and operability in mind. This can be done effectively by either the application architects or the non-functional engineering team. The reviews should be focused on the following elements of design and implementation:

- Memory management
- Transaction management and boundaries
- Code efficiency
- SQL code design for performance
- Data model simplification and design for performance (based on key high-volume queries)
- Error and exception management
- Recovery code after failure events

All of the above early detection methods should be considered for inclusion in the scope of the overall non-functional work to be conducted by the development teams and the non-functional engineering team.

Estimating Effort and Resource

Once the scope of testing has been determined, the project management team will be faced with the task of estimating the effort and resources required to complete all work within the defined scope. The key cost elements that should factor into the estimate are as follows.

People Resources

This category will include the non-functional engineering test team as well as any additional effort that is required by the development and project test teams. In addition, it is good practice to include any additional professional services and infrastructure implementation costs for net new infrastructure for new test environments as well as professional services associated with installation and configuration of test and monitoring tools.

Test Tools

This category includes software tools that are required to simulate load, create and execute test scripts, and report on test results. It also includes any required system resource monitoring tools for observing, measuring, and trending system resource utilization during capacity, sustainability, and failover testing.

Infrastructure Cost

This category includes all the hardware (HW) and software (SW) that is required to construct the required non-functional test environments.

The exact estimates will be driven by the actual scope of non-functional work defined for the project; however, the following guidelines and advice can be used for high-level estimates.

People Cost

Table 2.1   Non-Functional Effort Estimation

Function	Full-Time Equivalent Resource	Starting in Phase (Plan/Design/Build/Test)	Comments
Team Lead	1: All project sizes	Design	Should preferably be involved in the original estimation.
Test-Case Scripter	1: Small projects 2–3: Average-sized projects 3–5: Large projects	Build	Should have specific skills for the selected test tools.
Deployment Engineer	0.5: Small to average-sized projects 1: Large projects	Build	Assumes the existence of a formal application deployment team that is responsible for formal deployments.
Test Automation Execution Engineers	None: Small projects 1–2: Average-sized to large projects	Test	These are resources that are familiar with the operation and reporting function of the automated test tools.
Troubleshooting Engineers	1: Small to average-sized projects 2: Large projects	Build	These resources will be building the simulators/injectors and will troubleshoot the application during deployment and during test execution. They would also conduct some of the code and data reviews.

Test Tools

Many organizations make central investments in enterprise-wide software tools. In such cases, the project may benefit from existing licenses or may have to only be charged brown dollars (via internal allocation) rather than spend money on new licenses. It is important to review the set of tools existing within the organization and ensure that these will satisfy the requirements for non-functional testing for the project.

In the event that test tools are not already available, the project may elect to commit to a long-term investment in industrialized products that would benefit the organization post-project or go with open-source tools to minimize direct cost to the project.

In general, the number of licenses required should be calculated based on the expected transaction rate and the concurrent user load required to satisfy the application's business utilization models.

Infrastructure Cost

This is the cost associated with the construction of the necessary non-functional test environments. Later in this chapter we will discuss the various non-functional test environments, the characteristics of each environment, and the conditions under which these environments are required. Table 2.2 is a list of environments for non-functional testing, their intended use, and basic cost considerations.

A common oversight is to forget the cost associated with running, supporting, and maintaining these environments. Make sure to include all resource costs for support and batch operation for these environments as well as deployments, currency updates, and software licensing costs.

Table 2.2   Non-Functional Test Environments

Environment	Intended Use	Cost Considerations
Performance	Testing performance characteristics of the application and systems being implemented.	This environment needs to allow for extrapolation to production sized environment. It must be built with the same clustering and configuration as production but can be sized at half or quarter of the capacity. Depending on the level of activities and timeline, there may be a need for more than one of these environments. There may be a need for a separate batch performance environment given the length of testing duration for batch operations.

Table 2.2   (*continued*)

Failover	Testing failover and recovery of all identified failover points and components.	This environment must be isolated with all its components to allow for destructive and failure condition testing without impacting any of the other nonproduction environments. It must contain all the components participating in the failover testing in a configuration that is similar to production. The size of the environment can be much reduced because the test scope would not include a large volume of transactions.
Certification	Certifying performance, capacity requirements, and sustainability testing in a productionlike environment.	The environment must be identical to production (to the best degree possible). It must have data that simulates production volumes. It can be used as a DR environment to reduce overall cost.

Estimating the Delivery Timeline

The scope of the non-functional testing would clearly drive the delivery timeline; however, there are many other constraints that also drive the timeline, including the following.

- **Code availability**—Initial testing can be done with early versions of the code, but final certification must be conducted with the final (or close to final) code to be deployed in production.
- **Code and configuration fixes**—When an issue is identified in non-functional testing, in most cases it will require a code fix or configuration change, some of which will require the development team to produce.
- **Environment shakedown and troubleshooting**—Once a non-functional environment is deployed, it needs to be shaken down for functional verification. In the event that the scripts cannot execute there may be a reliance on the development team to assist in troubleshooting the environment.

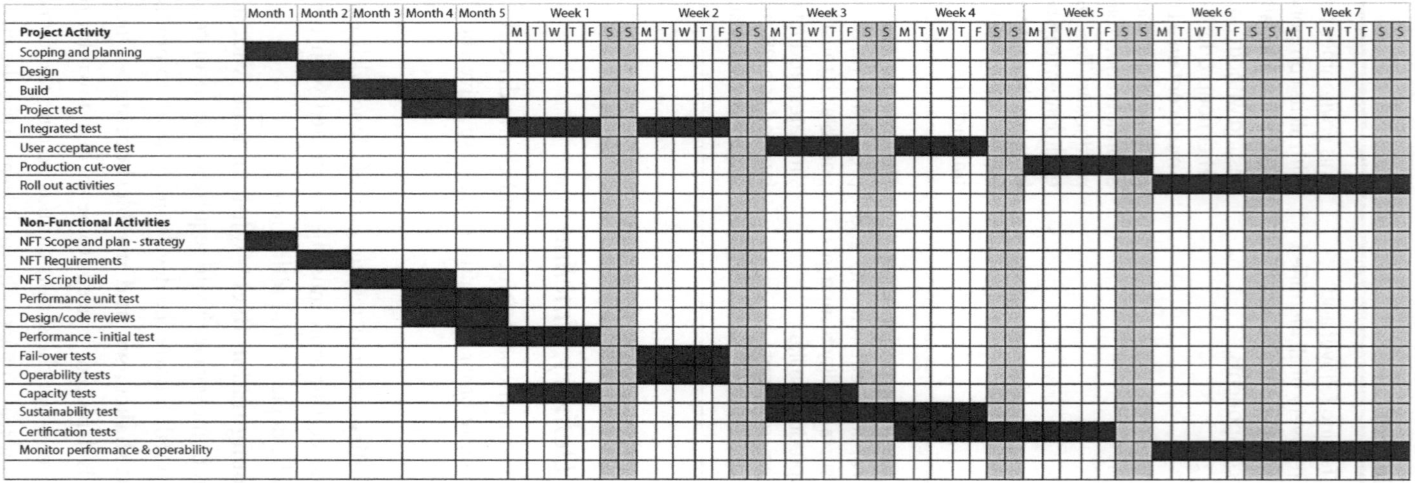

Figure 2.1   Aggressive non-functional test schedule and timelines.

- **Knowledge gathering**—The development of scripts and simulators requires some level of functional knowledge of the application; once again, this results in a dependency on the development team

In light of the preceding dependencies, the planning for non-functional testing must be aligned with the overall testing schedule in the program/project.

Below you can find two views for planning. The first view represents an ideal plan in the event that time is not a hard constraint or that you are early enough in the planning cycle to allow you to influence the overall project timelines. The second view is an aggressive delivery-minded view that is achievable but high risk in terms of meeting the deadlines. Both views must be aligned with the test scheduled, which also drives the delivery timelines for non-functional testing.

The aggressive delivery view is shown in Figure 2.1. The schedule shown in Figure 2.1 is designed to maximize the opportunity to conduct parallel activities, thereby reducing the overall schedule. It is, however, quite aggressive from a timeline standpoint and could easily be thrown off schedule if any of the key assumptions are not met, such as:

- Early code review and architectural reviews for non-functional aspects of the application had been conducted successfully
- Early non-functional unit testing had been successfully executed and reported by the development team
- The application code entering the integrated testing cycles is sufficiently stable to allow for non-functional testing
- No major redesign is required based on the results of the non-functional tests
- Multiple environments are in existence to support both functional and non-functional test activities

The key areas of parallelism that are accomplished by the above plan are as follows:

- Failover and operability tests are conducted in parallel with integrated functional testing; early code and architectural reviews will ensure that the development team has invested the right level of focus and effort into making the application operable and respondent to failover conditions.
- Final capacity testing is conducted in parallel with the first cycle of user-acceptance testing (UAT); this is supported by an early cycle of capacity testing that will confirm that the required system resources are available.
- Sustainability test is conducted in parallel with UAT, leveraging the code that had been frozen as entry criteria into UAT. A potential code refresh can be considered upon start of the second cycle of UAT.

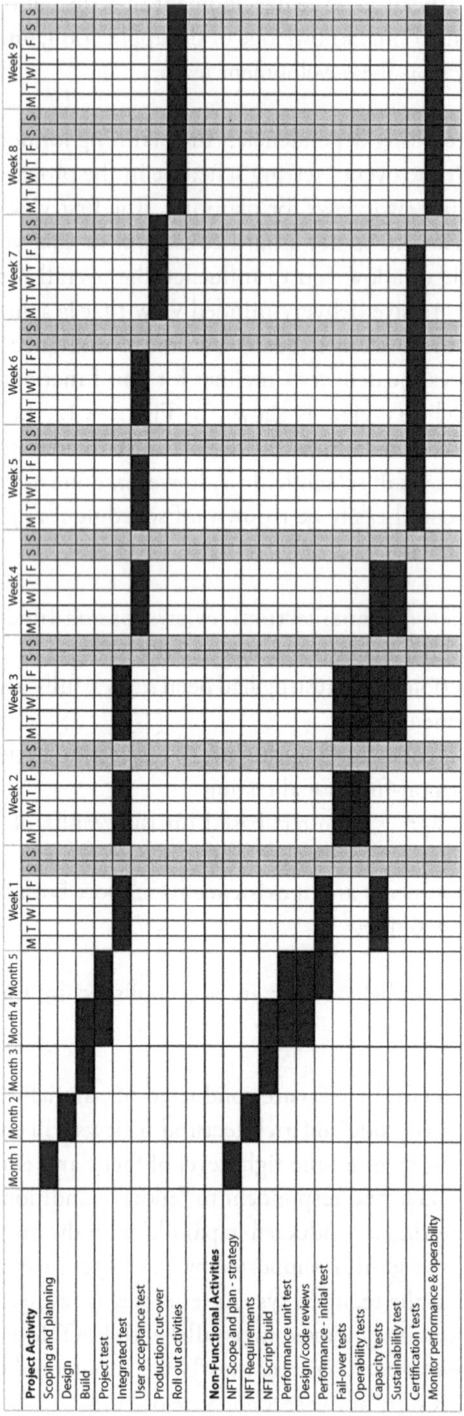

Figure 2.2 A less risky schedule for non-functional testing.

■ Certification testing is conducted in parallel to the second cycle of UAT and during the production cut-over week. This assumes that there are little to no changes (code fixes or configuration changes) between the first and second cycle of UAT.

The less risky plan for non-functional testing is shown in Figure 2.2.
The key differences from the preceding schedule are as follows:

■ Addition of an extra week of integrated testing to allow for any work required based on the findings from performance, operability, and failover testing.
■ Addition of an extra week of UAT to allow for the certification tests' first (and most likely final) cycle to complete prior to the end of UAT.
■ Extension of failover, operability, and capacity testing schedules as well as allowing an extra week for certification.

If time permits you may want to consider moving the certification testing for post-UAT activity, thereby ensuring that certification is the last testing activity and is conducted on a fully frozen code and configuration.

Test and Resource Planning

Test Types and Base Requirements

The following is a short description of each of the non-functional test types and the key considerations when designing and executing these tests. Subsequent chapters of this book include a detailed discussion regarding planning and executing of these tests.

Operability Testing

This is a test of likely production conditions that may affect the application/system in an unpredictable way. The objective of the test is to identify the key operability test cases with the highest potential impact to the system and the business using the system, and test the application behavior under such conditions. Some examples of operability tests include:

■ Behavior of the application when an external system interface is not available
■ Recovery from outage conditions
■ Application handling of bad data (ill-formatted)

Failover Testing

This is a test designed to verify the failover design, configuration, and process by simulating failover conditions. The objective of the test is to ensure that the systems can failover as designed under load with full in-flight transactions recovery and to ensure that the failover detection is triggered appropriately. Key considerations for this test include:

- Ensuring that the test is conducted in an environment that is identically configured like production
- Run a sufficiently varied load through the system to observe transaction recovery
- Measure success by accounting for all initiated transactions on the failover server/component and the continued service availability on the secondary server
- Cover as many triggering failover events as possible (application shutdown, OS failure, hardware failure, etc.); failover may behave differently depending on the triggering event

Capacity Testing

This test is intended to confirm and validate the capacity model that is developed by the non-functional engineering team based on business utilization information provided by the business requirements teams. The objective of the test is to run a simulated production load for a sustained duration and monitor the utilization of all relevant system resources. This test will finalize the hardware sizing requirements (i.e., the CPU, memory, disk, etc.); it would also confirm any additional configuration of resource allocations. Key considerations for this test include:

- Ensuring application resources are being monitored (i.e., connection pools, thread pools, memory utilization inside the container, etc.)
- Capture all base system resource utilization (CPU, memory, disk, I/O)
- Overlay the usage measured during the test with the current production usage (especially for shared environments)
- Ensure capacity test is run in isolation on an infrastructure that is identical or that can be projected to the production environment
- Run a mixed load at peak levels during the test to ensure capacity will be sufficient to sustain peak volumes and user levels
- Ensure that measurement tools are instrumented only for the key metrics you are looking to measure, such that the tool itself does not add load to the system

Performance Testing

This test is intended to test the performance of online response as well as bulk and batch operations. The objective of the test is to measure response time under load and verify that it meets user requirements. For batch and bulk operations, the objective is to test full data-load execution within the processing window defined in the non-functional requirement. Key considerations for this test include:

- Invest in scripting of the test cases for consistency in execution, data buildup, and measurement
- Invest in tools that provide for scripting and execution/results capture
- Test performance under simulated peak load
- Test and monitor performance in a sustained environment (environment that has been running for a sustained period)
- Invest in preparing a data bank that would simulate 6–12 months of production buildup

Sustainability Testing

This test is intended to measure and observe resource utilization in the application and the infrastructure environment over a sustained period of time during which daily load is simulated. The objective of the test is to identify any anomalies in resource utilization over time or any trending utilization information that may suggest a potential issue (such as memory leak, thread, or connection leak, etc.). Key considerations for this test include:

- Conduct the test in an environment that is replicating the production configuration
- Identify the sustained period to run the test, by considering processing cycles and availability requirements
- Ensure that there is a good coverage of the various business operations based on the detailed business utilization model

Certification Testing

This test is intended to verify all configuration settings in a production-like environment. At a minimum this test would include a subset of the performance test cases and a complete set of failover tests. In some cases the scope of a certification test would also include a capacity test to ensure that capacity is calculated based on production identical infrastructure. Key considerations for this test include:

- Test to be conducted in a controlled environment which is identical to production
- Configuration of the application stack and the infrastructure must be identical to production as the prime objective of the test is to test such configuration
- Include the execution of documented procedures in your test as part of the recovery, failover, or any other manual activity

Test Environments

Table 2.3 lists the test types, and the target environments in which these should be executed. In addition, the table states the minimum requirements for such test environments.

Table 2.3   Test Types and Target Environments

Environment	Requirements	Test Types
Performance Development	Capacity to run all test scripts from a CPU, data, and disk standpoint. Tools for load and automated testing available.	Script verification testing Performance execution test run
Performance (Online and batch may be separate environments)	Full capacity to run load testing. Tools for load and automated testing available. Architecture is identical to the production environment but configuration may be smaller in size.	Online performance Batch performance Operability Failover test run
Certification	Identical replication of the production environment. Same capacity, size, and configuration as production. Controlled environment fitted with monitoring tools for obtaining test results.	Certification Sustainability

Table 2.3 (*continued*)

Development Integration Test	Base requirement to allow for deployment of end-to-end functionality. No need for capacity, load, failover, or any other production-like configuration.	Development integration test
Integrated Functional Test	Deployment of full complement of applications end to end. Include interaction with test environments for external systems. Minimal capacity, no need for failover or other production-like configuration.	Integrated functional test
User-Acceptance Test	Controlled environment to ensure change control is proper. Deployment of full compliment of applications end to end. Include interaction with test environments for external systems. Minimal capacity, no need for failover or other productionlike configuration.	User acceptance test. Ensuring that functional application behavior meets the functional requirements

The Test Team

The test team consists of several key roles; some of these roles can be fulfilled by the same set of individuals. The roles and their descriptions are as follows.

The Non-Functional Test Lead

The non-functional test lead provides overall management for the team and is the key planner and interface to the rest of the project teams. Included in the scope of this person's work is:

■ Non-functional test strategy
■ Review and sign-off on non-functional requirements
■ Definition of non-functional test scope

- Non-functional test plan
- Test-results reporting for management

Code Deployment Engineers

Code deployment engineers are responsible for the deployment of all applications and simulators as well as setting up test data banks for all non-functional environments. Included in the scope of their work is:

- Manual deployments to test environments
- Scripting of automated deployment
- Automated deployment to test environments
- Troubleshooting of deployments
- Data backup and restore as well as test data initialization

Test Case Scripters

This group of individuals is responsible for building the test scripts for performance, sustainability, operability, and failover. Included in the scope of the group's work is the:

- Design of test cases
- Scripting of test cases
- Verification of test scripts

Test Automation Execution Engineers

This group is responsible for executing the tests and reporting the results. Included in its scope is:

- Test script execution in various target environments
- Troubleshooting of script execution
- Collecting and reporting the raw results

Simulator Developers

This group is responsible for the development of all simulators and injectors that are required to simulate external systems behavior and to seed data into the applications or generate load. The team would typically have a good code development background, with specific knowledge of databases, messaging systems, Web services, and other interface methods.

The Test Data Manager

The test data manager is responsible for developing a plan and managing test data throughout the test execution, and would be responsible for the following:

- Defining test data requirements
- Sourcing the data required for testing
- Managing the data for each test environment
- Establishing the backup and restore procedure for test data

Troubleshooters

Though this group is sometimes forgotten, its function is key to ensuring the smooth execution of the test pack. Typically the project teams are too busy to provide any significant support for troubleshooting non-functional test environments. Having a troubleshooter on the team that can dissect the problem and pinpoint the area where the issue resides will allow the team to move forward, bypassing the issue or getting more focused help from the project team.

Communication Planning

Setting Expectations

As with any delivery-based work, setting the expectations up front is a key to success. The non-functional test team must invest in setting the expectation right from the start with two distinct groups; the project teams and the management/steering committee of the program.

Project Team Expectations

It is important to set the expectations regarding the required inputs from the project teams, as well as the expected outputs, and reporting back to the project team. The project team should be aware of the following:

- The project team will be required to produce a detailed non-functional requirement based on a template provided by the non-functional test team
- The project team will be required to develop a business utilization model along with the business users that will help drive the volume calculations
- The project team will be required to assist in troubleshooting of the application in the test environments on occasion
- The non-functional test team may identify non-functional defect with the application that may require some redesign or tuning of the application

- Defect may be identified late in the delivery cycle due to the nature of testing
- The project team is expected to identify and test performance hotspots early in the development test cycles
- The non-functional test team may conduct code review and make recommendations for tuning and code performance improvements
- The non-functional test team will require its own environment that cannot be shared with the functional testing activities

Steering Committee and Executive Expectations

This group has to be communicated with in a very clear fashion regarding the following items:

- Scope of testing: what is in and what is out
- Risks associated with elements that would not be tested and the mitigations for such risks
- Budget required for all non-functional testing
- Review of all test environments to make sure management clearly understands the need for multiple environments
- Schedule and plan for non-functional testing and the gating criteria for testing of the application
- The potential for late defect discovery
- The size of team and the individual functions within the team

Summary

This chapter demonstrates the need to advance the scope and planning of the non-functional activities that are often overlooked when a project is initially business cased and budgeted. The planning required is extensive, and includes elements of budgeting, business casing cost and risk, determining scope, sizing the team(s), determining the required environments and schedules for testing.

Engaging the technology leads early in the planning process will ensure that all the considerations mentioned in this chapter are addressed head-on and will provide for accurate planning and budgeting for execution.

Chapter 3

Non-Functional Requirements

Many software projects fail as a result of flawed functional requirements. Defining a complete set of requirements for a complex system is difficult. People have been building software for decades but it is still common for projects to falter during this critical phase. Defining an effective set of functional requirements requires prescience for how the completed system will function and operate.

Functional requirements, however, only define part of the overall puzzle. Failing to capture accurate non-functional requirements exposes your project to the same risks that the failure to document a complete set of functional requirements does. We begin this chapter with a set of observations that are common for many software projects:

- Many projects omit to define non-functional requirements
- Many projects do not correctly understand what is meant by non-functional requirements
- Many projects fail to define the full scope of non-functional requirements
- Many projects leave non-functional requirements definition too far into the development lifecycle

For projects where these observations are applicable, non-functional requirements are not determined correctly and system quality in this area is left to the best efforts of the implementation team. This usually means that performance is an afterthought, and features such as operability are built into the system on a priority basis once the support team begins escalating the difficulties they are experiencing to management. A reactive approach to development builds bad blood between the user community, the support organization, and the development team. It can also introduce sloppy errors and vulnerabilities into a system. Reacting to crisis after crisis in your production environment is not an efficient way to build or maintain software, and will end up costing your organization money, resources, and possibly its reputation.

Consider a scenario in which end users and the development team proceed under the optimistic belief that the software will perform to an acceptable level. But what is *acceptable*? What if the development team confidently releases software that performs a given business operation in 2 seconds but the business is accustomed to 0.5 seconds for the same operation? The day *after* you launch a new system is not a good time to reconcile differing expectations.

From an end-user perspective, it is self-evident that the software must run fast, that it must never crash, and that it must be free from any and all defects. In the real world, we know that systems rarely meet these requirements with perfect efficacy. Like any engineering activity, all system characteristics need to be specified in writing to ensure that they are implemented and tested as part of the solution. Documenting non-functional requirements serves the following critical benefits:

1. **Serves as a basis for constructing a robust System Design:** During design and development, the implementation team knows exactly what behavior is expected from the system.
2. **Serves as a prerequisite for Non-Functional Testing:** Non-functional requirements give the QA (quality assurance) organization clear objectives and the input it needs to generate representative test cases. Like any requirement, a non-functional requirement cannot be considered met until it has been thoroughly tested.
3. **Defines a Usage Contract with the End Users:** The business users understand that the system is tested and rated to meet requirements for a designated load. If the end users triple the number of people using the system, then they can no longer expect the same level of service if that load is outside of the documented usage parameters.
4. **Provides a Basis for Capacity Planning:** Depending on your application, your system may or may not accommodate increasing volumes over time. For many business applications, the level of usage is expected to increase as the business itself expands. In these situations, capacity planning will need non-functional requirements as input to infrastructure planning activities.

In this chapter we will define the types of requirements that are included in the non-functional realm and we will look at how these requirements are derived from business inputs. Important considerations will be illustrated using the example of an online banking system. We will also visit the topic of roles and responsibilities, where we see how an organization should approach the formulation of non-functional requirements. At the end of this chapter, you will be familiar with the scope, definition process, and terminology required to write meaningful non-functional requirements.

What Are Non-Functional Requirements?

Before we continue, we will take a moment to review some of the content that was presented in the introduction to this book. Non-functional requirements describe the behavior of your system across the following categories:

- **Performance requirements** specify the throughput capacity and response times of your system. Performance requirements are only meaningful in the context of expected usage or load as we shall see later in the chapter.
- **Operability requirements** indicate robustness features and required behavior under specific failure scenarios.
- **Availability requirements** define the service level that the system must meet in order to support the business usage for the system.
- **Security requirements** provide guidance on authentication, access control, and privacy measures necessary to satisfy business concerns. Security is a topic deserving of a book unto itself. Accordingly, the authors have chosen to omit coverage of security-related topics in this book.
- **Archive requirements** specify the retention period for data that is generated, collected, and stored by the system.

In this chapter we shall see that non-functional requirements need to be documented by producing two different artifacts: the *business usage model* and the *non-functional requirements narrative*. The business usage model establishes key metrics for the usage of the system, including load volumes and usage distribution over time. In the context of the business usage, the narrative defines concrete objectives for the system. For example, a performance requirement for a specific business operation may be stated as an average time response of two seconds. This requirement is only meaningful if we understand how often that business operation will be executed and under what circumstances. As we will see, the usage model establishes the circumstances under which non-functional requirements are valid.

Do I Need Non-Functional Requirements?

In the introduction to this book we committed to being pragmatic in determining what is and is not mandatory. In the real world, software systems serve a variety of functions and user communities. If you are building a software system that supports ten users who rarely use the system concurrently, you may decide that the cost of formulating non-functional requirements is not justified for your application. If the system you are building is supported by other redundant systems, then non-functional requirements and testing may not be justified in your budget. If your end users can tolerate a prolonged period during which the application is not available without this having a significant business impact, you may decide to be more selective in documenting non-functional requirements.

In this chapter we make the assumption that your system meets most or all of the following criteria in order to illustrate a formal, structured approach to defining non-functional requirements:

- Your system functionality and technology base is complex. As such, it includes a variety of human interfaces and/or to software that interfaces directly to other systems.
- Your system is business critical and outages entail significant financial or reputation impact to your business.
- Your system has a large user population and usage fluctuates with time of day and season.
- Your system supports a large set of different, unrelated business operations.
- The end users for your system have demanding performance requirements.
- The projected usage for your system is expected to change over time.

Roles and Responsibilities

Building a software system is a team effort requiring both business and technical participants. Traditionally, business participants define the requirements while technical resources implement a solution that meets those requirements. Unfortunately, expressing non-functional requirements in a way that can be implemented and tested is a non-intuitive activity that requires close collaboration within your team.

In order for your requirements phase to produce a meaningful output, we strongly recommend the following role designations:

1. **Designate a Business Analyst as the Non-Functional Requirements Lead:** Preferably, this person is an individual with previous experience in this role. If you do not have such a person available, ensure that the designated person invests some time in understanding the materials in this book or another comparable reference.
2. **Designate a Technical Non-Functional Test Lead:** If you do not have a technical resource who can participate in non-functional test cycles, the technical lead from the development team is usually the best candidate. This person will work with the business analyst to ensure that business inputs are properly translated into requirements that can be tested and implemented. This can be a technical architect or a designer that is able to take a higher view of the project's overall requirements.

The business analyst will be responsible for producing non-functional requirements documentation; the technical test lead will work closely with the business analyst to vet the documentation to ensure it is complete. The technical test lead has additional responsibilities as follows:

■ Coaxing variations in the business usage out of the business analyst, i.e., asking leading questions to populate detail into the business model
■ Challenging the defined requirements to ensure that realistic targets are being proposed for the application
■ Helping the business analyst to understand where details are important in order to properly test the system
■ Helping to provide detailed content for the business analyst to include in the requirements documents

Challenging Requirements

Requirements are generated by analysts who do their best to document what users want, but users may not always know what they want—or they may change their mind after seeing a product. Furthermore, analysts do not always ask the right questions, nor do they always interpret the responses they receive accurately. Subject matter experts and consultants, in general, are notorious for imposing a view of the world on users who may or may not fully agree with the picture that is being presented.

Requirement swapping is a term invented by one of the authors after many years of trying to implement badly formulated requirements. There were many times when a requirement clearly expressed intent in a way that was technically complex to implement. An implementer could offer an alternative that would satisfy the user's intent but not necessarily meet their requirement verbatim. For cases like this, a proposal to swap a complex requirement for a simple, more natural requirement that in many cases the user likes even better can build consensus. In many circles this activity is part of a broader activity referred to as *requirements engineering*.

If you take the time to review requirements with the technical team, you will usually avoid future disconnects that result in wasted effort. In general, the amount of time that the technical team spends implementing a requirement should be proportional to the value of the requirement. Performance requirements can be great illustrations of this concept. A business user may arbitrarily decide that log-in should take no more than one second for any request. In the technical design, there is a robust, reusable log-in service available from another system but it only supports a two-second response time. In talking to the sponsor, most users will log in once or twice a day at most. Users are internal, so we don't have to worry about a competitor offering a faster login. In this case it should be easy to convince the sponsor to relax the one-second login requirement, especially if the technical team is willing to commit to a faster response time for another part of the system that is more frequently accessed.

In some instances you may have to explain to the users what it is exactly they are asking for. We have encountered situations in which the users were expecting a thousand people to use the system concurrently and therefore expected the system to have the capacity to handle a thousand transactions per second. It is only after explaining to the user community that each user had to fill in a lengthy form for each transaction—which would take them at least a minute and therefore was physically impossible for them to submit one transaction per second—that everyone agreed to a more realistic requirement of 16 transactions per second (1,000/60).

Non-functional requirements can be expensive to test and accommodate in the technical design. It is prudent to ensure that all parties with a stake in the system understand the effort and expected benefit for each requirement.

Establishing a Business Usage Model

Quantifying Human and Machine Inputs

Human behavior can be unpredictable. If you ask people to describe how they think they will use a system in the future, what they describe will be at best a rough approximation of their actual behavior based on what they are currently doing—or think they should be doing.

If you are going to test software systems against non-functional requirements, your foundation is your usage model. The usage model specifies the number of users who have access to the system and an estimation of the types of activities in which they will engage. For systems that are replacing or upgrading existing systems, there is often an opportunity to measure usage directly. For example, a new software solution that replaces an existing system likely means there will be an opportunity to report on historical transaction volumes and use these numbers as the basis for usage estimates.

Consider an online banking application for an established bank. If the bank is upgrading their current solution, they can expect similar initial volumes to the legacy system when they again "go live." The number of people who check their account balance online each day is unlikely to change when the new solution is implemented. For B2C (business-to-consumer) applications, on the other hand, customer usage is often difficult to predict. Will online banking users enthusiastically adopt the enhanced online banking solution? Will customers use the system more as a result of the enhancements? Will users tell their friends about the improved banking experience, spurring new customers to begin using the system? Will additional customers be attracted to the new system and switch banks to take advantage of the enhanced banking platform? These questions cannot readily be answered by technologists or business users, but they will impact the load profile of the system.

If you are introducing a new software product or service, you may have no empirical basis whatsoever for establishing a usage model. In this case, the usage model is entirely theoretical and based on predicted adoption and usage.

Some aspects of human usage are very difficult to estimate without actual observation of users on the new system. If you give users two buttons to press that perform slight variations of the same function, which button will they press? If you give users a suite of new functionality based on a consultative requirements gathering process, which features will they actually use and in what proportions? Users themselves can only tell you how they *think* they will use a software system. To make matters worse, the users who participate in your requirements gathering may or may not represent the perspective of the majority of end users. If consultants or management have the majority influence in the functional specification of the system, they may totally misrepresent the behavior of the user community when the system is actually in production. Malcolm Gladwell, in his book *Blink*, makes convincing arguments that in a very large number of situations, users make totally inaccurate predictions of their own behavior.

The subtleties of human interaction with a user interface are difficult to antici- pate; however, the number of business transactions that users will initiate is usually measurable—or, at least, more readily predictable. We consider business transac- tions as *coarse inputs* in the usage model. The number of times that users click a button or the number of times that users encounter validation failures is incidental to the number of coarse inputs. If a customer is using an online banking system to pay a bill, each bill payment is a good example of a coarse input. A coarse input is a high-level functional activity. It includes all the nuances of how each customer pays a bill.

Software systems often have nonhuman inputs. Machine inputs to your system are equally important aspects of your usage model. Many complex systems func- tion based on a combination of human and machine inputs. Machine inputs can be continuous feeds or can come in batches. Continuous feeds are requests or data inputs that arrive on a continuous and unscheduled basis. Batch inputs are a bulk series of requests or inputs that usually arrive and are processed as a single unit of work. Batch inputs are often, but not necessarily, scheduled interactions with your system. The characteristics of batch inputs may be predictable or unpredictable in nature. Consider a scenario in which an insurance company must process car insur- ance applications and make approval recommendations on a nightly basis. Such a system may involve the collection of application requests from multiple channel front-end systems. Will the number of applications be constant over time? Will the number of applications be subject to seasonal or time-of-month variations? In the real world it is likely that the size of the batch input to the system will vary with time. Again, this variation needs to be accounted for in your model. A usage model that fails to anticipate a surge in insurance applications at month-end is not a rep- resentative usage model.

The first step in establishing your business usage involves quantifying it for both human and machine inputs. This can be done by answering the following questions:

Human Inputs

- For human inputs, what is the operations window for the software system?
- For each class of user, how many users are in the user population now? Projected in one year? Projected in five years?
- For each class of user, how many coarse inputs do we expect on average and as a maximum in the operations window?
- For each class of user, what is the distribution of coarse inputs in the operations window?
- In particular, what is the busiest interval for the system with respect to the creation of coarse inputs?

Machine Inputs

- For machine inputs, what is the operations window for the software system?
- How many interfaces support the input of machine inputs?
- For each interface, what is the expected and maximum number of coarse inputs now? Projected in one year? Projected in five years?
- For each interface, what is the distribution of coarse inputs in the operations window?
- In particular, what is the busiest interval for the system with respect to the creation of coarse inputs?

We can consider an online banking solution as an example application to illustrate how these requirements might be documented. We will start with human inputs.

The operations window and user community parameters can be expressed as follows. Because this system offers services to retail customers, it is not surprising to see that the system is expected to be available 365 days a year and 24 hours a day. The user volumes could become considerably larger than the current ones. The bank has built an aggressive business strategy to attract customers to its lower-cost Internet channel. The one- and five-year projections represent significant increases over the current numbers. Customers are divided between retail and business clients, with retail customers enjoying a significant majority over business clients.

Table 3.1 shows example requirements against the usage attributes for the items in this example.

Table 3.1   Example Requirements for Usage Attributes

Usage Attribute	Requirement
Operations window	12:00 AM to 11:59 PM, Monday to Sunday
Number of users by class	Personal banking: 3,250,000 Business banking: 420,000
Number of users by class, one year from now	Personal banking: 3,850,000 Business banking: 675,000
Number of users by class, five years from now	Personal banking: 6,380,000 Business banking: 1,120,000

Based on historical business reporting for the legacy online system, coarse inputs for each class of user are expected to be as shown in Table 3.2. The data is shown by month.

In scrutinizing historical data, it is clear that there is seasonal variation for a number of coarse inputs. Logins remain constant throughout the year, but bill payments are highest in January and lowest in July and August. Not surprisingly, it appears that people are on holiday during the summer and pay bills most actively following the busy Christmas shopping season, in January.

In looking at the weekly volumes, it also appears that peak usage is from 12:00 PM (noon) to 1:00 PM during the day. During this interval, 30% of the daily volumes are typically completed. The busiest day of the week is Friday, as this corresponds to the day following Thursday, when many employees receive weekly paychecks. This one-hour period qualifies as our busiest interval in the business usage for human input. Non-functional design and testing is all about worst-case scenarios. If the bank's systems can accommodate the busiest hour of the busiest day of the year, then we can be confident that it will handle all other intervals. We add this parameter, the busiest interval, to the business usage (as shown in Table 3.3).

To the best of our abilities we have adequately quantified the usage of the system based on human interactions. However, we are not done yet. We must also describe the system in terms of machine inputs. The new online banking platform is expected to have at least three interfaces that will accommodate machine coarse inputs. A nightly job is expected to extract a report that captures all online customer actions for business analytics. Further, another job is expected to produce an extract file that captures all bill payments made on the online banking platform for

Table 3.2 Example Coarse Inputs by Month: Online Banking System

Coarse Input	Jan	Feb	Mar	Apr	May	June	July	Aug	Sep	Oct	Nov	Dec
Login	65,645	65,656	66,547	6,875	45,353	47,765	76,576	65,474	76,586	56,363	47,574	74,547
Account Inquiry	4,535	45,435	52,451	52,534	75,676	76,575	76,576	75,766	76,757	65,656	65,463	45,654
Bill Payment	45,345	56,433	36,363	64,463	74,756	45,356	65,533	5,646	65,465	5,353	45,645	63,635
Funds Transfer	63,463	53,646	5,346	6,346	36,361	63,446	63,356	63,535	36,635	65,363	65,346	43,213

Table 3.3 The Busiest Interval

Usage Attribute	Requirement
Busiest Interval	12:00 PM to 1:00 PM, Friday; 30% of heaviest day's business volumes
Login	2,309,039
Account Inquiry	1,209,049
Bill Payment	529,143
Funds Transfer	210,985

fulfillment. Finally, a backend system is loading customer-specific marketing messages that are displayed to users when they login to the application.

We capture parameters for the model for each machine input, starting with the nightly reporting extract. All business reporting is constrained to run during periods of lesser user activity (i.e., at night). In this case, the report is expected to run at 02:00 AM each morning, seven days a week.

In this case, we derive the expected and maximum number of coarse inputs from the human inputs. For each human coarse input there will be a record in the output report. Consequently, we calculate the average and maximum coarse inputs for this machine event as 1,304,309 and 6,029,309, respectively. In other words, on a Friday in January, the busiest day of the banking year, the business analytics report will extract 6,029,309 records. Table 3.4 shows the machine input usage attributes for our example.

The bill-payment fulfillment job is similar in its characteristics to the business analytics report. This job also runs off-hour; however, this job needs to run and be complete no later than 10:00 PM in order to meet the cutoff imposed by the backend fulfillment system. It is required that customers be able to pay bills up until 6:00 PM. All bill payments made up until 6:00 PM must be fulfilled that night. At this point, the requirement says only that the job cannot start until 6:00 PM and can be complete no later than 10:00 PM. In this case, the job schedule will be derived during design and testing based on performance results and failed job-recovery procedures. For now, we can record the requirements in as much detail as we have available (as shown in Table 3.5).

The last machine input is more difficult to describe. We expect marketing messages to be sent to the application, but we don't have details for how this requirement will be met in the implementation. Because marketing messages will be

Table 3.4   Example Batch Input: Online Banking System (Business Reporting)

Usage Attribute	Requirement
Machine Input	Business reporting
Input Type	Batch
Operations Window	02:00 AM, Monday to Sunday
Typical Coarse Input	1,304,309
Maximum Coarse Input	6,029,309 (third Friday in January)

Table 3.5   Example Batch Input: Online Banking System (Fulfillment)

Usage Attribute	Requirement
Machine Input	Bill payment fulfillment
Input Type	Batch
Operations Window	Must start after 6:00 PM and complete successfully before 10:00 PM, Monday to Sunday
Typical Coarse Input	687,095
Maximum Coarse Input	4,687,095 (third Friday in January)

available continuously from the source system, we will designate the machine input as continuous. The source system only operates from 7:00 AM to 10:00 PM daily, Monday to Friday. The source system enjoys a maintenance window nightly from 10:00 PM to 7:00 AM and on weekends.

The business analyst has met with the customer marketing organization, and they have provided the expected and maximum number of marketing messages as a percentage of the total number of users. On a typical day, they will forward marketing messages to the system for 5% of the registered customer base. On a busy day, they will send messages to the online banking platform for 20% of the registered customer volume (as shown in Table 3.6).

Table 3.6 Example Business Input: Online Banking System (Marketing Messages)

Usage Attribute	Requirement
Machine Input	Customer marketing messages
Input Type	Continuous
Operations Window	7:00 AM to 10:00 PM, Monday to Friday
Typical Coarse Input	115,451
Maximum Coarse Input	461,807 (third Friday in January)
Busiest Interval	12:00 PM to 1:00 PM, Friday; 30% of heaviest day's business volumes

An important aspect of the usage model is the number of human users who will be active on the system. We have just finished a discussion in which we divided load between human and machine inputs. Consider a login scenario in which 30% of the peak daily login volume constitutes 692,712 login operations in a single hour. What does this really mean? Does it mean that a single person is serially logging in to the application 692,712 times? Or does it mean that 692,712 people are logging in to the application once? Or is it somewhere in between? Or does it even matter?

The purpose of a usage model is to accurately reflect the expected production usage of your system. The usage model will drive the load scenarios that you use for testing most of the non-functional requirements for the system. In reality, for many systems the number of users executing business operations is just as important as the number of operations that are executed. For stateful systems, and any system requiring authentication is stateful to some extent, the number of active concurrent users is highly meaningful to the accuracy of the test. Many systems maintain state information as part of a user session. Each concurrent user will have a corresponding user session. The true performance characteristics of the system can only be measured if we are executing business operations with a representative number of concurrent users.

Let's introduce the notion of user volumes as an additional attribute of our usage model (as shown in Table 3.7). The business is asked to provide a statistical view of this attribute for the busiest day of the year over a 24-hour period.

As we will see, user volumes are an important attribute when we go to apply load to the system to achieve the target rate of business operations.

Table 3.7   User Volumes

Usage Attribute	Statistics
Maximum Concurrent Users	5,100
Minimum Concurrent Users	300
Average Concurrent Users	1,800
Busiest One- Hour Interval	12:00 PM to 1:00 PM, Friday

Expressing Load Scenarios

Once you have quantified the usage of your software system, you will need to design scenarios that emulate the actual usage of the system in order to conduct testing. We call these *load scenarios*. The objective of these scenarios is to achieve a load profile that accurately reflects the expected usage of the system. In designing load scenarios, the subtleties of human usage become important. If a load scenario describes the submission of an online request to a system, the number of validation errors that a typical user is expected to encounter is a meaningful aspect of the scenario. The load scenarios must achieve the target number of coarse inputs without over- or underemphasizing any aspect of the system behavior.

When defining functional requirements, a common practice is to document *use cases* to express the functional behavior of the system. Use cases describe a comprehensive interaction between *actors* and the *system*, and they typically specify every aspect of the system functionality. The non-functional equivalent of use cases are load scenarios. Load scenarios as defined in business usage are the business analyst's estimation of how coarse inputs are generated in the system. In many cases, load scenarios will be equivalent to the normal flow for use cases defined in the functional use case requirements.

In documenting load scenarios, it is acceptable to refer to use cases in the functional requirements, supplementing the use case with additional information where required. Load scenarios are not a comprehensive description of system capabilities, but they are an important component of the non-functional business usage.

Load scenario definitions are required for both human and machine inputs. The following elements are required for each load scenario of either type:

Human Inputs

■ Which coarse input(s) are achieved in this load scenario?

- What variety of data/input is critical to this load scenario?
- How much time does it take on average to input the data (also referred to as "think time")?
- What explicit steps are required to emulate this load scenario?

Let's continue our example of an online banking application. A typical load scenario can be found in Table 3.8.

The number of load scenarios is defined in response to the following considerations:

- How many unique scenarios are required to achieve the total number of coarse inputs?
- Are specific scenarios required to certify specific performance requirements?
- What are the cost and budget constraints that will impact the number of load scenarios that are devised?

Table 3.8 Example Load Scenario: Online Banking System

Parameter	Setting
Coarse Inputs	**Login:** Balance inquiry Bill payment
User Classes	**Customers:** • personal • business
Explicit Steps	**Login:** • 10% of users have one failed password attempt Select primary account for balance inquiry Select bill payment: • 20% of users initiate a bill payment for amount varying between $50 and $200 from primary account • 20% of users initiate a bill payment for amount varying between $50 and $200 from primary account •10% of users cancel operation without making a bill payment **Logout:** • 50% of users abandon session • 50% of users actually logout

Albert Einstein is renowned for the statement that "everything should be made as simple as possible, but no simpler." This very much applies to the specification of load senarios. The objective is to provide enough detail to accurately model the system, but detail for the sake of detail offers diminishing returns. Too much detail will be difficult to implement and maintain. At the same time, an oversimplified view of your system will increase the likelihood of real problems going undetected.

In many situations, performance requirements may require the specification of additional load scenarios. We will discuss this topic in more detail later in this chapter.

As you increase the number and complexity of load scenarios in your usage model, you will also increase your costs. When you are generating the load profile, it is preferable to describe the business usage in as much detail as possible. When it comes time to test, you will usually take a practical view of your load scenarios and adjust them. We will discuss this activity further when we describe testing approaches in Chapters 6 and 7.

Non-Functional Requirements

An Important Clarification

We have been using the term *non-functional* as an adjective since the first chapter of this book. On the topic of requirements, there is an important clarification that we must make. For many people, there is a perception that non-functional requirements are *technical* requirements. However, this is a misleading and inaccurate perspective.

Non-functional requirements are still *business* requirements. Like any other set of requirements, the technology team will interpret and translate non-functional requirements into a concrete implementation. Non-functional requirements need to be defined by a business analyst as part of the same exercise as functional requirements. We will illustrate the distinction between good and bad non-functional requirements with some examples. The following requirements may sound appealing, but are out of context in a non-functional requirements document.

1. The system must verify the integrity of all file outputs that are generated for customers by inspecting the first and last record in the file.
2. The system must log the username and time for each user login to the system to a file.
3. All application code must include in-line documentation for support purposes.
4. Performance testing must be conducted for a sustained period of at least eight hours at 200% peak load.

Each of these requirements is trying to express a valid consideration in the design and implementation of a system. Let's look at each of these requirements in detail to understand how they are flawed.

The first requirement sounds appropriate; verifying the integrity of files that will be transmitted to customers sounds entirely reasonable. The problem with this requirement is that it is overspecified: this requirement expresses a business concern *and* a technical recommendation. Our statement has been that non-functional requirements are business requirements and we need to adhere to that here. By instructing the technical team to meet the requirement in an overly restrictive way, the business is actually attempting to design the system. Software design is best left to the development and design teams who have training and experience in this area. Overspecified requirements are restrictive and will often lead to inferior systems. This requirement is more appropriately phrased as, *All system outputs must be verified for compliance with agreed upon output formats before transmission to customers.* This wording is superior because it allows the technical team to select the most appropriate means of verification. We have also recast the requirement to reference *system outputs* rather than *files*. This is a more inclusive requirement that better reflects the business concern.

The second requirement in this example is also overly restrictive. It is actually a functional requirement for audit purposes that is better aligned with the underlying business concern when it is reworded as, *The system must record audit information for every user authenticating to the system.* In this new wording, the technology team can implement an audit feature using a database that is more secure and offers more flexibility with respect to reporting.

The third requirement in this example makes a reference to the level and type of documentation that is required for the solution. Again, the business requirement is that the solution be documented so that it can be efficiently maintained. Depending on the platform, in-line documentation may or may not be appropriate; consequently it is better to leave this type of decision to the implementation team.

Many organizations maintain enterprise-wide development and coding standards. These types of standards typically describe coding best practices, documentation standards, and other maintainability concerns. There is tremendous business value to organizations that create common standards. Such standards ensure consistent quality and readability across different systems. Among other benefits, standards make it easier for employees to learn and support new applications when they are based on practices with which they are already familiar. Improvements to the wording of the example might be expressed as either *All aspects of the solution must adhere to the company's enterprise development and coding standards* or in the absence of an existing standard, *Technical documentation must accompany the solution sufficient for the application to be supported.*

The last requirement in our example is inappropriate because it does not describe the end state of the solution itself, but the means by which specific non-functional requirements are to be verified. As we will see in Chapter 6, the test strategy and plan is the appropriate place for describing the detailed test case composition. Adding this type of requirement to your scope will convolute the intent of your requirements. Furthermore, stakeholders who sign off on non-functional requirements are seldom in a position to evaluate your detailed test strategy. For this part of the example, our recommendation is to omit the requirement completely.

As you can see, there is a temptation to make non-functional requirements a broad, all-encompassing container for requirements that don't seem to fit anywhere else. The scope of non-functional requirements should be limited to true business requirements that reflect genuine performance, operability, and availability concerns. It is not efficient to communicate other topics like testing, delivery process, or technical design in what is supposed to be a business requirements document. There are more appropriate vehicles for this content such as test strategies, project charters, and technical design documents in which business participants can be asked to provide sign-off if required.

Performance Requirements

Performance requirements are usually the most prominent type of non-functional requirement in a software implementation. Users readily understand that systems that perform slowly will keep them waiting. More than likely, users have firsthand experience with systems that perform badly and are anxious to avoid similar experiences with any new system.

Performance requirements specify what should happen and how long it should take. Describing this in a meaningful way is usually more difficult than it sounds. We usually refer to "how long it takes" as the *response time* and "what should happen" as a *transaction*. This type of requirement will vary greatly depending on the type of application.

For an animation or graphics-intensive application, performance requirements will usually be expressed in terms of the refresh rate of the screen. The human eye can distinguish 1,300 frames per second. In general, anything faster than this will be acceptable to end users. In this case, each frame refresh is considered to be a transaction.

For Internet-based applications, the screen refresh rate is typically based on the amount of time it takes for a server component to generate a new screen and send it over the network to the end user. Users are accustomed to Internet applications and a threshold of under two seconds is usually acceptable for screen refreshes for applications of this type. For this example, the time it takes to request and then fully render a Web page is considered to be a transaction.

If a system is responsible for generating a complex report, users may be comfortable waiting hours for the report to be available. The generation of the report in this example can be referred to as a *transaction*.

For transaction processing systems, requirements may be a function of service levels with external systems. For example, a system that brokers health insurance claims on behalf of insurers may be contracted to respond within one second in order to meet front-end user requirements on the insurer's administrative systems. The service of this request on behalf of the insurer is a transaction.

Despite the differences in these types of performance requirements, there are some unifying characteristics across each of them. First, a performance requirement must be statistically defined. By this we mean that the acceptable transaction response time must be expressed in terms of average, maximum, or percentile performance. The average is taken as the measured performance across all inputs in an interval. For most applications this is the most common type of performance requirement. Our online banking application may require that the average user login take an average of two seconds or less. If there are 2,000 logins in a day to the online banking application in one hour and the average response time is 1.2 seconds, then the system meets the requirement. This is simple enough.

Next, let's consider the worst-case or maximum accepted performance for the system. In some cases, users may specify a maximum acceptable response time. For the online banking application, the business sponsors may decide that under no circumstances should any screen response take longer than ten seconds. In some cases this requirement is driven by user experience, and in other cases this is a hard requirement imposed by other systems. For example, in our insurance adjudication example from the last paragraph, the insurer may impose a timeout of ten seconds on all requests to the system. A consequence of this is that any request that takes longer than ten seconds will mean that the requestor has stopped waiting for the response and has reported an error to the user.

For some systems, an average by itself is not a sufficiently strict requirement to ensure acceptable user experience. It is common for users to demand performance results based on a percentile. A requirement of this type states that 90% of all transactions must have a response time of three seconds or less. From your sponsor's perspective, this requirement ensures that 90% of their customers will never have to wait longer than three seconds for a transaction to complete.

We now look at example requirements for the online banking application (in Table 3.9). This is a retail customer-facing application, so performance is a critical factor for the business sponsors.

In general, it is not productive or recommended during the requirements phase to specify requirements for individual transactions based on your best guess at system performance. For applications where response times need to be assigned for individual transactions, it is preferable to create categories. See Table 3.10 for an example of such classifications.

Light transactions are transactions that are critical and expected to perform at the highest service level. *Medium* and *heavy* transactions are reserved for less frequent transactions or complex transactions where users are more willing to tolerate additional latency.

Table 3.9   Transactions

Transaction	Average	90th Percentile	Maximum
Login	2 seconds	3 seconds	5 seconds
Account Inquiry	1 second	3 seconds	5 seconds
Bill Payment	2 seconds	3 seconds	5 seconds
Funds Transfer	2 seconds	3 seconds	5 seconds

Table 3.10   Transaction Classifications

Transaction	Average	90th Percentile	Maximum
Light	1 second	2 seconds	5 seconds
Medium	2 seconds	3 seconds	7 seconds
Heavy	3 seconds	5 seconds	10 seconds

Using this approach, all transactions are classified as either light, medium, or heavy. This is easy to understand and avoids confusion during the testing and validation phase of the software development lifecycle.

In assigning transactions to categories, you must agree on the range of inputs for which these performance requirements will be met. From a user's perspective, viewing account details is the "same" type of request for every user. From a technology point of view, rendering account information may vary significantly depending on any one of the following factors:

■ The number of accounts that the customer possesses
■ The type of accounts that the customer possesses
■ The last time that the user accessed their account view
■ The type of customer (retail or business)

Before you decide that an account inquiry is of medium weight for all users, you may consult the technical team and determine that the weights shown in Table 3.11 are more appropriate.

Table 3.11   Classification Weights

Transaction	Classification
Log-in	Light
Account Inquiry: Fewer than Five Accounts	Light
Account Inquiry: Five Accounts or More	Medium
Bill Payment	Medium
Funds Transfer	Medium

Does this mean that we are done? No; we are missing a critical piece. Performance requirements are only meaningful in the context of *load*. A response time of one second may be met easily if only one person is using a system. Meeting the one-second requirement becomes much more difficult if there are hundreds or thousands of requestors accessing while attempting the same transaction simultaneously. Fortunately, we completed the business usage model for this application earlier in this chapter. Users will expect performance requirements to be met under all circumstances. Accordingly, we must select the most strenuous interval in the business usage and use that as the basis for our performance acceptance.

In the previous section, we identified the interval in the business usage as from 12:00 to 1:00 PM on the third Friday in January as the busiest interval. This means that we will test for our performance requirements using this load profile. In order to be more specific, we calculate a transaction rate for the load profile. The transaction rate can be expressed as transactions per minute or transactions per second depending on the volumes for your system.

The busiest interval for our banking application processes 3,400 bill payments in one hour. We can then calculate the transaction rate for bill payments as follows:

$$Transaction\ Rate = \frac{Transactions}{Interval} = \frac{3,400}{3600s} = 0.94TPS$$

We refer to the transaction rate for the busiest interval as the *peak transaction rate*. Assuming we conduct a similar exercise for each of the other transactions for which performance requirements are specified, our example requirements evolve as shown in Table 3.12.

Table 3.12 Target Transaction Rates

Transaction	Classification	Target Transaction Rate (in transactions per second)
Login	Light	1.06 TPS
Account Inquiry: Fewer than Five Accounts	Light	1.87 TPS
Account Inquiry: Five Accounts or More	Medium	0.30 TPS
Bill Payment	Medium	0.94 TPS
Funds Transfer	Medium	0.71 TPS

When combined with the load scenarios defined in the business usage, we are well positioned to prepare test cases and conduct performance acceptance for this application from a requirements perspective. We will see more of the testing challenge in Chapter 6 and 7.

Operability Requirements

Business users do not specify the majority of operability requirements. Not surprisingly, the stakeholders for most operability requirements are the operators of the system. These types of requirements take into consideration the ease, robustness, and overall availability requirements of the software solution.

Component Autonomy

Complex systems are often implemented as a set of dependent components. Systems may also have dependencies on external systems. Robust, highly available systems typically meet the following minimum requirements:

■ If an infrastructure component is unavailable, services provided by dependent components should only be impacted insofar as they depend on the unavailable component. If a Web-based portal application serves as a gateway to four independent subsystems, if one of the subsystems becomes unavailable, there should be no impact to the portal itself or a user's ability to access the other three subsystems.

■ If a component needs to be restarted, re-deployed, or otherwise taken out of service, it should be possible to reintroduce that component without having to restart, re-deploy, or alter any other components in the system. Consider the example of an enterprise service that provides securities pricing information to a number of applications at an investment firm. If the enterprise service is taken out of service and then reintroduced, there should be no need to restart any of the dependent applications.

Trace Logging

Problems that arise in production environments are often difficult to troubleshoot because processing can be distributed across many disparate systems. If different systems are responsible for different components, it is difficult for any one support organization to reproduce the problem. When an external system does not respond in an expected way, it is critical to be able to provide a log of the request and response from that system. The exchange of data between systems can be logged at the level of the database and/or the file system. In most cases, the performance trade-off of this logging is well worth the increased visibility that it provides. Systems that include good trace capability are easier to test and support. If performance must trump operability for your application, consider asking for a configurable switch that enables trace logging selectively for specific components. In this way, logging can be introduced when a problem is suspected or in (quality assurance) environments only.

Communicating Outages and Maintenance Windows

Software systems are expected to be available during their operations window. In the real world, applications do not always meet their service level agreement (SLA). It is to your advantage to define how the system should react when it is unavailable. For example, a Web-based application can be manually configured during an outage to present all users with an error page. This informs the user that the service provider knows there is an issue and is working in all haste to correct the problem.

If an unscheduled outage occurs, you will want to prevent users from using the system. If the system is failing, additional user load will usually make matters worse; it can also delay recovery of the system. There is also no guarantee that the system will process user requests in the same way a healthy system would. For some applications, this can have grave results. For machine interfaces to other systems, it is also important to evaluate whether interfaces should be similarly disabled during unscheduled outages. It is usually better to reject new requests than to accept them when there is a risk that they will not be processed. The appropriate behavior can only be determined in the context of the application.

A variation of this same capability will be required when the system is being upgraded and/or maintained. In this case, the communication should tell the user when the system will once again become available.

Exception Logging

From a requirements point of view, every system should log exceptions with enough detail that the cause of the failure can be investigated and understood by technical resources. Error logging can be a critical aspect of production monitoring for the system. It is also desirable for the error to be presented to the user in a way that can be tied to additional technical logging at the level of the file system. We will look at exception handling and logging in more detail in Chapter 4.

Failover

Availability is achieved by increasing quality and redundancy of software and infrastructure components in your system. In the real world, even the best quality hardware will fail, and it is critical that you discuss the implications of such failure with your users. In the event of a failover, is it sufficient that service is still available for the initiation of new requests? Or is there a more stringent requirement for in-flight requests to be processed successfully. Is it sufficient for the request to be processed when the failed component is recovered, or does a redundant component need to recognize the failure and stand in to continue processing?

The behavior during a failover will depend on the criticality of your system and the sensitivity of the users that are using it. Consider the example of an end user who must complete a multi-screen form process that required input of over 200 fields. If a system component fails when the user is inputting the 199th field, is it acceptable for the user to have to start the process over? Depending on the system, there will be a cost to implementing failover for this scenario and it may or may not be warranted for your application. Before stipulating failover requirements, it is recommended that you consult with the technologists who will be designing the system. It is quite likely that these types of requirements were already factors in the infrastructure and software decisions that were made in the planning phase of the project. If the target platform for your system does not provide support for failover, then it is unwise to allow your users to specify requirements for this feature.

Fault Tolerance

Fault Tolerance requirements describe what the system should do when it encounters a failure. In many cases, these requirements should be described as alternative flows in your use case documentation.

Availability Requirements

Availability is typically expressed as a percentage of time that the system is expected to be available during the operations window. It is usually documented as a critical metric in the SLA with the user community. Availability is a function of application inputs, application robustness, and infrastructure availability. If your magnificently designed application runs on servers that are only available 80% of the time, then your application will be available, at best, 80% of the time. Conversely, you can invest in the most redundant, fail-safe hardware the market has to offer, but if your application is fragile you will not meet your availability targets.

Like so many things, quality comes at a price. As you invest in both infrastructure and software quality, you will asymptotically approach 100% availability. However, no seasoned engineer will ever expect or promise 100% availability. At best, the "five nines" are touted as the highest possible availability: a system at this level is available 99.999% of the time. For a 24-hour application that operates 365 days a year, this means that the application is meeting its SLA if it experiences *less than* 5.256 seconds of unscheduled downtime in a year. There are very few applications that require this level of availability, and you should speak candidly with your user community to discuss the cost/benefit trade-offs associated with availability at this level. In later chapters, we will look at infrastructure, software, and test-case design to support availability requirements. Table 3.13 illustrates typical availability for common system profiles.

Archive Requirements

End users rely on business systems to access information, and depending on the nature of the business, there will be a requirement for how long that data must be accessible to them. Some data must be available for the life of the software system. As an example, most businesses require customer profile information to persist forever. Alternately, some business data has a more short-lived requirement. *Transactional data* is data that accumulates steadily over the life of the system; it is required over the course of the business transaction and may be required for reporting purposes in the future. In general, transactional data is transient in nature and there is no requirement for business users to have access to it historically. As data accumulates in the system, this introduces ongoing storage costs and can degrade performance over time. As a result, it is important for non-functional requirements

Table 3.13 Service Availability and Typical Applications

Availability	Description	Examples
99.999%	Full hardware and software redundancy for all system components. Full-time dedicated monitoring and application support infrastructure. Support response time is 15 minutes or less for all incidents.	Securities trading systems. High availability customer self-service portal.
99.9%	Hardware and software redundancy for most system components. Full-time dedicated monitoring and application support infrastructure. Support response time is 15 minutes or less for all incidents.	Midrange availability customer self-service portal.
98%	Hardware and software redundancy for some system components. Unattended monitoring and application support infrastructure. Support response time is 30 minutes or less for all incidents.	Enterprise back-office operations platform.
95%	Full hardware and software redundancy for some system components. Unattended monitoring and application support infrastructure. Support response time is 4 hours or less for all incidents.	Noncritical business intelligence reporting platform.

Table 3.14 Archiving Requirements

Data	Accessible through the Application	Archived to Long-Term Storage
Supplier Profile Database	Indefinitely	After 1 year
Invoice Database	For 13 months	After 7 years
Audit Log	For 13 months	After 3 years
Materials Database	Indefinitely	After 1 year

to specify the retention period for the different types of data in the system. An example set of retention requirements is provided in Table 3.14.

In this example, these archive requirements are for a procurement system used by a manufacturer. From a business perspective, there are different retention periods for different types of business data. The supplier database is a permanent record of all organizations that supply the manufacturer with materials.

Summary

In this chapter we've seen that the definition of non-functional requirements encompasses many different topics spanning performance, operability, availability, and expected business usage. We've also seen that different projects have different needs in terms of the scope and depth of non-functional requirements. Pairing an experienced business analyst with a technical resource is the recommended staffing approach during requirements formulation. As we move forward, we will next look at how non-functional considerations influence software design.

Chapter 4

Designing for Operability

In the previous chapters we examined the initial phases of the software development lifecycle—namely (1) the planning phase; and (2) the requirements phase. In this chapter we turn our attention to software design, which traditionally follows the first two phases, and is often driven out subsequent to software architecture within the same high-level phase.

Software design has been raised to the level of high art by many who practice it. Good software design accomplishes many things including quality, flexibility, extensibility, and development efficiency, many of which are non-functional requirements or characteristic of these.

Over the years, there have been major enhancements in the process and approach to software design. Notable milestones include object-oriented and pattern-based design. Pattern-based design was introduced to a wide audience by the famous "gang of four"—authors Erich Gamma, Richard Helm, Ralph Johnson, and John M. Vlissides—in their book *Design Patterns: Elements of Reusable Object-Oriented Software.*

Design patterns are powerful because they are language-independent approaches that apply to recurring scenarios in software development. Many design patterns are so indoctrinated with developers they expect to see common patterns in each others' code. Software is easier to understand when it has been designed using a mutually understood set of concepts and terminology.

In this chapter we make our own contributions to the growing catalog of available design patterns. We will illustrate our patterns using current technologies and demonstrate how they are useful in achieving non-functional objectives. If you are a developer, you may find these techniques useful in writing quality software. If you are a manager or architect, you may find that these examples help you to challenge your development team to write better and more defensive code.

Error Categorization

As part of any software design activity, you should agree on standard error severities. Too often this decision is left until late in the implementation, after individual developers have agreed on an assortment of error severities, each having their own unique understanding of what this means.

Every project has its own unique needs, but the authors of this book have found the following categorizations (shown in Table 4.1) to be useful and widely adopted.

Table 4.1   Widely Used Error Severities

Error Severity	Context	Implication
Fatal	A core component, service, or resource is failing. Developers should assign this error level to events that are expected to impact an entire application or suite of functionality.	Indicates service is down and likely not available. Immediate and urgent resolution is required.
Error	An individual transaction or unit of work has failed for an unexpected reason. Error events may occur as a result of a fatal event in the infrastructure in which case a single fatal event will correlate to many error events.	In general, error events will not trigger immediate investigation by support. However, a high frequency of independent error events may be escalated into a fatal event by the monitoring infrastructure.
Warn	A configured threshold or assertion has been reached and a problem may be imminent.	Warning events do not reliably reach the attention of operations but are useful in development and QA (quality assurance) environments.
Info	An event occurred in the system that although not critical to the system warrants informational output. It may, for example, be useful to log the attempt of someone to transfer an amount of money larger than what they are allowed to transfer. If this pattern is found repetitively in the logs this may warrant investigation.	Informational messages are not meant for operations but can be used by log scrapers to detect unexpected usage patterns or by the support team to determine the cause of a problem.

Many people may recognize these severity levels as standard for many vendor software products and source-code frameworks. What is not standard is the meaning and implication of each of these error severities. As we will see in a later chapter in this book (Chapter 9), standardization of error types is especially important from a monitoring and operations point of view.

Design Patterns

One of the candidates for this book's title was *Designing Software that Breaks Properly*. Despite our fondness for this title, we decided on a broader one that reflected the full scope of the book. Nonetheless, this title is highly appropriate to the content in this chapter. The basis for operability design patterns is that they anticipate and design for problems. When problems happen, these design patterns ensure that the software breaks in a predictable and acceptable way.

Retry for Fault Tolerance

When an error condition is detected, you have two reasonable choices as a developer: you can return an error to an end user or you can log an error to an interface that is being monitored. Developers sometimes opt for a third choice: ignore the error or log an obtuse error message. On rushed implementations that lack code review procedures, this undesirable third choice can become very popular.

When an error occurs it is important for system operators to be notified in near-real time so that appropriate action can be taken. Once someone has been alerted, that person can investigate the health of the infrastructure, inquire on the health of third-party systems and validate the state of the application itself. However, this process is expensive. The person who must investigate an error may need to involve numerous other people to inspect resource health. The operator may need to contact third parties to confirm availability of other systems.

In the end, a series of communications may result (as shown in Figure 4.1). All of these communications may involve numerous people and multiple iterations. The point we are trying to make is that it is *expensive and time-consuming to respond to application errors*. This reality is not always fully appreciated during software design and development.

An obvious perspective on this scenario would be to correct the defect that caused the error event in the first place. Unfortunately, this perspective will only apply to a subset of scenarios. Consider an example in which a transaction processing system is asynchronously posting a message to a third-party system. It is possible that the software cannot post the message because of a system defect that causes the system to fail for specific message contents. It is also possible that the software cannot post the message because the third-party system is unavailable. In

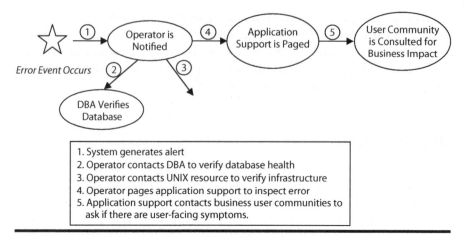

1. System generates alert
2. Operator contacts DBA to verify database health
3. Operator contacts UNIX resource to verify infrastructure
4. Operator pages application support to inspect error
5. Application support contacts business user communities to ask if there are user-facing symptoms.

Figure 4.1   Operations response to an application alert.

this case, there is no opportunity to fix a defect and avoid the problem, but there is an opportunity to introduce a feature.

Retry capability is not a novel or new concept. Most network protocols use retry extensively when sending data over a physical network. If an acknowledgment is not received within a specified time threshold, the message is re-sent until a configured maximum number of send attempts. A slow network is often a network that is experiencing frequent packet loss, requiring multiple send attempts for a good portion of the packets. Such a network is *slow* but *working*, which most users will prefer to a network that is not working at all.

This concept is also appropriate for many software scenarios, also, but in some cases will require more effort on the part of the software developer. Wherever your application initiates complex, asynchronous processing, it is worthwhile to consider a retry capability as part of the solution. The most obvious example is when your system is completing work in tandem with a third-party system. In such a scenario, you need to consider the following before you embark on such a scheme:

1. **Is the third-party system capable of processing duplicate requests?** If you are attempting to send the same request multiple times, you are assuming a risk that the destination system will receive the message more than once. Depending on the system, this may entail duplicate processing, which usually has adverse business consequences. For systems that cannot manage duplicate submissions, there may be an opportunity to selectively retry processing depending on the error type that is detected. If the error is clearly part of the communication to the external system (e.g., obtaining or testing a connection) then you may want to permit retries for errors of this type only.

2. **Is your operations window large enough to allow for multiple retry attempts?** What are the business requirements for processing? If the business is expecting you to process the message within one minute or less, it may not

be helpful to retry delivery of the message. In fact, the business may expect the message to be discarded as its contents will expire if it is not delivered within this window. On the other hand, if the business is willing to wait 48 hours for processing to complete, then your scenario is a good candidate for retry processing.

Assuming that your scenario is appropriate for retry processing, you will need to answer the following questions.

1. **What time interval makes sense between retry attempts?** This is a decision with two opposing factors. The smaller the retry interval, the more likely you are to process successfully with a minimum level of delay. However, if your system is processing high volumes, you may flood the system to which you are posting. If the system is not acknowledging replies or appears to be unavailable, you may be compounding its difficulties by resending at a high frequency.
2. **For how long should you retry?** Business requirements will factor heavily in choosing this setting. The retry window should be as long as your users can tolerate without experiencing business impact *minus* some contingency during which you can manually process if the retry capability is not effective. If a business user is expecting a transaction to be processed in no longer than 48 hours, and the message is still not processed after 24 hours, it is likely that you need to escalate and manually intervene.

We illustrate this thinking with the following equation, which indicates that the allowable retry period should be the sum of the maximum system recovery and expected manual recovery.

$$\text{Time}_{\text{Retry Period}} = \text{Time}_{\text{Maximum System Recovery}} + \text{Time}_{\text{Manual Recovery}}$$

It is also worth mentioning that these settings should be configurable and externalized from your application code. Once your system is in use, you may decide to fine-tune these settings to provide a higher level of service. You may in fact need to turn the retry capability off completely if you discover that a third-party destination system cannot handle duplicate requests, as originally believed.

Once you have determined the conceptual retry characteristics for your system, conceptually you will need to implement a mechanism (as shown in Figure 4.2). Figure 4.2 shows that there is a clear separation between the source application, the fulfillment service with retry, and the third-party service.

If the invoking application requires an immediate initial response, then the queuing service can be implemented to invoke the fulfillment service directly. In this case, the queuing service would log the request to the queue as completed. As we will see later in this chapter, it is often important to have a trace of request/response messages for troubleshooting and reporting purposes.

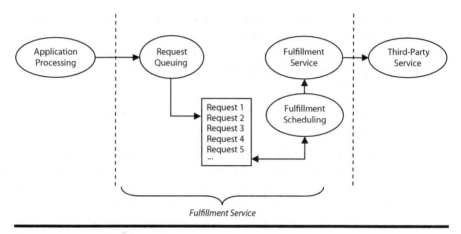

Figure 4.2   Fulfillment services.

If at any point the retry mechanism proves not to work as expected, it can be disabled by configuring the retry attempts to zero.

An important characteristic of this solution is that the queue is transparent and can be viewed by an application support resource. System transparency is a critical support characteristic for any system that is maintainable. At any point, a technical resource should be able to answer the following questions:

1. How many requests are pending?
2. What is the oldest pending request?
3. When was the last time a request was successfully fulfilled?
4. When was the last failed fulfillment request?

Each of these questions adds valuable insight to any troubleshooting effort. In the solution we have presented, a database implementation of the request queue would answer each of these questions.

Ensuring transparency of the request queue also creates opportunities for monitoring. You may decide that a properly functioning system should never have more than 50 items in the queue. You could then choose to introduce a monitoring mechanism that alerts operations whenever the pending items count exceeds 50 items.

Software Fuses

Most people are familiar with the concept of a fuse. When a threshold or error condition is reached, the fuse blows and halts processing. This same concept is applicable in a software environment. A familiar example in the software realm is the user-account lockout. As a security feature, many software systems only allow a finite number of authentication attempts before "locking" the account. No further authentication attempts are permitted until the account is unlocked by an administrator.

To illustrate this concept further, let's look at the example of a payment system that charges credit cards on a monthly basis for accumulated usage fees by users. This function occurs on a scheduled basis once per month and may process up to 25,000 individual user accounts. Credit card providers such as VISA typically charge on a per-transaction basis. VISA will assert its fee whether the transaction is successful or not.

The payment job first calculates the amount owed for each user and then queues the requests for payment authorization and settlement. Once the job begins settlement transactions on individual credit cards, it will proceed serially until all of the records have been processed.

In this example, we consider two types of failures. A *system exception* is an unrecoverable error affecting software resources complicit in the processing. An *application exception* is more likely to affect processing of an individual transaction. Because credit card processing results in actual customer charges, sensitivity is required during processing. The following thresholds are determined:

- **System Exception Handling:** If a single system exception is thrown processing will be stopped.
- **Application Exception Handling:** During serial processing, if the application encounters more than 25 consecutive application exceptions, a system exception will be raised and processing will stop.

Since there is a real possibility that this job will halt processing, it is critical that the software implementation conform as follows:

1. Return an error code and/or generate a fatal event for monitoring.
2. Ensure the system is in a state such that the job can be rerun without risk of duplicated or partial processing. Barring the possibility to have the system in a consistent state, you will need to provide a mechanism to compensate for the system's inconsistent state before or after resuming the job.
3. Ensure that the system has generated sufficient output that a technical support resource can reliably determine which records have been processed and which records have not.

Software Valves

When a system is experiencing errors, a typical reaction is to stop all processing until the problem is understood. Through communication and restriction of user access, you may be able to prevent human users from creating inputs to your system.

However, if your system participates in interactions with external systems, shutting down access may be difficult unless it has been designed into your application.

In some cases, you may be able to shut off inputs to your system by disabling components in the infrastructure. For example, a Web-based application might be disabled by bringing down the content switch through which incoming hypertext transfer protocol (HTTP) requests are routed. For asynchronous message-based systems you may be able to prevent external systems from posting messages to your application's input queues, but how will these applications react when their submissions are denied?

Another option is to bring your entire system down. The disadvantage in this approach is that it may deny service to healthy functionality in your application. This is also an abrupt way to deny service to applications that may depend on your system as a service provider. If you are trying to diagnose a problem with your application, you are abandoning any opportunities you may have to observe the state of the system before it is shut down. Further, restarting the system may be time-consuming once you are confident that you have resolved the error condition.

From an operations standpoint, as an alternative to each of the previous suggestions it may be necessary to introduce a logical shut-off valve for your application. To illustrate this, we will consider an archiving solution for a transaction processing system. As systems age, transactional database tables accumulate records over time. Eventually these records may impact application performance; and even if performance was not an issue, these records consume storage, which has an associated cost.

After an agreed upon period of time, we may wish to archive old records off of the non-production system or delete them altogether. After consulting with the business stakeholders for the system, we reach an agreement that we are allowed to purge records once they are at least 24 months old. Archiving these records is nontrivial as each record type has a complex set of business rules that determine relationships to other records. We can only archive a record if it is 24 months old *and* each of its related records is 24 months old. Unfortunately, this can only be determined by programmatically navigating the relationships between record types to make a correct determination.

The software designers in this case have implemented a solution in two parts. The first part of the solution identifies transactions that meet the criteria for archival. The second part of the solution actually archives each transaction. Visually, the system looks like that shown in Figure 4.3.

Identifying the transactions for archival is accomplished using an appropriate set of database queries. The actual archival of each record is performed asynchronously on the other side of a message queue to ensure proper logging and transaction handling for each record.

In this solution we expect the first part of the archival process to be completed on a scheduled basis each weekend starting at 10:00 PM on Sunday evening. This part of the process is expected to take 15 minutes or less, while the archival of all

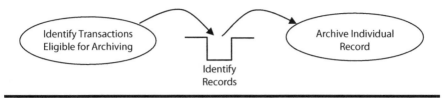

Figure 4.3   Record archiving system.

qualifying records is expected to take up to two hours for the largest forecasted weekly volume. However, our operations window requires the system to be available again the next morning at 7:00 AM. All archival must complete in the nine-hour window between 10:00 PM and 7:00 AM. If the system performs to specification, archiving should never last beyond 1:00 AM, but if there is one thing that this book has tried to impress upon you is that *should* is a word you need to remove from your vocabulary.

What if the system goes down at 11:00 PM, unexpectedly? What if database backups are scheduled during this window at some point in the future and the archival solution runs eight times slower? What if the forecasted business volumes are wrong, and the peak volumes are in fact much higher? What if the first part of the solution doesn't run successfully at 10:00 PM and a well-intentioned operator runs it at 6:00 AM? All of these hypothetical scenarios make this solution an ideal candidate for the introduction of a valve. We do not want archiving to run beyond the window allocated as it has an unknown impact on online usage of the system.

A software valve is introduced at the point of message consumption. A configuration table is introduced or extended to indicate whether archiving is allowed or disallowed for a given point in time. The first task in the archival process is to enable archiving. The process listening for archive record requests checks the archive-enabled flag prior to processing each record.

If the archive flag is enabled, it processes the record. If the archive flag is disabled, the listener discards the message. It is acceptable to discard the message because processing will be repeated the next time the selection job is run. It is not business critical that records be archived immediately after they qualify. In this way, we ensure that archive activities run only during the designated window (as shown in Figure 4.4).

As another example, let's revisit the retry pattern from the previous section. If the third-party service is down, our system will quickly enter a state in which there

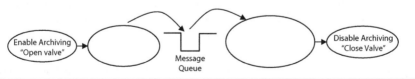

Figure 4.4   Example software valve: record archiving system.

are many outstanding requests, each of which is generating retry attempts. Assuming that the third-party is now aware that they have a problem, they may request that we stop sending additional requests until they have resolved the issue. Unfortunately, our fulfillment service schedules retry events on a per-record basis; we have no way of shutting this off unless it is designed into the solution. Obviously, a software valve is also appropriate for this scenario. Let's look at the revised solution with the addition of a valve (as shown in Figure 4.5).

If the valve is open, the request is queued again for another retry. In this case the number of retries is not incremented. Again, the software valve is nothing more than a configuration parameter that is dynamically checked by the fulfillment service before making each request.

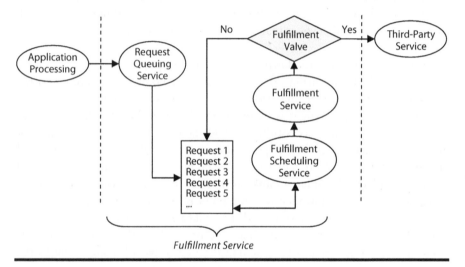

Figure 4.5   Fulfillment service and valves.

System Health Checks

A major deficiency in many software systems is that they are unable to tell you what is wrong with them when they malfunction. For each failed operation the system may create error outputs that can be helpful in diagnosing the problem but will not be helpful in replicating the exact system behavior under the problem condition. It would be an added benefit if we could poke and prod the system—much like a doctor attending a sick patient—and collect symptom information on our own schedule. There is no reason why applications cannot be built to meet this behavior; they just need to be designed this way in the first place. We refer to this capability as a *system health check*.

A system health check is a detailed series of tests that allow an operator to verify overall system health. This is often implemented as a single interface to the system that, when invoked, reports a detailed status on health. Typical attributes that are verified by a system health check include the following:

1. **Connectivity to interdependent systems:** If your system requires connectivity to other systems to function, it is worthwhile to verify and clearly report status on this connectivity. This type of health check will verify that the network connectivity and remote system availability are intact.
2. **Availability of major subsystems:** If your application follows a component architecture in which components can be deployed independently of one another, but are still dependent through loose coupling, it is worthwhile to verify that all subsystem services are installed and available.
3. **Availability of database and file system resources/connectivity:** Most complex software systems have a dependency on database or file-system resources. A good health check will verify these resources to ensure storage is available.
4. **Performance of critical operations:** If your application is time-sensitive, discrete health checks can always be implemented and timed to report the execution time for key subsystem operations.
5. **Statistical rollup of transaction-level errors:** If your system logs failed transactions to a persistent storage, you can report on the number of transaction-level errors that have occurred.

A system health check should be as expansive in its coverage as possible. You should not feel limited to the example diagnostics that we have listed in this chapter; rather, you should prepare a list of all resources and dependencies that your application requires to function correctly. For each item on your list you should consider the introduction of a discrete health check.

Health checks can be bundled with your application or they can be implemented as stand-alone processes or scripts that are deployed to the same platform. The advantage of a stand-alone health check is that its availability is not dependent on the availability of your system. However, a stand-alone health check will not be able to report on the health of application resources with the same accuracy and granularity as a health check that is actually embedded in your system. If your system health check is part of your application, there is the possibility that the health check will not be available if it depends on an application resource that is not available. A menu-based health check that allows a technician to select individual health checks for execution is a valuable approach to mitigating this risk, but requires more design and development effort.

The Characteristics of a Robust System

A robust system exhibits characteristics that allow it to self-diagnose and ask for assistance so that the system can remain functional and operational against a variety of different types of impacts. These characteristics are described in this section.

Simple Is Better

Intuitively, most people would agree that the simpler something is, the less likely it is to break. Generally speaking, this is true; the probability of failure is the sum of the component probabilities of failure in a system. Richard Manicom, the executive responsible for the Canadian government's federal tax processing systems through most of the 1990's, once articulated a valid point to the authors with this anecdote. Consider the scenario of a twin-engine aircraft flying across the Atlantic Ocean in which you are a passenger. Do you feel safer because there is a redundant engine in the plane? What if you were told that the likelihood of an engine failure is *twice* as likely for a single engine plane? In order for this to make you feel safer, you must have confidence in the ability of the plane and its pilot to recover from an engine failure. In other words, you are accepting additional complexity in the system and trusting that it will improve the overall reliability of the aircraft. The relative safety of single vs. multi-engine aircraft has been a topic of ongoing debate in the aviation industry since the 1960's. Dick Collins was the first to point out that statistically, multi-engine aircraft are involved in more fatal plane crashes than single engine planes in Flying Magazine. This statistic makes it tempting to conclude that single-engine planes must be safer, but an equitable comparison requires consideration of many more factors than we are able to discuss here.

Complexity is often a requirement in order to achieve the objectives of the system you are building. In the real world, there are many factors that can cause complexity to increase and as a systems designer, you must ensure that you are accepting complexity in your design for the right reasons. You may make well-intentioned choices in your design that are meant to improve operability or availability, but if the complexity you introduce is not properly designed, tested and implemented, it may have the opposite effect from what you intend. As a general rule, you should strive for minimal, simple designs and accept complexity only when you have the means and the commitment to implement it properly.

Isolation

Many large organizations support hundreds of different information systems. In an effort to control costs, businesses are increasingly adopting strategies to operate multiple applications on shared hardware. This is often referred to as a shared services model and it can be a cost-effective way to manage infrastructure costs. A shared services model allows an enterprise to make large, bulk purchases in infrastructure and then distribute this cost amongst different applications and lines of business. Managing your infrastructure as a shared service also creates opportunities to simplify and streamline your support organization. However, these attractive cost-savings often come with a hidden cost. If you are implementing multiple applications on a shared hardware platform, you are exposing yourself to the potential for undesirable interactions between applications. For example, if your production applications are deployed such that they all rely on a single network path, you are accepting the risk that a single misbehaving application could impact all of your production applications. As a general rule, you should strive for dedicated infrastructure for applications that require high availability. Applications that are isolated from interactions with other systems will be simpler to operate, more straightforward to troubleshoot and will enjoy higher availability.

Application Logging

Historically, developers have had two means of understanding the runtime behavior of their applications. They can look inside the application while it is running, or they can rely on the outputs the application creates while it is running. The former is usually referred to as *runtime debugging* or *application profiling*. The latter is referred to as *application logging*.

Runtime debuggers for many software platforms are sophisticated and incredibly useful. Debuggers allow the developer to run the program line by line, inspecting and changing variable values and influencing the runtime behavior to understand the program. Debuggers tend to be intrusive in that the software must run in a special container or allow the debugger to connect to the software itself on a specified interface. In production environments, it is usually not feasible to run the application in a mode that permits debugging. Debugging is usually a single-threaded activity and may seriously impact the performance/availability of your system.

Application logging is non-intrusive; it is compiled into the code and is capable of creating output during the normal execution of the system. Good application logging is a critical element of any maintainable software solution. Time and time again the authors of this book have seen good return on investment in development, QA (quality assurance), and production for application logs. The following guidelines have proven to be effective.

1. **Ensure your log level is dynamically configurable:** Many modern programming platforms have logging frameworks available that allow you to dynamically toggle logging on and off or change the log level. Log4j for the Java platforms is perhaps the most pervasive example.

2. **More is better:** In general, the operations benefit of application logging far outweighs any performance penalty. This is true assuming you avoid unnec-

essary string concatenation in message formulation unless the message is actually being logged.

3. **Debug logging:** This refers to log statements that provide a running commentary of the program execution. Developers frequently introduce debug logging as part of their own programming efforts. The authors suggest that you institutionalize debug logging as part of the development deliverable. Tell developers in advance that obtuse debug messages that are meaningful only to them will not be acceptable in their code. Debug logging is a mandatory requirement in the code that is delivered.

4. **Performance logging:** Instrumentation for performance can be a critical component for some applications. Because logging is often the least intrusive way to observe a system, performance logging can be your best bet for resolving difficult application performance issues.

5. **Trace logging:** In the operability requirements discussion in Chapter 3, we introduced the concept of trace logging. The authors recommend that all interfaces with external systems support a trace log that captures all input/output messages. The trace log should be independent of any other application log. If it is practical for the number of external interfaces you support, we recommend an individual trace file for each physical interface.

When new software systems are launched, they are usually afflicted by at least one of the following two problems:

1. **Insufficient and/or obtuse error logging:** Logging good error messages is a topic we will discuss in the next section of this chapter.

2. **Gratuitous logging.** Messages are frequently logged at the wrong severity level. Often, this is not caught until the system is in or near production. During test cycles, cluttered application logs are often attributed to open defects. It is also common for developers to ask that the QA environment run with debug logging enabled. If debug is enabled, it is harder to spot debug messages that are mistakenly being logged as errors.

In order to mitigate the problems described above, we recommend two courses of action:

1. The development team should designate an individual to be responsible for monitoring the application logs in non-production environments. This resource should raise defects against log messages that are badly formed, incomplete or have a mistaken severity.

2. At least during the final user acceptance test cycles, you should ensure that you are running the application with the same log levels configured as you expect in production. When defects are raised, the development team should ensure error logging is as expected as part of the defect fix itself. The development resource mentioned above should closely scrutinize application logs during these cycles.

Application logging, like so many topics in this book, is usually an afterthought in the implementation of most software systems. If you institutionalize logging best practices and set clear expectations with your development team, you will see the returns in support and operations activities down the road.

Transparency: Visibility into System State

As we will see later, troubleshooting a defect in a QA cycle or resolving an urgent production issue starts with information gathering. The choices you make during the design phase can impact the information you have available when you need to solve a problem.

At this point, we'd like to highlight an antipattern that can cause serious grief for any software system. Storing and transmitting data in a binary format is sometimes a requirement, not an option; however, where there is flexibility the authors strongly encourage you to exchange messages between systems in clear text.

XML has been a widely successful and adopted technology largely because it is text-based and transparent. Developers can inspect an XML document and understand it. XML is often self-describing when the attributes are given meaningful names. Consider the following login request message in three possible formats:

1. XML Format

```
<?xml version="1.0" encoding="ISO-8859-1" ?>
<login-request>
   <username>Tove</username>
   <password>jgd0s75h540hr03hnfep9srhf934</password>
   <encryption>PROV_RSA_SIG</encryption>
   <timestamp>09:11:06 Jul 12, 2006</timestamp>
</login-request>
```

2. The Delimited Format

```
Tove|jgd0s75h540hr03hnfep9srhf934|PROV_RSA_SIG|09:11:06 Jul 12, 2006
```

3. Binary

```
<not-printable-characters>
```

To a developer, the advantages of clear-text XML-based messaging require no further elaboration.

It can sometimes be tempting to store data in binary format. Java object serialization makes it easy to store data in a single database column. From a programmer's perspective, the data is structured because it can be marshaled back into the original Java object. In this case, the programmer does not need to maintain a matching database layout for the coded object. If an additional attribute is required, the new object type is serialized back into the table with no database changes required.

Though tempting, there are two serious drawbacks to this approach that make this type of design counterproductive.

1. **Visibility:** Once you have stored data in a binary format, you relinquish all hope of querying/reporting on this data once it is in storage. The only means to access it is through the code that serialized it into the database. When an end user calls to report an issue with a specific database record, it will be inconvenient to say the least to look at specific attributes of the serialized object.

2. **Compatibility:** If you are relying on your platform's native capabilities for marshaling/unmarshaling serialized objects, you must ensure that changes to the software object remain backwards compatible with data that was previously serialized with the earlier code. This is error prone, and requires that you test with production data in order to be certain you are not introducing a problem.

Except in very unusual circumstances, the authors of this book recommend that you avoid binary transmission between systems and storage of data. In this way, you achieve the architectural advantage of clear separation between your chosen software platform and your data model. If you decide to rewrite your application for a different platform, you are more likely to preserve the data model intact.

Traceability and Reconciliation

Traceability and reconciliation enable the location of data. Systems with good traceability allow you to find a transaction quickly based on a variety of search criteria. Reconciliation efforts establish whether the number of inputs matches the number of outputs at key junctures in the system flow. We will discuss both traceability and reconciliation in more detail next.

To establish traceability in your system design, you need to find a way to link the business input to a transaction identifier that will be propagated throughout your system. In most cases, you will find it convenient to establish a system-generated identifier for each business request. The advantages of establishing a universal internal reference are as follows:

■ This request identifier can be displayed to users who can use this identifier to refer to their request in the event of problems.
■ This request identifier can be propagated into all data structures that contain data related to this request. It is convenient as a foreign key into all database tables that house related transaction data.

- All error and application logging should reference your system request identifier. This makes it easy to scan logs for all messages related to a specific request identifier.
- Where possible, your design should propagate this identifier to external systems in requests that your system makes. Again, when possible, you should ask that the external system include your request identifier in response messages.
- In fulfilling the business request, if your system must interface with systems that are not capable of maintaining a reference to your unique identifier, you will need to maintain a local mapping of your request to the transaction identifier that is used by the uncooperative external system.
- You should maintain state for all business requests using appropriate data structures. For example, if your processing requires you to make an asynchronous request to an external system, the request status should reflect that a request has been successfully made and that the system is awaiting a response. Again, the global request identifier should be at least part of a composite key to such a data structure.

If you adhere to transparent design for your data as discussed in the previous section, consistent use of a global request identifier will allow you to determine the state of a request and to extract any and all data related to that request. This is an indispensable ability when you are troubleshooting an incident on any system. Even if the information is not immediately useful to you in your investigation, it is critical that you be able to inform the business users of the exact status of their request. If the business users have accurate information, they can take steps to mitigate the impact of a lost request outside of your software system (although they will probably not be happy about it).

For highly traceable systems, designers will even go one notch further: not only will each request be traceable, as mentioned above, but the data model will also be structured so as to maintain a history of the changes made by various requests over time. In these systems each version of a data element is maintained separately or each change to a data element over time is maintained. The request identifier is appended to each revision of the data element together with the timestamp for the change.

Reconciliation is normally a batch activity with an objective to ensure that system state is correct based on the inputs that have been received up until that point. Consider the example of a client-server call center application in which customer service representatives (CSRs) are taking orders for telephone customers. Each order that is placed results in a database entry on the call center application server. Whenever an order is received, a separate subsystem reads the order and initiates a fulfillment process to the inventory and fulfillment system, which is hosted centrally for the organization.

This same fulfillment system services a number of channels including Web mail, regular mail, and a small number of brick-and-mortar offices. For this business, customer service is based on the successful initiation of a fulfillment order for every order that is taken at the call center. Both the fulfillment system and the call center application have been implemented by a highly conscientious technical team, but despite their best efforts, orders taken at the call center do not always translate into fulfillments. In order to mitigate this risk, the organization has initiated a nightly reconciliation process in which reports are generated from both the fulfillment and call center applications. If the number of orders taken does not match the number of fulfillment requests, the discrepancy is investigated. Since introducing the reconciliation reporting, the technical team has seen two distinct types of failures:

■ An order is placed in the call center system *that is never fulfilled.*
■ An order is placed in the call center system *and the order is fulfilled twice.*

The purpose of the reconciliation report was to monitor for the first type of failure; however, the technical team quickly realized that they had two problems on their hands. In some cases, the fulfillment system was generating duplicate orders. Customers were being sent (and potentially billed for) the same order twice. The reconciliation process not only informs the technical support team when orders do not equal fulfillment but also where the discrepancy lies. This system adheres to our advice on the topic of traceability. Not only is every order assigned a unique system-generated identifier, but this identifier is propagated to the fulfillment system.

When the reconciliation report does not match, it shows exactly which orders have been omitted or exactly which orders have been fulfilled twice. The support team can use the problematic order identifiers to interrogate the system for order status and correct the problem before the call center or the customer is even aware that there was a problem. Of course, each time an issue is identified in the reconciliation, the root cause for the discrepancy is investigated and a code fix is made to eliminate this scenario from ever happening again. In this case, the reconciliation is a part of the monitoring and continuous improvement strategy for the organization. The important design observation is that reconciliation approaches are not possible if the system is not designed in a transparent and traceable way.

Resume versus Abort

Your application will experience errors. If your design is sound and your test coverage is thorough, then hopefully errors will occur rarely. When an error occurs, the support team needs to be focused on two key actions: assigning root cause to the problem *and* resuming the failed business function. The stakeholders for your system tend to be more concerned with the latter. This part of the chapter will focus on recovering individual failures.

A common approach to managing exceptions is to strand the failed transaction and prompt the user to initiate a new transaction. This approach works provided the failed transaction does not leave the system in a state that blocks the second attempt. For example, if your system processes customer address changes and only allows a single address change per customer at one time, the failing address change would need to be invalidated manually by an operator or canceled by the users themselves. This level of processing is simple and adequate for many software systems.

The retry philosophy applies to scheduled jobs also. If a job is run once per day during off hours, if the job fails the operations staff needs clear direction on how to intervene, if at all. In the age of outsourcing and reducing costs, many organizations have adopted a model in which operations staff is not familiar with the application. In the spirit of "simple is better," a scheme that works well is to ensure that failed jobs can always be rerun without detriment to the system.

In more complex cases, you may have no choice but to resume the business transaction. Earlier in this chapter we looked at an example in which a retry capability was added to an interface between our system and an external dependency. Let's revisit this example and ask the question, What if the number of retries is exceeded for a large number of transactions between our system and the third-party restored service? In such a situation, it may be impractical or impossible for the business to input new transactions. In such a case, it is far more preferable for us to resume the transactions that are already in the system. Because we have adhered to the transparency guideline discussed earlier, we can readily report on the number of transactions that are in this state in our fulfillment queue. If the fulfillment scheduler is designed to poll the request queue and retry transactions that are below the retry threshold, we have an option to simply reset the number of retries on these records. Assuming such a design of the scheduler component, the retry solution meets three of our criteria for robust systems:

1. It attempts to do **automated recovery** through a configurable number of retries.
2. It is fully **transparent**. At any point in time, we can interrogate the number of transactions in each state.
3. It can be **resumed**. If the number of retries is exceeded, we can reset the system for all or a subset of transactions with a single database statement.

Exception Handling

An entire book could be written on the topic of exception handling. A core feature of any programming language is its native exception-handling capabilities. We would like to avoid a technology-specific discussion, so in this section we will define some general guidelines and then move on.

In our experience, the three most problematic and recurring themes for software systems are as follows.

1. Insufficient error checking in code.
2. Insufficient detail in error messages when they are logged.
3. No reliable way to correlate user events with logged exceptions.

We will now visit each of these topics in the context of another example. Our concern is how errors are handled by application code so this example will reference an example code fragment in the Java programming language. For we will consider the implementation of a business operation that calculates an insurance quote. In our example, the method *calculateQuote* takes an object of type *QuoteRequest* as its argument and then performs the required business operation, ultimately returning an object of type *QuoteResult*. The implementation of *calculateQuote* is shown below.

```
public QuoteResult calculateQuote(QuoteRequest qr) {
    QuoteResult quoteResult = new QuoteResult();
    String applicantName = rq.getApplicantName();
    Address applicantAddress = rq.getApplicantAddress();
    try {
        verifyAddress( applicantAddress.getLine1(),
            applicantAddress.getLine2(),
            applicantAddress.getCity(),
            applicantAddress.getState(),
            applicantAddress.getZip()
            );
    exception (AddressInvalidException aie) {
        logger.debug("Address Invalid");
        rethrow aie;
    }
    /*
    . . . other business logic to generate the quote
    */
    return quoteResult;
}
```

In this example, if the address attribute of the QuoteRequest object is not defined, this code will throw a runtime system exception. Because this exception is unchecked, it will throw this exception back to the caller, who may in turn rethrow it. In fact, it is entirely possible that this exception would be thrown all the way back to the end user's display:

```
Exception in thread "main" java.lang.NullPointerException
at com.auerbach.nfd.example.insurance.QuoteEngine (Unknown Source)
at com.auerbach.nfd.example.insurance.web.QuoteAction (Unknown Source)
```

One of the results of writing defensive code is that you get the appropriate error messages. This is the first problem with the application code in our example. There is no checking on the address attribute before dereferencing. As a result, a system exception is thrown and the opportunity is missed to log a much more meaningful exception. We could easily have avoided this by checking the address attribute as follows:

```
QuoteResult quoteResult = new QuoteResult();
String applicantName = rq.getApplicantName();
Address applicantAddress = rq.getApplicantAddress();
If {applicantAddress==null) {
    throw new InvalidQuoteRequest(quoteRequest);
}
```

By checking for this error condition and rethrowing a typed application exception, Java will force the calling object to handle the checked exception. This greatly improves the chances that the end user will see a genuine error message and not an incomprehensible system exception.

In addition to arguement checking, it is important to log as much information as possible. Here is an example of a good logged exception:

```
Tue Jul 10, 2006 09:08:22 -- ERROR -- QuoteHelper.java:67 "InvalidQuoteRequest
exception being thrown for request: 9342432. Address is null. QuoteRequest object
is: [9342432,"Emily","Ford", . . .]
```

Here is an example of what is all too often logged instead:

```
Tue Jul 10, 2006 09:08:22 -- ERROR -- QuoteHelper.java:67 "Error calculating quote"
```

In the first example log message, we get two key pieces of information that are absent in the second example. First, we know why the exception is being thrown: the address attribute has been checked and found to be null. Second, we are able to correlate this error to an actual user request. If three users report issues calculating insurance quotes on a given day, we use the error logs to derive exactly *which* users experienced *this* particular problem.

We can look at the same code fragment again with each of our recommendations implemented:

```
public QuoteResult calculateQuote(QuoteRequest qr) {

    QuoteResult quoteResult = new QuoteResult();
    String applicantName = rq.getApplicantName();
    Address applicantAddress = rq.getApplicantAddress();
    // 1. Check for potential error conditions
    If {applicantAddress==null) {
```

```
      // 2. Log a detailed record of the error
      logger.error("InvalidQuoteRequest exception
      being thrown for request: " + qr.getApplicantNo() +
       ". Address is null. QuoteRequest object is: " + qr);
      // 3. Throw a typed exception that forces the
      calling application
      // to handle it
      throw new InvalidQuoteRequest(quoteRequest);
       }
   try {
      verifyAddress( applicantAddress.getLine1(),
        applicantAddress.getLine2(),
        applicantAddress.getCity(),
        applicantAddress.getState(),
        applicantAddress.getZip()
        );
   exception (AddressInvalidException aie) {
      logger.debug("Address Invalid");
      rethrow aie;
   }
   /*
   . . . other business logic to generate the quote
   */
return quoteResult;
}
```

To many developers reading this book, what we suggest in this section is sound patently obvious. We make these remarks because a vast number of software systems have been built (and continue to be built) that do not meet this standard. If you are an architect, technical lead, or development manager, you need to insist that this level of error handling be accounted for through the code review process for your deliverables.

Fortunately, emerging technologies continue to make appropriate error logging and handling increasingly easy to implement. For example, exception handling is a major improvement over the developer obligation to properly implement return codes. More recently, aspect-oriented programming (AOP) approaches make it easier to crosscut broad swaths of your application with consistent behavior and handling. Error handling is one of the most often referenced applications of AOP constructs. If you are a Java technologist, you are encouraged to investigate the Spring framework invented by Rod Johnson, at time of writing, the most popular AOP framework for this platform.

Infrastructure Services

The short answer is that you shouldn't expect anything from the infrastructure. It does not matter what promises are made around the quality and availability of the infrastructure; the application needs to be coded in a way that is resilient to infrastructure failures.

That said, the technical team must be aware of the features in the software platform that are expected to provide resiliency. For example, if the chosen software platform provides redundancy between clustered servers, the development team should review vendor documentation for this feature to ensure that the design of the solution is compliant with vendor recommendations.

A good example of where this is applicable is in the BEA Weblogic Application Server. This product supports failover in a clustered environment, but only if session-based application data conforms to the java.io.Serializable interface. Without this understanding, it would be easy for a development team to invalidate this vendor feature.

Design Reviews

Design reviews are needed to confirm that standards and guidelines are followed and are going to meet the requirements, both functional and non-functional.

The Design Checklist

In the preceding sections, we've looked at some key elements of successful software design. We are also including a list of questions that you can use to audit your own implementations. At the conclusion of the design and implementation phases, you may find it worthwhile to sit down with a representative from the implementation team and pose the following questions.

1. Are error severities documented and understood by the development team?
2. Is there a defined service level for all work that the system is completing asynchronously? For each point of failure, has automated retry recovery been considered as a robustness strategy?
3. When exceptions are thrown, does the system leave processing in a state that can be resumed by an operator or by the user directly?
4. If the system is experiencing problems, how do I gracefully shut off additional inputs? Does the system have flexibility to selectively disable individual functions?

5. If there is a surge of inputs or errors against critical functions, what is the expected behavior? In what way will this impact unrelated processing in the same system?
6. For all batch jobs, is there a simple, reliable, documented recovery procedure if the job fails during processing?
7. For each external interface, does the application support dynamically configurable trace logging?
8. At any point during processing, can a technical resource inspect the system and see all data and state information for any individual unit of work to support troubleshooting efforts?
9. Has the development team conducted code reviews with attention given to logging and exception handling? Were actual defects raised as a result?
10. Has a technical resource completed a review of all application logs from the last functional test cycles? Are all error messages meaningful and complete?

The Operability Review

Once your application design is complete, a worthwhile activity is to conduct an operability review as an aspect of the overall design review. An operability review looks at your design from the perspective of discrete failure points, with a goal of predicting the expected behavior. A common artifact of software design is the sequence diagram, (shown in Figure 4.6). A sequence diagram illustrates the sequence of system calls that achieve a given business operation. Sequence diagrams

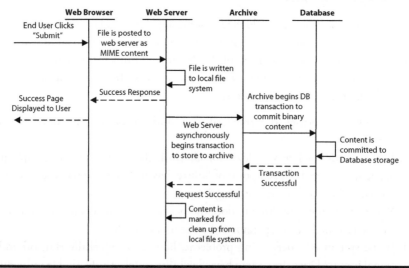

Figure 4.6   Example sequence diagram: multimedia upload application.

can be written at the object level for your application as well as at the software component level for the total software system. Let's consider a view of an application that allows users to upload multimedia content to a web site which stores this content on their behalf in a repository. We will use this simple example to illustrate the purpose of an operability review.

In the operability review, there are two principles that will guide us. They are as follows:

■ If something can go wrong, it will go wrong.
■ The word *should* is stricken from our vocabulary.

Let's take a pessimistic view of our sequence diagram (shown in Figure 4.7) with these guiding principles in mind. We will use the symbol ⊗ to indicate a failure point.

In this view, we see that there are 12 discrete failure points for the application. We generated these failure points on the assumption that for each arrow in the sequence diagram it is possible for a failure to occur at either of the end points or to the system call itself while it is in flight (e.g., network error). Let's put these types of failures into familiar scenarios and language.

For each of the failure scenarios that you enumerate in the operability review, you should discuss the expected application behavior. During this process, remember not to use the word *should*. If you are using the word "should," it means that

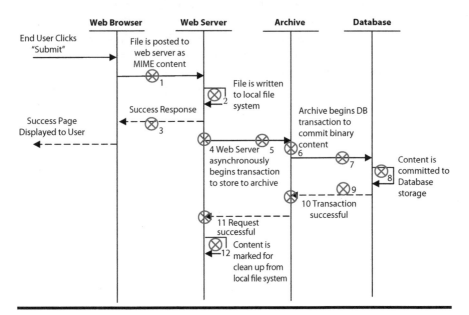

Figure 4.7   Example sequence diagram with failure points: multimedia upload application.

you don't really know how the application will behave—as in, "The archive server *should* roll back the transaction and return an error status." Alternately, it might mean that you are assuming that a failure scenario will never happen—as in, "The Web server *should* never lose connectivity because it is directly attached to the same switch as the archive server." You need to avoid this type of thinking in the context of an operability review. Remember, things will go wrong, no matter how unlikely that may be, and you need to know with confidence how your system will react when they do.

If you are uncertain of the application behavior, you are encouraged to devise a test to find out. Through this process, you may find that you need to revise your design or build additional robustness into the application. At the same time, depending on the likelihood of the failure scenario, the criticality of the business operation, and the process for detecting and correcting the incident, not all scenarios may require design intervention. For these cases, it is important to identify them as a team and make a collective and documented decision to address them or not.

Summary

Good software design can be applied to achieve a host of benefits: flexibility, extensibility, readability, maintenance, and quality. Successful projects are often projects with strong technical leadership that insists on a thorough design phase. In this chapter, we've argued that some of the most tangible benefits of good software design are in the area of operability. Extensibility and flexibility are important but loftier benefits. You may need to extend or change direction in your software, but in the real world, applications that recover gracefully from errors will earn accolades sooner and on more occasions.

In the next chapter we will look at effective techniques and guidelines for building scalable, high-performing software systems.

Chapter 5

Designing for Performance

The goal of this chapter is to help you to better architect, design, and develop software that meets the performance requirements of your system. We will focus on the different aspects of the solution design that will inevitably influence its performance, or at the very least the perception that the end user will have of the application's responsiveness.

In our experience, performance considerations need to be part of every step of the development process. Projects that delay performance considerations until late in the software lifecycle are at significant risk when it comes to their non-functional test results.

Requirements

The performance requirements of a system are gathered as part of the non-functional requirements of a software solution, as discussed in Chapter 3. In what follows we will highlight how performance considerations should be looked at as an influencing factor of the requirements gathering process.

The "Ilities"

Performance is intrinsic to a system, whereas some of the capabilities (further referred to as "ilities") of a solution—although not all of them—can be added as an afterthought. Performance will also have a major impact on the "ilities" so much so that for some systems, some of these "ilities" will have to be sacrificed in favor of performance. Note that the reverse is also true, and that performance may have to be sacrificed for one or more of the "ilities." The important thing is to determine where performance is critical and how thoroughly it is allowed to affect your overall system because of its criticality.

> "I am personally a big fan of BMW motor cars. What I like about BMW is how over the latter years they have made performance an integral part of their car design. PErformance in a BMW is not about a big engine, but rather about squeezing the most out of the engine. IT is also about making the driver feel secure in using the power at his disposal and doing so in an environment that is easy and comfortable to use."

In what follows we take a look at how performance and the capabilities of a system can be intertwined. We have chosen the "ilities" we discuss based on our experience with how these aspects of a solution are interrelated. These do not, by far, cover all of the capabilities associated to computer software (a search for "ilities" on Wikipedia lists more than 50 possible "[capab]ilities"); however, they should convey a sense of the type of questions that need to be answered when analyzing the requirements for a system that will be highly sensitive when it comes to performance.

Scalability

The first thing that will come to mind for many people when talking about performance is system scalability. This property does not relate so much to the performance of a system but rather to its capacity to uphold the same performance under heavier volumes.

The requirement for scalability must be considered in relation to the need for future growth of the business function that is supported by the software solution.

As a rule of thumb for a business with a moderate or slow growth rate, vertical scalability of a system will be sufficient as long as Moore's law holds true, which it seems will be the case for still a number of years to come.

It is notable, however, that chip makers have started concentrating more efforts on multicore central processing unit (CPU) solutions, and we would argue that today software solutions should be built to scale horizontally in order to sustain business demands at affordable costs in the future.

Scalability can influence performance in different ways. In distributed systems, scalability will usually be the result of load-balancing requests coming into the system, so that they can be processed by multiple nodes. The load balancing will carry with it a small overhead that should be taken into account during specification, especially if load balancing occurs for each tier in the distributed solution.

Distributed databases or application servers will, in some cases, provide caching mechanisms to speed up data lookups. Although the cache will drastically accelerate data access in some cases, it will also require synchronization of the data across all nodes, which does not come for free. Whether the system is mostly to be used for reading data or for writing data will need to be assessed in order to define the appropriate caching strategy (more about caching follows on p. 109).

Grid-computing solutions have multiple computers act as one; however, this is not fully transparent and will require data synchronization to occur during specific points of the processing. This will also add overhead to the total performance and must be factored in when defining the system.

Usability

Making a system that is both enticing and easy for people to use, is a complex task, worthy of a library in itself. Consequently, we will limit our interest here to the impact usability requirements can have on performance.

Everyone will agree that a poorly performing system is not usable; people will get frustrated and very soon abandon the application as a whole, even if the performance issues are only related to one functional area of the entire solution.

The solution architect and business or usability analysts must therefore collaborate in order to come up with usage patterns that are both efficient for the end user and computationally viable for the system under construction. The architect's role will be to provide input regarding the technology options available to the team, whereas the usability analyst will ensure that these technology options are used in a context most suitable for the end user.

Both should ensure that the user is not subjected to long waiting periods. Expensive computations should not be performed while the user is waiting; they should be removed from the user interaction flow and handled separately so that the user can go on with her work.

A contemporary example of this is the use of Web 2.0 technologies in order to execute front-end validations that would previously have taxed the backend systems.

Another example is the use of asynchronous processing and exception handling using workflow systems. Using this paradigm, processing errors are not reported to the user immediately but through some form of a notification mechanism. This type of processing is advantageous in environments where the user's error rate is very low and rapid response times of the essence.

Extensibility

The extensibility of a system can on occasion jeopardize its effectiveness.

In order to make a system extensible, designers and developers are often forced to add additional controls and decision logic into the computational model, which will quite often lead to performance degradation.

In all instances a design should be kept simple, except if the requirements explicitly mandate the need for an extensible solution. In the latter case the requirements will also have to provide guidance on the specific conditions under which the solution should be extensible, and not simply make a high-level statement about the need for extensibility.

An interesting example of the impact of flexibility on performance is the Enterprise Java Bean (EJB) framework. The EJB framework by its very nature had to be designed with extensibility in mind. In its prior iterations (versions before 3.0), every component that was built for the system had to elicit characteristics of security, transaction support, etc. As a result each EJB call had to go through some wrapper code to handle these aspects of the component. This was because the notion of extensibility had been baked into many aspects of the standard. As of EJB 3.0, the standard changed rather fundamentally: instead of baking things into the way components were defined it was decided that components should be built with no or very little knowledge of the framework, and extensibility would be handled by injecting the capabilities mentioned above using techniques of aspect-based programming.

Securability

Networks, and the Internet in particular, have opened up the door for many threats to the enterprise. As a result, many companies became conscious of the need for tighter security and especially for building security into all aspects of their software solutions.

Tightening security rarely happens without an impact on system performance. Therefore (and as with each theme in this section) securing your system needs to be done in a way that neither degrades the performance of your solution nor disrupts the operation of its functions.

In order to do so, the stakeholders, business analyst, security architect, and solutions architect will need to work together to determine the scope of the security measures that are required for the specific purposes of the system.

Here are some of the questions that will be important to determine which principles will underpin the security architecture:

- How many users will be using the system?
- What is the access perimeter of the system: a local area network, distributed across regions on an intranet or the Internet?
- Do people with different profiles or roles access different functions of the system?
- Does the system manipulate data that is highly confidential or of a sensitive nature?
- Is there a need to trace back all actions/changes made via the system to an originator?

These questions are important, as they will allow the security architect to determine:

- The need for encryption or not and if said encryption should be hardware accelerated, which may be necessary if many concurrent users have to be supported or if elevated volumes of data require encryption.
- How to implement access controls. The demand for heavy access verifications will obviously impact overall system performance; hence this quality of the system may require the implementation of cached access control lists, or other optimizations around such checks.
- Non-repudiation is another security measure that will impact the responsiveness of the system, given that each transaction requiring non-repudiation will need signing. It is advisable to limit the requirements for non-repudiation to only those specific transactions that may be legally binding.

It is not uncommon to find your business stakeholders demanding "as much security as possible." An important part of your job as a technologist is to educate them on the performance trade-offs they may have to accept in order to achieve the desired level of security.

Operability and Measurability

We have combined operability and measurability, as these system features will most often coexist.

Mission-critical systems will usually need to report information about their state and overall sanity back to an operations team. The type of information required may be as simple as providing a log of any significant malfunctions in the system or as complex as providing measures of the system performance, averages on the number of errors per hour, real-time alerting through monitoring protocols such as simple network management protocol (SNMP), and a variety of other measures and informational data.

The data required to provide a defined level of information about the system will have to be captured by the system, and hence add additional constraints of computation and input/output (I/O) to the system.

The overall impact of these additional system constraints can be limited by allowing reporting on the data to occur separately from the actual data gathering. This may not always be feasible, especially when dealing with real-time systems, but should be considered whenever the performance considerations outweigh the need for immediate notification.

On the data-gathering side, care must be taken to limit the number of data items that need to be captured. In that respect it is important to define the reason for capture of the items as well as the lifecycle requirements of the items. Data required for trending and long-term analysis may need to be captured on permanent media, whereas for data that is needed only at system runtime it may be sufficient to keep a transient in memory copy.

With today's technologies it is, in certain cases, even possible to benefit from runtime instrumentation, which allows adding or removing instrumentation to an application while it is running.

Maintainability

The ability to maintain a system will not really have an impact on its performance. Source code comments and design documentation do not impact system performance, although we have sometimes wondered whether some development teams believed so, given the scantiness of documentation and comments provided for some of the solutions we had to review.

The reason we wanted to cover this topic is to stress the fact that design and code documentation are important, and even more so when dealing with algorithms that have to be heavily optimized. In many cases when optimization is required, algorithms become either very complex or unreadable—or both. Therefore, particular attention should be taken to the documentation that will surround such artifacts.

Recoverability

When a process will take a considerable amount of time to execute, you will usually want the capability to recover from a failure in the middle of the process without the need to rerun the whole process. The capacity to recover will depend on what information is available to recover, and maintaining this information will by all means impact the overall performance of the process.

The rule of thumb is clearly that recovery should not take longer than resuming the process, if indeed the process can be rerun. If either the process cannot be rerun, or the recovery is faster than resuming the process, the price of maintaining recovery data is acceptable and it will have to be incorporated into the capacity requirements for the system.

The system's architect should ascertain with the business analyst that there is indeed a requirement for recovery. In some cases data is perceived to be critical to a system, when in fact the data is either transient or maintained as part of another system. In those cases it is most likely that recovery of the data is not mandatory, and therefore the performance penalty of recoverability should not be incurred. For instances in those cases you could, for instance, think of disabling the database features that will maintain recovery logs.

Architecture

When taking a critical eye to a system's architecture in order to figure out how to design for performance while at the same time keeping to the projects' timelines, there are two important parts to your approach.

First of all you will have to determine which parts of the solution will need a more thorough look to determine whether special measures are needed to ensure the required level of performance. We call this activity the "hotspot" analysis of the architectural picture, which we'll examine in more detail in the coming section.

Secondly you'll gain time by applying standard architectural patterns to the performance issues that are specific to your problem. We will try to help you in this regard by introducing you to a set of common performance patterns, as well as their antipatterns.

Finally we also encourage you, when defining the architecture of a system—whether it has high performance requirements or not—to take a pragmatic approach as outlined in our personal note. Whenever possible, use the K.I.S.S. approach: Keep it Simple and Stupid. On many occasions we have seen development teams come up with designs that were far too complicated and circumvoluted for the problem at hand. This seems to stem from a perception of the designer that if the solution is too simple then he hasn't done his job right. In our experience it is better to reward people for coming up with simple, elegant solutions rather than overly complicated ones that address more than the requirement. It is up to the manager to clearly communicate this to the team.

Hotspots

When defining the architecture of a system it is important to clearly identify those parts of the system that are liable to cause performance bottlenecks. These areas of the system are quite often referred to as *hotspots*.

The determination of hotspots within an architecture will be achieved by mapping the non-functional requirements for the system onto the logical architecture. Doing this will provide the design and architecture team with a view of which parts of the system will require particular attention when it comes to the technical design and even the implementation of the solution.

We suggest that you approach hotspot mapping as follows:

- Make sure that the non-functional requirements of the system have been accurately articulated with as much detail as possible around volumes and response times.
- Map each input or output channel of the system to its associated non-functional requirement(s) and determine whether a hotspot would result from the volumes or response requirements expected from said channel.

- Make sure each component of your architecture has its input and output flows defined. The throughput and response requirements of a component are a combination of the requirements for all of its in- and outflows.
- Based on the throughput or response requirements for each component, identify those components that are potential bottlenecks. Start with the components that only have in- or outflows from or to external entities, and then only those components that receive their inputs and outputs from other components of the system.

Patterns

Divide and Conquer

By "divide and conquer" we understand the need to split up the work in smaller parts. It is our opinion that the divide and conquer pattern is one that engineers cannot live without in light of the increasing complexity of the systems that they are tasked to build in today's world.

When designing for performance this pattern is specifically helpful for tackling the following problems:

- The identification of hotspots is made easier, and the analysis of said hotspots is straightforward when one only has to concentrate on the inputs and outputs of the problem area.
- In many instances, the computation of all parts combined will take the same amount of time and resources as the computation of the total problem, but in many cases splitting up the computation of certain parts will give the impression to the end user that the system performs more efficiently.

Load Balancing

Load balancing is a typical pattern used to achieve horizontal scalability in a system. A typical load balancing setup is shown in Figure 5.1.

In order for such a setup to achieve optimal scalability on requests made to the system, these requests should be independent, and short-lived. When every request is independent, each one can be processed by any hardware node in a server cluster or farm, as long as the same application is deployed on each one of these servers. This is an ideal solution, as it allows the load balancing mechanism to choose the least busy server to execute the request, thereby optimizing overall resource usage.

Moreover, if every request is short-lived and will consume approximately the same system resources whatever the request, the mechanism to load balance does

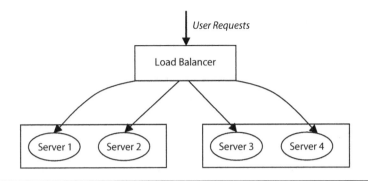

Figure 5.1   Simple load-balancing scheme.

not need to be complex, and a simple "round robin" approach will usually suffice. Typically serving up static Web pages falls into this category.

Most applications are not that fortunate, and will have varying resource requirements for each request as well as requests that are not totally independent of each other. A typical Web application will maintain a user's session, and all requests coming from that user's session will need to share his session's state. State is generally maintained on the server, thereby binding requests to the server(s) on which said state is memorized.

When faced with long-running requests and/or dependent requests, load balancing can still be of use but will require more intelligent allocation of load. For instance, you may decide to direct the load of resource intensive requests to specific servers, which have been allocated and tuned specifically for the execution of such requests. You may want to send the load balancer information about current server utilization so as to route requests to those servers being less utilized.

Note that load balancing will quite often be used to support failover as well. This will require additional mechanisms to be put in place in order for the load balancer to be aware of dead nodes in a cluster, as well as which nodes have a replica of any state information required to fulfill a request.

In the end, the more intricate the strategy to decide where to send the load of a request, the more impact the load-balancing process will have on end-to-end performance of your requests. Depending on your specific requirements, you will need to find the right balance between the complexity of a good load-balancing mechanism and the benefit it provides you in terms of overall scalability of your system.

Parallelism

Whereas load balancing deals with the execution of unrelated requests in parallel, this topic will cover the parallel execution of related computations. We decided to keep the two topics separated, though we could have handled load balancing as a subtopic of this one.

Even with today's fastest computers, some calculations may still take a long time to complete. Hence, if either the hardware does not exist to speed up your computations, or buying the hardware that would allow faster computation is economically not viable, dividing the problem into parallel computations is your only remaining option (short of dropping the problem altogether) in order to up the performance of these computations. Note that if this is true for the CPU usage of your solution it can also be true for its I/O usage. In one case the solution is said to be "CPU bound" whereas in the other case it is "I/O bound," in both cases making things run in parallel will help.

Before thinking of parallelization you will need to identify which parts of your application would benefit the most from it, and if these parts can be parallelized at all, meaning whether the algorithms exist to handle the task in parallel.

Once you have defined which parts of your solution will be benefiting from parallelism you will have to evaluate the overhead cost of the parallelization algorithm in order to determine the boundary conditions under which parallel processing will be triggered or not.

In many instances parallelized processing is only interesting as of the moment certain volumes of data need to be manipulated, but does not make any sense for small data volumes. For instance, when performing a parallel sort, the time of each parallel sort together with the time needed to aggregate the results of these parallel sorts should not exceed the time it would have taken to sort everything without parallelism (as shown in Figure 5.2).

Now that we have defined the criteria that should guide you in answering the question—To parallelize or not to parallelize?—we will look at some examples of where to use parallelism when a system is I/O bound.

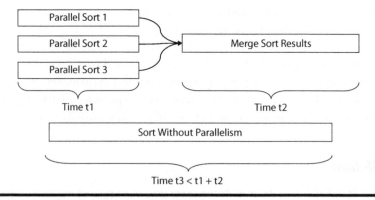

Figure 5.2   Using parallelism in a sort algorithm.

Scenario 1: Poor Query Performance

An application is required that allows business users at a distribution facility to search historical order information. A national database exists that stores order information. This business manages order fulfillment for a number of online businesses, so the record volumes are large. The database design has used the native database capabilities to do date-based partitioning on the order fulfillment table. In the current production database, there are between 4 and 6 million records for each business day. This strategy allows different partitions to reside on different parts of storage reducing contention for I/O reads. A prototype is built for the application that implements a variety of the queries indicated in the business requirements. The proof of concept is a success, with the exception of a subset of queries that include wide date-range criteria. These queries span a massive amount of data in order to execute, and all indications are that the query performance is very slow. The development team profiles the query execution and observes that the query plan is optimal, but that the query is slow because the database system must do a large number of physical reads from disk in order to fulfill the request.

In this case, the query performance is limited by the physical constraint of disk speed. Earlier in this section we stated that your objective is to refine your implementation to the point where the only constraints that remain are hardware constraints. Does this mean that there is nothing that can be done here? This would not be an interesting example if this were the case. In this example, if we look a little harder we realize that we have not truly reached the point of physical hardware constraints.

In the scenario description, it is mentioned that the database designers designed the order fulfillment table using a partitioning strategy specifically to take advantage of multiple physical disks. This is an advantage that we have not yet leveraged in our performance-tuning exercise. Many modern relational databases offer parallel execution capabilities. This means that the database optimizer will identify components of the query that can be subdivided and executed in parallel. Not all queries can benefit from this approach, but it doesn't take long for us to realize that it is perfectly suited to the problem at hand. By allowing the database to search different partitions on different disks in parallel, we can dramatically improve the performance. What was previously a serial activity with a difficult physical constraint (disk access speed) can now be executed in parallel. In this example, the implementation team was able to experiment with the degree of parallelism based on the physical database architecture and was able to successfully derive excellent performance gains.

Scenario 2: Aggregating Results from External Systems

A back-office financial services application is being enhanced to show bank employees a single, complete view of up-to-date account and balance information for a given customer. Account and balance information is maintained in up to 14 different backend systems, each of which has different response time targets for requests. The challenge facing the implementation team is how to interrogate each of the backend systems for information and report back within the aggressive response-time requirements set forth by the business. A paper exercise quickly shows that serially connecting to each of the backend systems will never meet the performance requirements.

In this example, a local database is not the performance constraint; but rather from the responsiveness of external systems. In this case, the theoretical best-case performance is constrained by the longest response time of any one of the backend systems. In other words, if we were able to make 14 concurrent requests, the longest we would have to wait would be for the time it took the slowest system to respond. Before embarking on a heavily parallelized solution, the design team looks at the problem and makes the following additional observations:

■ Systems 1–5 consistently respond in 60ms or less
■ Systems 8 and 11 consistently take between 1500ms and 3000ms to respond
■ System 11 may not need to be interrogated (depends on the response from system 4)
■ The remaining systems take approximately 100ms to respond

It may be tempting to introduce fourteen concurrent threads to access each system in parallel, but this would appear to be unnecessary. A more appropriate strategy would be as follows:

■ Thread 1: Issue a request to system 4 and then 11 conditional upon the response from system 4
■ Thread 2: Issue a request to system 8
■ Thread 3: Issue serial requests to the remaining systems
■ Thread 4: Impose a timeout on the aggregate request of 4 seconds

The performance-limiting step is thread 1 or 2, which we expect to take at least 1500ms to complete based on the known behavior for system 8. It is not an issue to make serial requests on the remaining systems because the aggregate of these responses is still expected to take less time than threads 3 or 4. Note that we have introduced a fourth thread to manage the overall execution and to impose a timeout. If the system does not provide a timely response (even if it is an error), users can become impatient and submit a large volume of repetitive requests, a process that creates risk to system availability.

Before we can consider this exercise complete, we should make a remark about maintainability. What if dramatic performance improvements are made to system 8, while at the same time system 3 undergoes a change in usage or platform that degrades its performance significantly? From an operability perspective, hard coding the parallelism strategy into the application could be a defeating strategy as systems evolve. An appropriate response to this design challenge would be to assign four worker threads from a pool to the completion of each consolidated request and allow them to complete the work as quickly as possible. In this type of scheme, if a thread takes longer to complete its work than expected, other threads can pitch in and off-load effort as soon as they become available.

Synchronous versus Asynchronous Execution

One of the central questions when developing for performance is whether to execute synchronously or asynchronously. Note that the answer to this question doesn't pertain so much to the resources that will be used to execute the code but rather to the perception an external consumer will have of the system's responsiveness.

Executing an algorithm asynchronously will give the external consumer an impression of fast responsiveness given that the brunt of the work is not done during the interaction with the consumer. This, however, is only a matter of perception, given that the resources required and the complexity of the system dialog is quite often higher for this type of solution. Remember however that in most cases the external consumer (whether human or not) is the party who will determine whether your system is a success or not, thus the extra effort may well be worth your trouble.

Consider an application in which business users must complete a series of forms to initiate a business request. Once the form has been fully populated, there are two steps to the fulfillment. The first step is to validate that the form inputs adhere to basic business rules and validations. Processing for this validation is lightweight and does not contribute to the duration of the fulfillment request in a significant way. The second step in the processing is to submit the request to an external system for further validation and acceptance.

The submission to the external system may take up to two minutes to process based on the complex business processing that is needed to verify the request. In the original system implementation, the application was designed such that users waited for the response and were presented with the request outcome once it had been completed. Business complaints and duplicate submissions led the technology team to introduce "please wait" messages and interface controls to try to manage user expectations during processing. Users submit approximately 6–10 such requests an hour during busy periods. If each request takes two minutes to submit, business users are spending up to 1/3 of their time waiting for requests when they are at their busiest!

Ultimately it was decided that a new paradigm was necessary. After consultation with the business, the technology team proposed that a new model be adopted, which is commonly referred to as "fire and forget." In the revised design, business users complete the form as before and then submit the request in the last step for asynchronous processing. The design team found that most input errors were being caught by the intraform validations and that the first submission rarely needed to be repeated. As a result, an inbox was added to the user interface that would populate with the request status once the request had been fulfilled. As a convenience feature, the team added an email notification that would allow users to be informed when their request had completed processing. An unexpected advantage of the alternative implementation was that when the backend fulfillment system was unavailable, business users could still submit requests asynchronously to the front-end system. This operability advantage improved the perception of system availability as well as performance.

Finally, whether to opt for synchronous or asynchronous execution will depend on the type of system you are building, the skills you have available, and many other parameters. In Table 5.1 we attempt to provide a series of guidelines that may help you to decide which way you want to go.

Deferred Processing

A subcategory of the asynchronous processing pattern can be dubbed "deferred processing." For the lazier amongst us this means *never do more work than you have to*—advice that is particularly relevant in today's climate of object-oriented implementation and component-based frameworks. Component development offers irrefutable advantages from the standpoints of extensibility, reusability, and maintainability. However, component usage can also lead to serious performance issues when not used at the appropriate times. It is common for a component to be designed for one purpose and then re-purposed for something else. The secondary usage of the component may not require the full component implementation, but it is more convenient to use the existing "as is" component than to design something new or change what is already available.

A typical example of this type of danger is the "User" object itself, which is a common object in modern software implementations. The *"User" object* is an abstraction of all characteristics of the authenticated user who is interacting with the system. The user object commonly includes attributes for username, full name, address, date of birth, email address, payment information, etc. When a user first initiates a session with the system, it is common to construct the user object and populate all of its attributes from storage. In some circumstances this may be entirely appropriate if the attributes for the user all reside in a single, local, and efficient data store. However, if the user object is a composite of information from different systems, the context in which the user object is being used may not require the object to be fully constituted. In this case, it may be prudent to defer the construction of the object until a request is actually made to the object for the specific attribute. Consider the example in which payment information for the user is stored in a different profile database than name and address information. For this example, we might propose an object interface as follows:

```
public class User {
public User(String username, String password) { ... }
public String getFirstName() { ... }
public PaymentInfo getPaymentInfo() { ... }
}
```

A user object is constructed when the user authenticates to the system and provides a valid username and password. In a deferred processing scenario, we would suggest that the object construction start by verifying the username and password against the authentication store. The implementation may also load the user's personal information, including name and address, but the object construction would not necessarily load payment information for the user. This independent initialization is deferred until the application calls the *getPaymentInfo()* method at some point in the future.

Caching

Another mechanism that is commonly used to improve performance, or at the very least give the perception thereof, is caching. This is mainly used to improve the performance in scenarios requiring slow or voluminous I/O interactions, but can also be used in parallel computing to maintain local copies of shared data.

Caching is such a pervasive performance-improvement pattern that it is very common to have many layers of cache between the end user and the physical data storage. Let's consider the conventional three-tier architecture for a Web-based application and look at a subset of different caches that may be at play. A nonexhaustive example of how caches can be distributed is shown in Figure 5.3.

The main challenges related to caching information are twofold: 1) keeping the cached information in sync when the information is distributed or when the information can be modified by mechanisms that do not involve the caching mechanism; and 2) managing the memory used by the cache in a way that minimizes memory use but maximizes the use of the cache (in other words, choose the caching strategy that will maximize cache hits).

These, however, are technical challenges, and solutions exist. For instance, most application servers will use one or more caching mechanisms, and some will even allow you to provide your own caching strategy. There are also a number of free and commercial solutions available, such as Open Symphony OSCache or Gigaspaces.

Cache synchronization will ensure that the cache reliably reflects the contents of the primary data store. When cache contents become out of synch, the contents are referred to as stale. Depending on the nature of the data that you wish to cache, you will need to choose a suitable synchronization policy. There are a variety of choices, which we describe in Table 5.2.

Table 5.1 Guidelines for Synchronous versus Asynchronous Execution

Information about Interaction with the System	Synchronous Execution	Asynchronous Execution
A request requiring some form of validation feedback is executed.	Ideal for this kind of interaction.	Asynchronous treatment does not add a lot of merit, given that a reply is always due to the requestor. Using asynchronous methods in this case will add complexity to the implementation with no benefit likely. One notable exception to this that has proven its benefits is the approach taken by some AJAX-based implementations. In this case, validation feedback is provided to the user in real time while she inputs the data. The validation of the entered data is done asynchronously while the user continues to type in more data. Although overall this uses up more resources (due to the multiple asynchronous calls), it gives the system a much better user experience.
A packet of information is sent to the system. No results or feedback is required.	If absolutely no treatment of the information is required on the receiving end, then a synchronous interaction will be fine.	When some form of treatment of the information is required, it is best to put the information on a queue and perform the treatment when resources become available.
The interaction is very dynamic. Continuous requests/response exchanges are required.	Although not much different from the first scenario, this scenario will quickly put heavy constraints on the resources of your system. Synchronous interaction is only recommended if you have a lot of resources at your disposal.	If you have limited resources at your disposal, introducing some form of asynchronous behavior in this instance will allow the system to better manage resource consumption. Some middleware solutions will do this for you (see note below).

Table 5.1   Guidelines for Synchronous versus Asynchronous Execution

Note: Although we speak here of synchronous and asynchronous interactions, we are talking from the point of view of the system's designer and/or developer. At the level of the CPU, most executions will be asynchronous to some extent. This asynchronous behavior comes from the fact that the operating system will manage the execution of multiple processes and therefore pre-empt or queue the execution of some of these processes, thereby introducing a form of asynchronous behavior. Moreover, when running code on a transaction server or application server, the middleware will normally rely on one or more resource usage control mechanisms that will also introduce a form of asynchronous execution. These considerations are important either when defining the capacity requirements of a system that is running more than just one application or when troubleshooting performance issues on a shared production system.

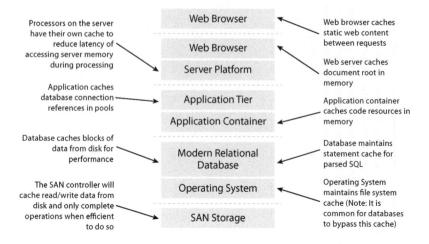

Figure 5.3   Caching is pervase in most system implementations.

In order to ensure that the cache is just a cache and not a full replica of your data store, the cache will have to be provided with a caching policy that will determine which elements to remove from the cache once the memory consumption of the cache has reached a certain limit. A list of commonly used caching policies can be found in Table 5.3.

Finally, one conundrum we have experienced with regards to caching on some of our projects could be dubbed "too much of a good thing." On many instances we have found development teams replicating cached information in various pieces of related code. Although we mentioned earlier that it was not uncommon to see caches at different layers of an architecture, we have to caution you that this does increase the chances of desynchronization between the various caches and the root entity that is being cached. And it also consumes a lot of memory, which is still a valuable commodity. The right places for caching must therefore be defined as part of your global system architecture and not left to the whim of each and every developer.

Antipatterns

Whereas design patterns illustrate proven approaches to common problems, antipatterns exemplify design flaws that consistently cause applications to have problems. On the topic of performance, the authors have seen the following patterns repeated over and over again without predictable results. As important as it is to "do the right thing," it is equally important to be able to recognize the wrong thing and be equipped to avoid it.

Table 5.2   The Cache Syncronization Approach

Cache Policy	Description
Time Expiration	The cache maintains a timestamp for each member and ejects members once they have aged to the configured timeout.
Write-Through	A write-through cache updates the cache as part of the operation to update the primary data store. This type of cache will preserve cache synchronization for updates initiated by the application but will not guarantee synchronization should external systems update the primary data store.
Refresh-Ahead	This is an enhancement to the time expiration strategy, in which members are refreshed once the expiration period has elapsed rather than being cast out of the cache altogether. Typically, this strategy would need to be combined with the least recently used (LRU) to manage cache size.
Write-Behind	This is a performance improvement to the write-through strategy. Effectively, the application writes to the cache and the write to the primary data store is deferred and completed asynchronously.
Optimistic	For complex cache members that may be updated by external systems, the only way to reliably guarantee synchronization is to verify the timestamp of the object in the primary data store. The drawback of this approach is that you still pay the performance penalty of seeking to the target object. The advantage is that you do not need to reconstitute a complex object if it is in the cache. Upon verifying that the object is current, the application can use the cached reference.

Table 5.3   Commonly Used Caching Strategies

Cache Policy	Description
FIFO **(First In, First Out)**	In this cache policy, members are ejected from the cache in the same order that they were added. This approach is basically a queue, and the primary advantage is simplicity.
LRU **(Least Recently Used)**	Members of the cache are ejected in order of maximum idle time. This strategy is a big improvement over FIFO and is also simple to implement. This strategy is the most common caching strategy.
LRU2 **(Least Recently Used Twice)**	Similar to LRU, with the variation that objects must be accessed twice before they are added to the cache. This makes the cache scan resistant, meaning that the cache is not overwhelmed with members that participate in a linear scan of the entire data store.
LFU **(Least Frequently Used)**	The cache maintains data on the frequency with which data is accessed and ejects members with the lowest frequency.

Overdesign

During the design phase of a project, it is easy to become enamored with performance strategies and build them into your solution design. The introduction of these strategies can quickly escalate the complexity of your application. The best advice that we can give you is d*esign to best practice and then performance tune to your bottlenecks.*

In other words, you may spend weeks perfecting your caching strategy only to find that the native I/O for most of your data retrieval is perfectly acceptable without a cache at all. To make matters worse, you may find that you have serious performance issues, but none of them are in the focus areas you invested in during your design phase. If you design your application flexibly and follow simple industry standards around performance, you are unlikely to have problems introducing tuning and enhancements into your design once you have identified concrete problems.

Overserialization

Innovations in technology continue to make it increasingly convenient to build systems based on distributed architectures. Support for distributed processing is a core feature in the two most common development platforms in use today: the J2EE specification and Microsoft's .NET framework. These frameworks allow you to develop objects, deploy them in a distributed way, and then access them transparently from any of the components in the distributed architecture.

The platform manages all of the implementation details associated with remote invocation, freeing the application developer to focus on the business-specific aspects of the system. This is a powerful advantage for any developer working with these platforms. However, this flexibility comes at a price. Anytime you exchange data over a network, the request data must be serialized into a stream and then transmitted over a wire. At the receiving end of the request, the remote implementation must unserialize the request data and reconstitute the request in object form. This process is usually referred to as marshalling and unmarshalling the request. The same process is required in reverse to transmit the response back to the caller. There are two performance exposures in this scenario:

- Work has to be done to serialize and unserialize the request/response.
- Work has to be done to transmit data over the wire between the remote and local implementations.

From a performance standpoint, you want your application to spend as much time as possible actually doing business processing versus overhead. The overhead of these two factors is easily managed if it is anticipated during application design. The most common design pattern that is used to address this factor is the use of value objects and coarse-grained interfaces. We will illustrate with a simple example. Let's consider an often-cited example for the J2EE platform: Entity Enterprise Java Beans (EJB). An entity bean is an object implementation for data that resides in persistent storage—most typically, a database. In our example, we'll consider a database table called ORDER for which there exists an entity EJB named OrderEntityBean. Here is the database entity-relationship (ER) representation of the ORDER table.

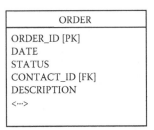

The OrderEntityBean has a number of object attributes, each corresponding to a column in the ORDER table. The object declaration looks something like this (in this example we are showing only the data access interfaces):

OrderEntityBean
orderId: Integer date: Date Status: String contactId: Integer description: String
+ create(): OrderEntityRemote + getOrderId(): Integer + setOrderId(): void + getDate(): Date + setDate(): void + getStatus(): String + setStatus(): void + getContactId(): Integer + setContactId(): void + getDescription(): String

Because OrderEntityBean is an entity bean with local and remote interfaces, it is undesirable to have remote clients calling a setter method remotely for each attribute on an order. We do not want to pay the performance overhead of remote invocation for each attribute update. As an alternative, and to avoid this problem, we introduce a value object and new interface on the order entity bean as follows:

OrderEntityBean	OrderValue
orderId: Integer date: Date Status: String contactId: Integer description: String	orderId: Integer date: Date Status: String contactId: Integer description: String
+ create(): OrderEntityRemote + getOrderId(): Integer + setOrderId(): void + getDate(): Date + setDate(): void + getStatus(): String + setStatus(): void + getContactId(): Integer + setContactId(): void + getDescription(): String + setDescription(): void + **getOrderValue(): OrderValue** + **setOrderValue(): void**	+ **OrderValue(): OrderValue** + getOrderId(): Integer + setOrderId(): void + getDate(): Date + setDate(): void + getStatus(): String + setStatus(): void + getContactId(): Integer + setContactId(): void + getDescription(): String + setDescription(): void

A value object is sometimes referred to as a transport object. Note that the value object is an ordinary Java bean—in this case with a plain constructor. The getter and setter methods for the order value object are referred to as *coarse-grained interfaces* to reflect the fact that they perform work in bulk on the object through a single interface. Similarly, the getter and setter methods for individual order object attributes are referred to as *fine-grained interfaces*. Now that we have introduced a value object, a client is able to construct a single value object and set all of the attributes on the order entity bean using a single-method call. Let's look at the before and after sequence of operations between the local and remote application tiers:

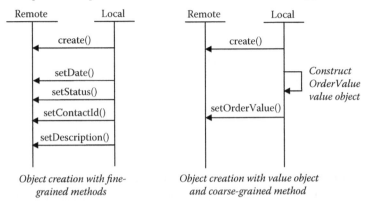

Object creation with fine-grained methods

Object creation with value object and coarse-grained method

The introduction of a value object allows us to avoid three remote method invocations that were required in the original implementation. This is a simple and widely used design pattern. Method invocation for EJBs also includes layers for security and transaction handling that introduce marginal overhead. In addition to avoiding serialization on each call, the value object implementation avoids these additional costs also.

Related to this topic, the EJB 2.0 specification introduced the notion of local interfaces for EJBs. This feature allows EJBs to defined local and remote interfaces. Local interfaces allow a calling application to pass arguments by reference instead of by value. Previous to EJB 2.0, all EJB method invocations had to be by value, meaning that a copy of the parameter data had to be serialized to the remote instance and unmarshaled. Using local interfaces, calling client code can now use these interfaces if the developer knows that the calling application code will be located in the same application monitor as the remote implementation.

Oversynchronization

Synchronization is an important implementation tactic for ensuring data integrity in software systems. The term usually refers to the need to ensure that only a single thread of execution is able to use a given resource at any one time. This is usually achieved by introducing a lock or semaphore that can only ever be granted to a single thread of execution at any one time. A good example of this is write operations for database records.

If a user is updating a record in the database, you do not want concurrent write operations to proceed simultaneously. In a worst-case scenario you might end up with a record that has been updated by a combination of two separate updates resulting in a serious data integrity problem. In order to avoid this, applications need to synchronize access to certain types of resources. Unfortunately, synchronization is fertile ground for the introduction of a performance bottleneck.

If an execution thread reaches a point where it needs to access a synchronized resource that is not available, the application thread has no choice but to wait. You are unlikely to meet your performance objectives if application threads are frequently waiting. Not only does this mean that you may have an end user who is also waiting, there may be other user requests that are not being serviced because a thread is not available to do so.

To avoid performance degradation due to synchronization, you should review your application design and implementation to ensure that you are avoiding each of the following:

- **Synchronizing resources that do not need to be synchronized:** It is not uncommon for a well-meaning programmer to introduce locks or synchronizations to resources for which this is not required. A common example is for an object or method that was originally designed for write operations to also be re-purposed for read-only operations. If the read-only requirement for the object introduces a high frequency of concurrent accesses, you will need to introduce an unsynchronized, read-only version of the object or interface.
- **Synchronizing a resource for longer than necessary:** An even more common scenario is for developers to demarcate the synchronized resource such that it includes far more resources than actually required. If the object or block of execution that is synchronized is defined to be overly inclusive, it will mean that the lock is held for longer, increasing the probability that a competing request will need to wait in order to execute.

Synchronization issues can be difficult to find once they have been introduced to a system. It is important to review your application design carefully prior to performance testing to try to avoid this type of bottleneck.

If your application has been built and you suspect synchronization may be causing performance degradation, this type of problem is often characterized by lower than expected CPU usage under load, for obvious reasons. Custom instrumentation and profiling is often required to isolate this type of problem.

User Session Memory Consumption

Most online transaction processing (OLTP) systems that provide a useful business function require users to work with the application over a series of interactions. As the user navigates, refines usage criteria, and provides data input, the server side of the system will usually need to maintain some record of the user's interactions in order to support business processing.

A language preference is a simple example of something that the server side of the system needs to "remember" in order to provide an accurate ongoing user experience. As the system accumulates user information, it typically adds this to a data structure often referred to as a *session*. Throughout the user interaction, the system will add, subtract, and modify the session to reflect current state.

In many applications there is a temptation to store session information in memory on the server and reference upon each user request. Unfortunately, for systems that support a large volume of users, this is not a scaleable design. Memory is a limited and critical resource for application processing. A common and unfortunate example of poor design is to store large query results in memory while a client application or user scrolls through the results. A search result may retrieve 500 records, but a typical user interface will only show 10–15 records at a time in a summary. It is a common mistake for the server to hang onto all 500 results in memory so that they are readily available for the inevitable subsequent requests to view additional pages of data. Databases are good at efficient data retrieval and buffering data that has been recently requested. In this example, you should forward subsequent requests to the database and let it do all the work between requests.

Because user interaction with the system is unpredictable and potentially complex, it is considered an antipattern to store user state information as part of the session on an application server. For OLTP systems, you are advised to push as much state information out to client systems as possible for purposes of scalability.

Algorithms

There is no denying that it is often more elegant to optimize a computer algorithm so that it will yield the appropriate performance rather than buying a bigger computer to handle a poorly conceived program.

It is not our intention to provide the reader with an exhaustive list of all of the incredible algorithms that exist. Not only would the list need revisiting on an hourly basis, but, when it comes to the basic algorithms that matter, Donald E. Knuth did a much better job in his *"The Art of Computer Programming* series than we could ever hope to achieve."[5]

Our aim is to make you aware that when it comes to performance programming you will need to surround yourself with professionals that understand the ins and outs of building efficient algorithms. These professionals will need at least some basic notions of computational complexity theory, and will understand the advantages, shortcomings, and pitfalls of the software libraries they will be using. In other words, they will be able to tell you whether an algorithm will take exponential time to compute or not, and which library function is best suited to support the execution of your algorithms.

For instance, when it comes to sorting algorithms that person will be able to tell you that a Quicksort algorithm has a complexity of $\Theta(n \log n)$ and that there are other algorithms such as Heapsort and Mergesort, which may be more adequate depending on the problem you are tackling. Moreover, if he is a Java developer he will also tell you the Arrays.sort method uses the Mergesort algorithm, which has the advantage over Quicksort that it provides a stable sort (it maintains the relative ordering of elements with the same comparable value). By relying on developers who possess these skills, you will require less investment into hardware capacity and what is certain to be a long and tedious non-functional test cycle.

Technology

Programming Languages

The chosen programming language will most certainly have an impact on the performance of your application. The choice of language must be a careful balancing act between the need for execution efficiency versus the need for programming efficiency; and in most cases, the need for companies to standardize on a set of standards will also be a factor.

From the standpoint of performance it is best to look at programming languages based on how the resulting program will be executed in the target environment rather than based on the language itself:

Compiled languages

Languages such as C++, Cobol, or Fortran, are compiled so as to execute using the instruction set of the target platform/CPU. This will usually yield the better execution times, given that the compiler can fully optimize the execution code for the target system. We will not futher elaborate on these languages, as it can be accepted that these are probably the most efficient languages from a performance perspective. But in many cases these languages do not yield the same level of productivity as more modern languages such as those we will discuss hereafter.

Virtual-machine-based languages

In this category Java and C# are probably the most prominent examples although many other languages are available that either run on a Java or .NET runtime, or have their own VM implementation.

Note that some parties may not agree with the statement that C# and the other .NET languages are virtual-machine based, but by our reckoning there isn't much difference between Java's bytecode and JVM approach and .NET's common language runtime approach except, perhaps, for the fact that the CLR is more language-agnostic than the JVM. From a performance perspective it has been demonstrated that there is little or no difference between both technologies.[6]

There is a price to pay for the use of a virtual machine. It will have a larger memory footprint than that of an average compiled program, given the need for it to house its own runtime environment as well as the extensions it uses to instrument or optimize code execution, such as a just-in-time or Hotspot compiler, or built-in monitoring capabilities.

The virtual machine will also have a slight performance cost. This performance cost is linked to a number of factors. First and foremost, there is the startup cost due to the need to convert the code targeted at the virtual machine (VM) to code targeted at the underlying CPU. The way this impacts performance may differ depending on whether a just-in-time compiler is used versus a Hotspot compiler (more about this below).

Then there is the fact that the virtual machine also serves as a "sandbox" for the code's execution. In other words, it will attempt to contain any malicious activity that may emanate from the code. This means that additional checks will be performed during code execution, which will also slow down the functions impacted by such checks. Note that if the code comes from a trusted source you can disable most of these checks, here you must find the right balance between security and performance (as discussed in the section on securability).

Finally, one of the main causes for performance degradation with VM-based languages is not so much related to the VM but to the fact that these languages make use of garbage collection for their memory management. Although memory managed through garbage collection proves conducive to faster development (given the fact that the developer "seemingly" doesn't need to care about how his use of memory gets managed), it is also the primary reason why some VM programs perform very poorly.

Many programmers will not think about memory consumption anymore when using a language that does all the memory management work for them. This, however, will result in the garbage collector having to do all the "thinking" for the programmer—at the cost of performance. Because of some of the constraints imposed on a garbage collector, it will stop a program's execution in order to collect the memory that has become unused. As a result, the program's overall performance gets degraded and in many instances the user's perception of this performance degradation negatively impacts the acceptance of a system. It is important for a development team to understand this issue and ensure that memory management remains a concern when using these languages.

Some of the techniques to alleviate these problems, such as object pooling, are well known and should be part of every programmer's bag of tricks. Although applying good programming practices will remedy the problem it is also noteworthy that research in the area of garbage collection has not stopped and that today new approaches to this complex issue solve some, if not all, of the performance impacts brought about by this type of memory management.[7]

Just-In-Time versus the Hotspot Compiler

In the early days of Java, the virtual machine approach was heavily criticized for its sluggish performance. In those days the Java bytecode would be fully interpreted and not translated to the target platform's CPU. This resulted in 10 to 20 times slower execution than an equivalent C++ program. As of the next generation of Java Virtual Machines (1.2), performance was greatly improved by the introduction of Just-in-Time (JIT) bytecode compilers. Note that Sun opened up the JVM architecture to support the inclusion of a JIT compiler, and different vendors such as IBM or HP have their own specific JIT compiler implementation, some yielding better results than others. The purpose of the JIT compiler is to convert Java bytecode to native machine code. Hence, by paying a small price at startup, important performance gains resulted at runtime. The improved performance was not yet at a par, however, with the types of performance optimizations achieved by compilers of languages such as C or Delphi. This is due to the reduced visibility the JIT compiler has of the execution logic of the program; bytecode does not convey as much information about a program's underlying logic as does a higher order language such as C, C++, or Pascal. Hence, the JIT compiler is unable to optimize loops or method calls to the same extent a "classic" compiler is. This is why the Hotspot compiler was introduced as of Java 1.3. Instead of taking a "brute force" approach to bytecode conversion, the Hotspot compiler runs the bytecode in interpreted mode long enough to understand its underlying logic. Once it has been able to "figure out" this logic it is able to decide which parts of the code are worthwhile, converting to native code and how to best optimize these parts. It may even decide to continue interpreting some parts of the bytecode if these are deemed not to have a fundamental performance impact.

Interpreted Languages

Although any language can be either compiled or interpreted, the languages that were built with an interpreter as the underlying engine usually have two things in common. They are either purpose-built to be efficient at one or more specific tasks or they have been conceived to be very dynamic in nature, and quite often they have both characteristics.

Most, if not all, so-called scripting languages are interpreted languages. The vast majority of scripting languages are purpose-built; for instance, shell script languages target the manipulation of operating system artifacts such as files and directories, Javascript is good at manipulating the object model underlying the Web pages rendered by a browser, and the AWK language was designed to work with text.

The interpreters for these languages are for the most part built in a way wherein the code is interpreted just prior to execution. This means that the code is quite often reinterpreted for each line that is executed. This is very sluggish, and clearly not performance prone, but it makes it very easy to change the code and reexecute it, which makes development and test cycles very rapid. These languages are therefore used in contexts where the ease of changing the scripts and the facilities provided by the language (such as file and directory manipulation in shell scripts) will give the development team an edge when it comes to speed of coding rather than speed of execution.

Other languages such as Ruby, Python, or Perl are also quite often associated with interpretation. However, these languages—or should we say, their execution platform—use a slightly different approach than scripting languages. The code for these languages is compiled to an intermediate representation just prior to execution or on an as needed basis. This will make it easy for the execution engine to translate the instructions in the alternate representation to operations of the underlying processor architecture. Although this mechanism will impact performance, it is faster than that used by scripting language and does facilitate the creation of dynamic languages, some of which are targeted toward specific problems. Perl, for instance, is a language that was developed to make string manipulations easier, which has made it an ideal language to develop dynamic Web content; after all, a Web page, in its simplest form, is a long string of text.

Your choice of such a language will need to be balanced between the need for performance versus the facilities provided by these languages. As an example, Ruby with the addition of Ruby on Rails makes the development of Web sites with a database backend a breeze; hence, if your Web site is targeted at short, low-complexity transactions, Ruby may well be for you.

Distributed Processing

Distributed processing can take many forms and has been around for quite some time. Before Web Services ever saw the light of day there was RPC, Corba, DCOM, RMI, and possibly other mechanisms to enable a software solution to execute function calls across a network.

These calls come at a great computing cost. Not only does the function call need to be translated into a format that is platform independent (remember the section on overserialization), but additional checks are required to verify connectivity, additional mechanisms are required to manage the lifecycle of remote objects or processes, security has to be taken into consideration, and possibly distributed transaction solutions might have to be involved. All of these will drain the capacity of your system for the sole purpose of making a call over the network. You must therefore make sure that this luxury is used sparingly and for the right purpose.

One of the greater benefits brought by Web Services is that this technology has put an emphasis on the notion of providing services rather than functions across the network. Services are of a higher order than functions and, when designed correctly, will illicit different usage patterns that aim at limiting the number of calls over the network. A service-oriented approach is the right approach to designing distributed solutions; it is a cause for thought as to why it has taken us so long to figure this out.

Make sure to keep this in mind when designing your distributed solution even if you do not use actual Web Services technology. Design with services in mind, rather than functions. Create services that represent actual business functions, and therefore have a real business value. Build the interfaces such as to limit the number of calls required during any given interaction.

The additional bonus you get from using actual Web Services is that you can rely on the actual infrastructure that was built for the Web. This gives you access to a whole plethora of solutions for load balancing hypertext transfer protocol (HTTP) requests, monitoring network traffic, and handling network failover.

Centralized versus Decentralized Processing

It is interesting to note how over the years computing has flipped back and forth between centralized and decentralized models of processing and how these have been related to the availability of processing power and the need for performance. First there was the central mainframe, one machine with tremendous amounts of power available. Over the years workstations started gaining in power and hence it became possible to off-load some of the processing toward the desktop, which is how the client-server decentralized model came about. In time, networking capabilities evolved and distributing processing across multiple servers, and the advent of the Internet made it desirable again to centralize much of the processing. These days the need to provide users with a richer Internet experience is pushing new demands of processing toward the browser using Web 2.0 technologies, which tend to indicate the resurgence of a decentralized processing model.

Distributed Transactions

If you have decided to go distributed you may be faced with a dilemma regarding the way to deal with transactions. Transactions are dealt with easily when a single resource is involved (e.g., a database); however, when multiple resources are involved, and these resources are moreover distributed across the network, the complexity of transaction processing gets multiplied.

Now the transaction manager has to coordinate multiple transactional resources across the network. In itself the "two-phase commit" protocol used to coordinate multiple transactional resources is already causing a lot of overhead, but it is even less efficient when it has to do its coordination work over the network.

Hence, although it may be easier for your developers to use distributed transaction management (they will have to put less thought into how to manage the transaction), it is definitely not the way to build a "lean and mean" system. Whenever possible, use transactions involving only one resource.

Note also that in our experience many systems that support distributed transactions do so poorly. They quite often depend on the good comprehension and interpretation of a distributed transaction management protocol such as XA. These protocols are very complex, and their errors due to misinterpretation or miscomprehension are not uncommon.

XML

In what follows we talk about all the declinations of the extensible markup language (XML) and not about a specific standard or a particular industry. Although it can be said that XML has done wonders to enable collaboration of widely disparate systems over the Internet, it is probably one of the worst technological choices when it comes to performance.

Given that the goal of XML (and its predecessor, standard generalized markup language [SGML]) was to create a language that was both readable by humans and by the computer at the same time, it is a structured language, but not one that is the most efficient for a machine to read. Humans require a verbose identifier and some formatting—such as spacing, line breaks, and tabulations—in order to be able to read and understand XML, whereas the computer couldn't care less and would be more efficient if it didn't have to read all the formatting characters and was provided with numerical identifiers that take up less space and can be more readily matched to records in a database or memory array.

By making the above statement we are not encouraging you to make XML more machine readable and less human readable, as this would defeat one of the main reasons for the use of XML. If you were inclined to do so, we would encourage you to look at other means for transporting data rather than using XML.

The message we want to pass on is that XML is a beneficial technology when it comes to the definition of messaging contracts between heterogeneous systems, but that it should not be used indiscriminately for any sort of communication, especially when performance is critical.

When you do end up choosing XML as the mechanism for communication of your application, the one thing to choose correctly is the parsing technology that will read the XML. A number of parsing mechanisms exist that are either more or less efficient. Choosing the one that is right for you will depend on what you need to do with the XML data. At different ends of the complexity spectrum you have mechanisms that are SAX (simple API for XML) based and those that are DOM (document object model) based.

SAX-based solutions will handle the XML piecemeal, one element at a time. The overhead of the parser is minimal but you have to do all the leg work yourself. The advantage is that you have complete control of the parsing and can stop it at any time if you do not require all of the information in the XML, or if the XML is incorrect.

DOM-based techniques will parse the complete XML and provide the developer with a document object model, which can be used to programmatically traverse the XML elements. The advantage here is that using the object model the developer has complete flexibility in the manipulation of the XML structure. It is possible to get a list of all elements with a certain name, to add or remove elements to the structure, etc.

In both cases the parser will usually give you the luxury to validate the XML for you against either an XML schema or an XML document type definition (DTD). Without detailing these two mechanisms—which is not within the scope of this book—we can, however, mention that a schema is more complex to validate than a DTD.

The right parsing mechanism is the mechanism that will perform exactly the amount of work that you require. In most cases SAX-based mechanisms will do the trick when all you need to do is read the XML once to transform it into some other format or object model, whereas DOM will be more useful if the XML structure needs to be traversed a number of times and possibly modified.

Software

This section will look at performance from the perspective of different software solutions found in the most common system architectures in the industry. Each one of these common software infrastructure pieces will require special attention when it comes to performance tuning. Our goal here is to provide some commonsense guidelines regarding the attention points for each of these systems when scrutinizing performance.

These guidelines will obviously not replace the expertise of a person specialized in the configuration and operation of these solutions, but should provide the reader with enough insight to tackle some of the more common performance issues found when dealing with these often used infrastructure components. However, when in doubt, hire a professional!

When building a system that will require a large amount of tuning and has some very stringent performance requirements, we are confident that you will require support from the software vendor(s) you have selected to support your system. Given that it is not unlikely you will need to ask your vendors for changes, fixes, or enhancements in their product if you are dealing with a performance-intensive problem, you would do well to ensure that the vendor will indeed support you to that extent. This is usually rather easy when you are a big corporation with million-dollar maintenance agreements with your vendors, but it may be a problem if you are a small outfit with limited resources. In the latter case you may want to side with either smaller vendors who will be willing to partner with you, or with open-source software that you will be able to tweak to your specifications when the need arises.

Databases

When it comes to databases, you can summarize the things to focus on when considering the performance of your database server in one word: *structure*. In what follows we will discuss relational database systems, since these are the systems that we the authors are most familiar with. We are confident that whatever the database system, the means to tune it will always deal with structure. Other database engines will likely use a different terminology to refer to their specific structures.

Storage Structures

The structure of your database will be important at different levels. Let us start at the lowest level, the structure of the data files onto the physical storage system.

Four main data structures normally compose a database system:

1. The system tables that hold information about the database structure itself, or what is usually referred to as *metadata* (data about the data).
2. The database tables and other objects such as stored procedures, views, and so forth.
3. The database indexes, which, although they are another type of database object, are considered separately given the essential role they play in making a database efficient.
4. The transaction logs, and other log files used to handle various aspects of a database's operations.

Each of the above structures is stored by most database solutions in one or more files. In order to optimize access to these files it is preferable to store them on different file systems, segregated across different disks. As a result, when these files are accessed in parallel by the database engine, disk access will also occur in parallel.

Index Structures

Once files are correctly structured, the next area to look into are the indexes. Indexes will allow the database engine to optimize query access to your data but they will slow down creation, updating, and deletion operations. Define your indexes with care and make sure to include the appropriate columns in each index. It is possible to combine more than one column into one index, which enables the engine to use this index for either column. You will have to give precedence to the most used column, however. For instance, in the example below, both index creation stanzas will allow the engine to optimize access based on the values of columns A and B. However, the first stanza will be better when the sort order or selection criteria favor first A and then B, whereas in the second stanza the opposite is true.

CREATE INDEX TABLE_T_IDX ON T(A,B);

CREATE INDEX TABLE_T_IDX ON T(B,A);

Depending on your database system, it may also be possible to define different types of indexes depending on the data you are manipulating. B-tree-like indexes are used in one form or another by most database solutions and are very efficient when the indexed data has a high degree of uniqueness, meaning that the entries are mostly different from each other. For data that does not vary as widely, other types of indexes will be more efficient. Check your database system for the types of indexes it has to offer.

Together with the proper index definitions you have to make the database engine aware of the sizes of your tables; this is usually referred to as the database's statistics. These statistics will allow the engine to determine if it is more cost-effective to use an index or simply to scan a table for the contents you require. For small tables it is most often more efficient to simply scan the table for the required content, but the engine can only do this if its information about the table contents is up to date.

After all of this, if you still need an edge on one of the indexes, you may consider pinning the index into memory, which is also an option provided by most databases. You would only do this if, first of all, the index is used very frequently and, second, the index size does not grow a lot. By doing this you will prevent costly I/O operations to occur if parts of the index are not present in memory.

Partitions

If you still do not achieve the desired performance after tuning all of the above structures, you may need to partition your data. Partitioning should only be considered when dealing with very large amounts of data, rule of thumb: more than a million rows in one table. When dealing with these types of volumes partitioning will allow you to apply a "divide and conquer" strategy. The data gets divided into smaller volumes that can be managed more efficiently. When a query has to take into account data across all of the partitions it is also possible for the engine to optimize execution of the query by accessing the information in the different partitions in parallel and then merge the results from all partitions together in the end. If the data that needs to be retrieved is not large, then this will be a lot more efficient than looking up the data in a linear fashion.

Other Ways to Improve Database Performance

There are, of course, other ways to improve your database's performance. You can use other structural tricks, such as materialized views, to improve data access for read-only data. You can tune the number of connections that can be made to your database, or you can tune the memory allocation for different caches and memory areas used by the database engine. These parameters will be very specific to each database engine and we invite you to discover them by consulting the manuals of your preferred database package.

Application Servers

As this book aims to be generic we will not try to discuss performance tuning of any specific application server on the market. There are definitely books better suited than this one for divulging all the tips and tricks of a specific vendor when it comes to their application server. Instead of giving you a grocery list of all the different parameters that can be used to get the most out of this or that application server, we will try and focus on those resources that will have to be tuned for any middleware of this sort.

Tuning of an application server could be referred to as "the tuning of the pools" given that the control of resources within such servers is usually managed by changing the size of a pool of resources. The pools that can normally be sized are listed in Table 5.4.

Messaging Middleware

Messaging middleware, also known as queues, plays an important role when it comes to asynchronous processing. Depending on the use you want to make of this type of middleware, your concerns should focus on different characteristics of these solutions.

- If you are looking for raw speed there are solutions (e.g., Tibco RendezVous) that will be very efficient in fast message delivery. These solutions will draw heavily on your network resources and will be highly dependent on your network topology. The purpose of these solutions is to deliver messages fast, but as a result they will not always guarantee actual delivery of the message, or the uniqueness of said delivery (the message might get delivered two or more

Table 5.4 Resource Pools

Resource Pool	Why Tune It?
Threads	This is the central resource of your application server. It will determine how many requests can be processed concurrently inside of the server. These requests will be either of the synchronous or asynchronous type. Note that depending on your server it may be possible to define more than one set of threads (also referred to as thread pools). Each set can then be associated to a specific request channel (e.g., one set for all HTTP online requests, and one set for all message-based asynchronous requests). It is important to understand the relation between threads and other resources in the system. In order for a thread to completely handle a request it will most likely need to access various other resources in the application server. Hence, if these other resources are not sized in a way that will guarantee a resource is always free when a thread needs it, the resource will be causing a bottleneck in the processing and introduce performance issues. It is therefore a good rule of thumb to have more of these other resources than there are threads. If many types of different requests are processed by the system it will be useful to divide the processing of requests between different sets of threads and size the resources used by these requests based on the sizing of the given thread set.
Connections	There are many different connections that can be managed by the application server. Database connections are the most common ones; however, there can also be connections to messaging middleware, connections to third-party applications, network connections to handle all sorts of protocols, etc.... As mentioned above you will have to size these connections based on the number of them that are required by a typical request multiplied by the number of parallel requests that can be handled by the system at any given time, which is equivalent to the number of threads that can process the request. Connections = ConnectionPerRequest * Threads + KK is a small constant that you'll add to account for errors in your knowledge of how many connections are required per request. Usually 5 is a good number. You will also have to be certain that the target system for the connections (database, third-party app), has sufficient capacity to handle the number of connections that you plan to set up to it. If this application is also application server–based, for instance, you may need to ensure that its threads are equal to the number of connections you have foreseen.

– continued

Table 5.4 Resource Pools

Objects	Although not true for all application servers, most modern ones use an object or component paradigm. In order to manage the memory usage of the server, it will not allow an unlimited creation of the base components into memory, but will rather rely on pools of objects that can only grow to a certain size. These object pools are a resource like any other in the system, and hence could be sized according to the same rules as the number of connections discussed above. We discuss objects separately because some application servers use the object pool not only to recycle old objects in order to create new ones, but also as a transactional cache. In this case the cache is used to maintain the state of objects during as part of the lifecycle of a transaction. For some types of requests it is possible that a large number of objects participate in a transaction and hence the size of the object pool should be based on the largest number of objects that may participate in a transaction of your request. PoolSize = ObjectsInTransaction * Threads. In this case you will have to verify that your system has enough memory to host all of the different object pools.

times). These are ideal when messages need to be broadcast very efficiently but actual delivery is not mandatory, and when the receiving system tolerates multiple deliveries of the same message.

■ If guaranteed delivery is what you are looking for, the messaging solution you will choose will have to include a mechanism to persist the data. This means that performance will be impacted by the additional I/O cost that will be incurred. Depending on the underlying persistence mechanism, the impact can be non-negligible. Many messaging systems (e.g., IBM WebSphere MQ) will use a database system as their persistence mechanism. This provides additional flexibility for the management of the messages—the messages can be indexed by topic or other criteria, or the transaction manager of the database engine can be used to enroll the message persistence activity into a transaction—but it does add additional overhead to the whole operation of sending a message. If all you are interested in is that your message is guaranteed to get from point A to point B, a simple file-based solution may be what you require.

■ Your requirements may also involve complex routing, in which case the throughput of your setup will be dependent on the routing rules you have defined and the associated network infrastructure. In the case of complex routing across multiple networks, the overall behavior of this type of middleware will be more dependent on network latency, network traffic, etc. rather than on the configuration of the middleware itself.

One of the nicer things about messaging middleware is that performance problems associated with these tools are fairly easy to identify: just find the location of where messages are getting queued and you've found where the problem is. This does not mean, however, that the problem will be easy to resolve.

ETLs

Now that we have discussed software that is used mainly in processing discrete units of work, such as messages and online requests, let's talk a bit about tools that are geared toward the processing of high volume "batch" units of work. This software family gets referred to as ETL, which stands for *extract, transform, and load*—in other words, *extract* a lot of information from one or more places (databases, files, or other storage media), *transform* it in some way, and *load* it back into (usually) another place or set of places.

ETLs are by their very nature very resource intensive. They will try to squeeze the most out of your system in order to extract the data as quickly as possible, transform it at blazing speed, and load it back to its target. Extracting and loading will put a heavy strain on your system's I/O capacity, whereas the transformation will drain memory and CPU. These tools usually offer an impressive number of parameters that will help you tune them so that they will solely use those resources that you want them to use.

The one thing to understand about this type of software is that it is mainly a way to ease the implementation of processes that conform to the pipe-and-filter pattern. The main characteristic of this pattern is that it is linear and does not automatically lend itself to parallelization, which would allow cutting the time necessary to perform the required transformations. This means that it will often be the job of the ETL engineer to determine how to parallelize the transformation process.

Parallelization of a pipe-and-filter process is straightforward in itself (as shown in Figure 5.4). All you need to do is split the data up so that it can be processed in parallel.

In practice, however, it is seldom as easy as we make it sound. It must be possible to split the data, which is dependent on a number of aspects of the data and the transformation process:

- Splitting the data and processing it in parallel must be less costly than processing everything linearly. In other words, the splitting process must be low-cost, and you must have sufficient CPU power to process the data in parallel.
- The data entities being split up must not be interdependent from the perspective of the filtering process, otherwise that process will not provide the proper function.
- When other data inputs are used within the same process, it must be possible to split those inputs as well or to replicate them so that one copy is available to each parallel process.

If you are unable to split up the processing into a number of parallel chunks, you may be reduced to finding the most appropriate ETL solution for you. As usual, the software landscape is rife with different kinds of solutions in this

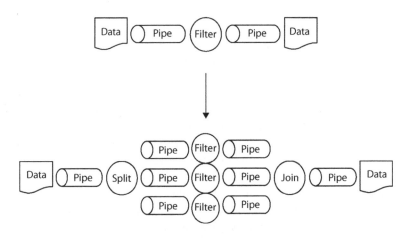

Figure 5.4   Parallelization of a pipe-and-filter process.

problem space. Some solutions will be very generic, favoring all sorts of transformations and ease of use but providing results that are not always optimal. Other solutions are targeted at very specific problems, e.g. sorting of data. Many database vendors also offer solutions to handle data extracted from their database; these solutions are usually not very user friendly or loaded with functionality, but they are designed to optimize the extraction and load process from and to the database, which is often costly due to its I/O nature.

Hardware Infrastructure

Phew! You've made it this far. You've made sure that your requirements were specified with performance in mind, you designed your application to use every bit of CPU and memory available to you, you optimized your code, and you tuned all of the software pieces you were reliant upon. And still you want more bang for your buck. It is now time to look at your hardware infrastructure.

Resources

When it comes to hardware, the problem of performance becomes a problem of managing the resources that you have available to you, knowing that most of these resources do not come cheap. You'll have to determine the configuration that will optimize your usage of CPU, storage, network, and possibly other hardware devices. Where to look first for optimization options will highly depend on the profile of your application.

If you are dealing with a computing intensive application you'll want to have the fastest CPUs, and possibly a lot of them as long as the application scales horizontally. For such applications, looking at network throughput and latency may only be necessary if you want to distribute the processing across multiple computer nodes, and communication between said nodes is intensive. Storage will likely be of little concern.

If you are dealing with an online transaction system, storage and network capabilities will likely be of the essence. You'll want to look at network hardware to distribute your load across multiple servers to make sure that your database and storage systems are properly tuned to minimize I/O latency and maximize throughput, and you'll want to do the same for your network. The network topology will have to be designed to minimize packet hops; preferably those computer nodes that exchange a lot of data should be on the same subnet and use gigabit connectivity (or better, if available). Storage will require direct channel attachments of the storage devices probably using technologies such as dark fiber.

If you are dealing with heavy batch processing, you'll have to be particularly attentive to the I/O capabilities of your servers. You'll want to ensure that I/O bandwidth can be tuned and that sufficient I/O channels are available on the machine to allow some level of scalability for I/O operations.

Whatever your challenge, you'll want to make sure that a proper capacity projection was done as part of your project, and that it is later substantiated by taking adequate measurements during your performance and sustainability tests.

Resource Sharing, a.k.a. Federation

Many companies these days are either looking at federating their hardware or are actively doing so. Companies look at hardware sharing primarily as a means to optimize usage of an expensive pool of resources and secondarily as a means to facilitate management of this resource pool. To support this, a number of vendors have come up with an offering that will allow their customers to request additional hardware power when the need arises (e.g., IBM's On Demand program).

There are different strategies that can be applied to federate your resources. You can use hardware capabilities to make this possible; one of the most prominent technologies in this area has been dubbed "blade" technology, which relates to the ability of hardware supporting this technology to be "sliced and diced" in a manner that will support the user's processing requirements. The advantage of this type of technology is that the split up of processing resources is done at the hardware level; hence, there will be no degradation of performance to a target system running on the partition of a blade server. This system will have its own dedicated processors, memory, and I/O busses.

A different approach to federation involves the use of virtual machine technology to create "virtual hardware," which uses the capacity of the underlying system for actual operations. This approach does impact performance of the system as a whole. Although the exact capacity consumption of each virtual machine is in most cases controllable (depending on which vendor solution you use), the code used to "virtualize" the hardware resources will always induce a level of overhead to the overall processing power of the system, thereby lowering its raw performance. This approach does have the advantage that it will allow you to deploy an image of a virtual machine on the target platform using a predefined set of virtualized hardware, which means that you can use a similar image to deploy to your development, test, and production environment. This has clear advantages for people wanting to tightly control the promotion process of a software solution.

Yet another approach that we have seen used is the federation of applications using application servers. In this case applications are deployed as packages (e.g., EAR files), onto the target application server, and it is the resources dedicated to the applications server (see page 125) that will be shared by the different applications. This is probably the most difficult approach to control from a capacity-management perspective. If applications deployed in this way are not well behaved and the application server resources they will use are not segregated, situations will arise in which one application ends up consuming all resources, thereby leaving the other applications with no processing power. It is therefore important, should you choose this approach, to impose strict regulations upon the application developers regarding the way they use application server resources, and how they configure their components. You should try and favor independent resource pool usages (see Table 5.4) as much as possible; this way each application will impact only its own resources.

Summary

Somebody recently told me, "presentation is 50% of success," and although he was talking about the clothes he was wearing I believe this is very true when it comes to presenting information to a user.

For the end user, the perception of performance is what counts; it is quite possible that the underlying system is doing more processing than what would be absolutely necessary, but if this gives the user the impression that everything is going very fast, you have probably done something right.

Today's AJAX solutions are a big help at making the user perceive things are going faster for instance. While the user fills out a Web form, his inputs are being checked by XML-based requests made in the background. Although the XMLs being sent back and forth between the Web browser and the server require a lot more capacity from the server systems than if one request was used for the whole validation process, the overall perception to the user is that his work, and therefore the system, is done faster.

Another one of today's technologies that can be used to give the user a perception of faster processing pertains to the use of work-flow technology. Using a work-flow system (a.k.a. an exception management system) you can refrain from executing tedious parts of the processing as part of the user's transaction. If a complex validation can be split up into a simple validation capturing 80% of the problems and a more involved validation that is required yet only triggers an error 20% of the time, the secondary check can be left for a later time and executed as a separate part of the work-flow process. When the error is triggered, either a compensating action can be taken or the user can be notified at that time that something went wrong. By using this strategy the user will not be bothered by the overhead of the difficult validation and will only be bothered by it, after the fact, 20% of the time.

These technologies may not be the right ones to solve your performance problems, but decoupling parts of the processing from the user's interaction process may well be what you need for some of them. So don't always think of performance; think of appearance.

Chapter 6

Test Planning

Non-functional test planning and execution is a challenge. Planning your scope, executing your tests, and interpreting results are tasks that require a delicate balance of business understanding, technical expertise, and objectivity. Whereas functional testing can be reliably mapped to functional requirements, non-functional test scope is derived from a usage model that is an approximation of how the system will be used.

To ensure effective test cycles, the following planning activities are important:

1. **Identify high-level non-functional scope:** In this activity, you identify exactly which requirements will be tested, to what degree they will be tested, and when they will be tested.

2. **Review and accept non-functional requirements:** If the business analyst and technical participants have completed quality non-functional requirements, review and acceptance of the requirements will be a short meeting. This is an opportunity to ask questions, clarify understanding, and gain an appreciation for where special emphasis may be required.

3. **Define core and optional test cases:** For complex systems, the nature of non-functional testing is such that it is very difficult to test every permutation of human and machine inputs. In this activity, the non-functional test lead proposes a set of detailed test cases that outline the test objective, required data, configurations, test steps, and supporting apparatus.

4. **Define test tools and supplementary software:** The last ten years have seen major advances in the variety and capabilities of software testing tools. In order to create artificial input volumes, you will very likely require a software package. There are a number of packages available and we will discuss them in this chapter.

5. **Determine resource and environment requirements:** Execution of non-functional tests is a technical activity requiring development expertise. You need to account for this in your resource model.
6. **Prioritize and schedule test execution:** Non-functional test execution usually requires most of the application functionality to be working simultaneously. If the development team is creating the system in a series of phased deliverables, you will need to accommodate this in your scheduling. There is also a clear advantage to bringing high-risk test activities as far forward as possible.

As you complete the planning activities listed above, you should record your decisions and intentions in a non-functional test strategy document. The strategy document is a good reference for yourself and other stakeholders who require a view of your test plan and methodology.

This chapter reviews each of the listed elements of the test planning phase. We illustrate examples of where poor planning has caused projects to incur delays or omit important test coverage. This chapter is mandatory reading for professionals responsible for ensuring that quality non-functional test coverage is executed according to schedule.

Defining Your Scope

It is tempting to take the position that you must test *everything,* but this perspective is impractical. In determining scope, your objective is to be pragmatic and weigh technical risk against business needs to arrive at a scope that adequately mitigates business risk. By definition, non-functional testing concerns itself with testing scenarios during which

- Things go wrong
- A number of things happen all at once
- Extreme conditions are reached (e.g., extreme data volumes)

As we shall see, there are hundreds of ways that things can go wrong. For complex systems, the permutations of human and machine inputs are virtually endless. In this section, we look at ways of coping with the magnitude of possible test cases that this reality presents for both operability and performance test types. But first we will discuss how to assign components inside and outside of your system boundary.

System Boundaries

Your test strategy must include a statement defining system boundaries for your intended scope. Components that fall within your system boundary are generally components that are being developed as part of the program or project under which you are working. For these components it is expected that you have access to a software vendor or in-house development team. It is also expected that you have an in-house testing environment along with the deployment capability to install and configure the application.

Components that are outside the system boundary are external systems and dependencies over which you have no control. In defining these components outside of the system boundary, you assume that they will meet an agreed upon service level in the production environment and do not require any direct testing as part of your efforts.

As we shall see in Chapter 7, for these components it is often necessary to simulate the external system with a homegrown component that stands in for the external dependency in order to support your test scenarios. Let's look at an example architecture, as shown in Figure 6.1, and apply the previous definitions to determine a system boundary.

The example shown in Figure 6.1 describes a CRM (customer relationship management) solution in which 500+ customer service representatives (CSRs) respond to customer telephone inquiries; these customer service agents are widely distributed geographically. Primarily, agents work from home on desktop computers that are provided to them for this purpose. The client application communicates with an application server using SOAP/HTTPS. A collection of services are exposed as Web services to the application server for shared functionality like sending email and faxes. Customer information is drawn from an enterprise customer database that is accessed over a MQ (message queue) series messaging interface.

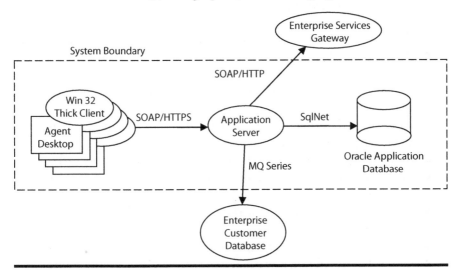

Figure 6.1   Example system boundary for a CRM application.

In this example, all of the components that are shown within the system boundary are being upgraded as part of a major system enhancement. The development team is actively engaged and can assist with scoping, deployment, troubleshooting, tuning. The enterprise customer database and the enterprise gateway tier, however, are existing services that have been previously tested. These systems are actually already in the production environment and support similar loads to that which will be imposed by the new system.

The organization has tested these systems well beyond the business usage model for the distributed call center. Both of these applications are in a support mode and do not have development resources available to assist with testing and development. Furthermore, these enterprise services belong to a different division in the organization. The bureaucracy required to include them within the system boundary would cause costs to multiply. In Chapter 7 we will see how our system boundary will influence our test execution.

It should be obvious that the elements within our system boundary are high risk and justify commanding the bulk of our testing efforts. The supporting legacy systems are outside our system boundary. You will need to make a similar judgment call for your application and document it in your test strategy as part of your test planning. Our next area of focus is on how to scope the coverage for the test case itself.

Scope of Operability

For even moderately complex systems, there are a myriad of ways that things can go wrong. Consider a simple example like database failure. Here is a list of different scenarios in which your application can experience database failures. We use an Oracle database as an example:

- The network fails and can no longer route responses back to the application
- The network fails and can no longer forward requests to the database
- The network cannot find the database server
- The network is functioning, but latency increases and causes 50% of requests to timeout
- The database is listening to requests, but is returning an authentication error
- All Oracle processes on the database are down
- The listener on the database is down, but the database is otherwise healthy
- The listener is running and accepting requests, but the shared server processes are down
- The database is experiencing performance issues and 50% of requests are timing out
- The database is refusing new connections
- The database is refusing new connections after a delay of two minutes
- The database is returning transaction errors

- The database is configured with *Real Application Clustering (RAC)* and one of the servers has stopped responding
- One or both of the servers in the RAC cluster experiences memory corruption
- One or both of the servers in the RAC cluster is unplugged
- One or both of the servers in the RAC cluster experiences kernel panic
- An Oracle shared server process crashes and creates a core dump
- Oracle server runs out of disk for table extents

In this list we have included only scenarios that are *external* to your software system. The client connectivity can also be subject to a host of potentially fatal types of errors. If you decide to conduct non-functional test scope for database failure, which of the above test cases will you include? No one would dispute that including all of these failure scenarios results in the highest-quality test coverage, but the testing may take four weeks to execute. Is this practical?

To make matters worse, the load profile for the system is also variable. For each of the failure scenarios above there are potentially hundreds of variations of in-flight requests based on time of day and season, not to mention the randomness associated with individual user behavior. Consider a scenario in which there are 12 distinct and unique scheduled jobs for your system. Are you going to test each and every job with each of the 20 failure scenarios above? This would result in 120 test cases *just for the combination of job execution and database failure.* We haven't yet considered human and machine online inputs in this planning.

As you can see, defining your test scope means making judicious decisions. A prudent approach includes consideration of the following inputs:

- How much business risk is associated with this functionality?
- From a technical point of view, how many unique test cases are associated with failure for this component?
- From a technical perspective, what is the likelihood of each type of failure?

This discussion can only be had by involving the business and technical participants who helped to formulate your non-functional requirements. If we revisit the list of Oracle database failure types from above, we can group them based on similarity to one another as follows:

Database Not Responding (50% Likely)
- The network fails and can no longer route responses back to the application
- The network fails and can no longer forward requests back to the application
- The network cannot find the database server
- The network is functioning, but latency increases and causes 50% of requests to timeout
- All Oracle processes on the database are down

- The database is experiencing performance issues, and 50% of requests are timing out
- The database is refusing new connections after a delay of two minutes.

Database Responding with Application Error (25% Likely)

- The database is listening to requests, but is returning an authentication error
- The listener on the database is down, but the database is otherwise healthy
- The listener is running and accepting requests, but the dispatcher and shared server processes are not running
- The database is refusing new connections
- The database is returning transaction errors on every commit
- Oracle server runs out of disk for table extents

Database Partially Available (25% Likely)

- One or both of the servers in the RA cluster experiences memory corruption
- The database is configured with *Real Application Clustering* and one of the servers stops responding
- One or both of the servers in the RAC cluster is unplugged
- One or both of the servers in the RAC cluster experiences kernel panic
- An Oracle shared server process crashes and creates a core dump

Basically, each type of failure belongs to one of three types: (1) the database is not responding at all; (2) the database is responding immediately with an application error; or (3) the database is only partially available.

If we agree that fundamentally the application should react in a similar way for each of the failure modes in any one of these categories, we can take the first step in defining our test scope.

In each of the three categories, we select the most representative failure mode for that category. For example, we may decide that the network configuration is static and reliable, so the most likely mode of failure would be a sudden performance/capacity event on the database in which all or the majority of database requests begin to timeout. We apply similar thinking to the remaining two categories and agree on mode of failure for these categories also.

Next we examine associated business risk. In dialog with the business and technical participants, we learn that 10 of the 12 jobs scheduled for this application are not critical. These 10 jobs perform housekeeping tasks that can be completed anytime within a one week window. If a job fails or does not run, its processing will be completed the following day. Further, these ten jobs run on a dedicated server that is isolated from the more critical online application. The remaining two jobs, however, are highly business critical. Architecturally, these jobs are constrained to share the online application server and, to make matters worse, they run at the end of the peak usage period for the online application. In this case, it is an easy decision to categorize these jobs as mandatory test cases for each of the three failure modes that we have defined. As a result of our analysis, instead of 120 test cases, we now have six test cases. Since the two jobs are independent of one another and run on a similar schedule, we may further optimize our execution to schedule a total of three tests in which each failure mode is tested for both of the jobs at the same time. We will talk more about optimizing test execution later in this chapter.

Scope of Performance

The factor that most complicates performance testing efforts is variability in business usage. In the same way that a business usage model approximates actual usage, our test cases will approximate the business usage model. How heavily you are able to invest in performance testing will be a function of perceived risk and expected cost. If time and budget permits, you should derive your test cases based on 100% of the load scenarios defined in the non-functional requirements. If this is not possible, you may need to sit down with business and technical participants to exclude scenarios that are

- **Low business risk** (For example, a feature is not frequently accessed and/or a business user can tolerate poor performance)
- **Complex** to implement because load scenario requires preconditions that are hard to achieve or require interactions with systems outside of your system boundary
- **Technically equivalent** to a scenario that has already been defined for your scope

If you do decide to exclude load scenarios, this needs to be clearly communicated to management along with the reasons for excluding these test cases. Be prepared to justify the expected cost for full scenario coverage versus your proposed coverage. Initially, it is difficult for most people to accept that 100% non-functional test coverage is infeasible for most systems. Part of your challenge will be to educate your stakeholders on the limitations we have discussed in this chapter.

Load Testing Software

Load testing software is available from a number of reputable software vendors. In this section, we discuss product features that we feel have been critical to the success of projects in our experience. We will also make some brief comments on products that are available at the time of this writing.

Product Features

A prerequisite for executing performance and operability tests is a solution for how you will create load in your testing environment. For applications having a large number of concurrent users, a software solution is required. It is impractical to create load manually with human testers.

Choosing the right software solution for your testing is a decision involving many factors, including the skill set of your testers, available budget, corporate standards, software platform for your solution, and whether your application will have an ongoing need for non-functional test capabilities. In this section we will enumerate a number of product features that are important in any solution.

1. **Randomness:** Many loading tools can create randomness in the execution of your test scenarios on your behalf. This is helpful because it allows you to execute load in a way that is generally consistent with expected usage, but that also allows for subtle variations expected in human usage. The most common implementation of a randomness strategy is through the concept of *think time*. Think time refers to the length of pauses between execution of steps in the load scenario. Think time simulates the time that a user or external system spends looking at a screen or otherwise contemplating/processing outputs from your system.

2. **Supported interfaces (web, wireless, client/server, etc.):** Some load testing solutions support exclusively web-based applications. If you represent the needs of a large organization, you should inventory the full range of applications for which testing will be required and make sure that you choose a solution that can support each of them. For example, only a subset of load testing tools can support client/server protocols necessary to simulate thick client interaction.

3. **Scripting and programmable logic:** Some solutions offer you a great deal of flexibility in terms of building logic into your load scenarios. Other solutions limit you to a record/playback capability in which there is limited means to make scripts intelligent. A single "smart" script may support three different scenarios using condition logic. A scripting language also enables you to include non-standard pauses and validation conditions. If you suspect that you will need to develop more complex load scenarios for your application, make sure that you have the required development expertise available. Products may employ widely used scripting languages like Visual Basic or Jython. Other products require use of their own proprietary language.

4. **Cost:** Predictably, feature-rich, industry-leading load solutions can be very expensive. In contrast, there are some very functional open source solutions that are free.

5. **Externalizing data from scripting steps:** A major part of the variation in many load scenarios is the variation in data. In the online banking example

from Chapter 1, we identified two types of users: retail and small-business users. In implementing load testing scenarios, it is preferable to implement a single script for functions like "login" that can be multi-purposed for both retail and small-business users. In many solutions, data like username, account number, and amount can be externalized from the script itself as part of a configuration file.

6. **Overhead and concurrency:** If you need to simulate 100s or 1000s of concurrent users, you will need a load-testing platform that is robust. The loading software needs to maintain state for each concurrent request and reliably report performance statistics and error rate to a central database as part of your results. Software packages capable of supporting high volumes do so by implementing a distributed set of controllers and agent processes that can create load from a scalable number of server machines. Software vendors with this level of support will charge customers based on the number of concurrent scenarios that they need to execute.

7. **Reporting capabilities:** One of the advantages of using a load testing solution is that reporting, including statistics like average, minimum, maximum, and percentile, is completed on your behalf. Depending on the vendor, many reports include detailed graphing capabilities and comparison against previous test cycles.

8. **Monitoring:** Some vendors include plug-ins for monitoring software components in your solution itself. Such plug-ins can monitor OS (operating system) parameters like memory, threads, and CPU (central processing unit). Plug-ins also exist for monitoring vendor-specific platforms that implement standards such as J2EE and .NET. The authors recommend leveraging the monitoring platform that is intended for the production environment as part of your testing strategy. Monitoring capabilities that are bundled with load testing software can be used to supplement, but not replace, the monitoring that should already be in your test environment.

Vendor Products

Selecting the right load testing software for your system will depend on many factors, including how you prioritize features described in the previous section. In this section, we include some objective opinion on some of the more popular load testing tools available at time of writing.

Mercury LoadRunner, now a part of HP's IT management product suite, enjoys broad market penetration amongst performance testing software. LoadRunner is a rich solution that provides all of the features listed in the previous section. For Web-based applications, LoadRunner scripts can be developed using a record/playback approach. The record/playback process generates a proprietary script that can be inspected and/or altered. LoadRunner also supports load testing for non-Web-based interfaces including client server, legacy, Citrix, Java, .NET and all widely known (enterprise resource processing) / (customer relationship management) solutions like PeopleSoft, Oracle, SAP, and Siebel. From a monitoring perspective, there is rich plug-in support for a number of platforms and vendors including J2EE, .NET, Siebel, Oracle, and SAP. Features and flexibility come at a cost. Mercury's product is the most expensive to license in the industry. Further, there is no synergy between the load testing solution and the automated functional test suite (WinRunner and QTP) so resources cannot rely on a common skill set in order to develop scripts for functional and non-functional scenarios.

E-Load, from Empirix, is a load testing tool, supporting each of the features listed in the previous section. The Empirix product is focused on web-based and call center applications, thus lacking support for the full range of systems that are likely to exist in a large enterprise. E-Load can scale to simulate thousands of concurrent users and uses a distributed architecture to do so. E-Load is based on the Jboss open-source J2EE application server. The authors have found that some tuning is required out of box to create significant loads. Also, the stability of the loading engine seems to degrade as scenario complexity and length increases. For tests that must run for longer than 2 hours, the authors have found that this tool may require careful monitoring and occasionally must be restarted.

If budget concerns are overriding for your project, there are a number of open-source contributions to the area of load testing software. Jmeter, from the Apache Software Foundation, is a popular Jakarta-based Java solution that can be used to create loads for different types of interfaces, among them: Web applications, Perl scripts, Java objects, database queries, and FTP (file transfer protocol) servers. Because Jmeter is open-source, developers on your project can extend/customize Jmeter as needed. For example, custom plug-ins can be written to create load for unsupported interfaces. During tests, statistics capture and graphing capabilities are highly configurable but do not have the same ease of use as other vendor-supported solutions. Jmeter is written in pure Java, and thus can run on any platform with support for a JRE (Java runtime environment).

Grinder, available from SourceForge.net, is another popular open-source load testing tool. Like each of the preceding three products, Grinder supports a distributed architecture for creating large concurrent volumes of requests. As of version 1.3, Grinder scenario execution is driven by Jython scripting. Jython is a scripting language based on Python that adds support for Java. Jython allows for great flexibility in scenario scripting but requires a developer's programming skill set. Grinder is a good choice for developers or technical resources in a QA (quality assurance) role who need to do discrete testing of services over standard protocols such as IIOP, RMI/IIOP, RMI/JRMP, JMS, POP3, SMTP, FTP, and LDAP, SOAP, XML-RPC, HTTP, HTTPS, and JDBC.

PureLoad, from Minq, is another offering in the area of loading testing software. Minq is the maker of the popular Java-based DBVisualizer database utility familiar to many developers. PureLoad includes a record/playback feature for Web-based applications and also supports authoring of scripts to test services exposed over standard protocols such as NNTP, FTP, SMTP, IMAP, JDBC, LDAP, Telnet, and DNS. Other standard features include creation and storage of test scenarios, statistics capture, and graphical presentation of results.

Additional Testing Apparatus

Simulators, Reflectors, and Injectors

There may be scenarios in which your software system must interact with external systems that are outside of your system boundary. For these cases, additional testing apparatus may be required in order to conduct non-functional testing. In the example earlier in this chapter, we determined that performance test cases that exercise the enterprise customer database are critical, but that there is no instance of this system available for testing. The only way to test these scenarios is to devise additional test apparatus to stand in for the enterprise customer database. This stand-in processing will need to mimic the enterprise customer database (ECD) interface in a manner consistent with the service level agreement (SLA) for this system. For example, if all requests over an MQ to the EDC system are guaranteed to respond in 2 s or less, then our additional test apparatus should also behave in this way.

In practice, there are three types of such test apparatus:

1. **Injectors:** Injectors are the simplest form of test apparatus; injectors create inputs to your system, but do not expect or require any response from your system. Injectors are used to simulate load representing machine inputs. Injection capability is often a supported feature of your load testing software.
2. **Reflectors:** Reflectors are used to stand in for an external system that participates in request/response with your system. A reflector is a "dumb" server process that listens for requests and reflects back a static or crude response. The goal of the reflector is to provide the minimum response needed for your loading scenarios to operate.
3. **Simulators:** Simulators are "smart" server processes that actually mimic a complex interplay between your system and an external system. A simulator may actually store state information and intelligently construct response messages based on the request or on previous requests. Some systems require a simulator in order for even the simplest test cases to execute. If you build a simulator, you may be able to cross-purpose the simulator to support functional testing and training purposes. Ultimately, an investment in a simulator is a technical activity requiring design and development; as such, it is the most complex and costly of these three apparatuses.
4. **Stubs:** A stub is a piece of application functionality that is embedded in your system and provides stand-in processing for an external system. A stub is like

a *simulator* or a *reflector* except it is part of the run-time code for the application itself. Typically, stubs need to be configured to override the intended production configuration for the application. Stubs can be a very convenient means of substituting for an external system but because of their embedded nature, they will compete with your application for resources. An externally hosted simulator or reflector will yield more accurate performance and capacity results but will be more cumbersome to implement and maintain.

If you decide that additional testing apparatus is required, you will need to staff a custom development activity. In most cases, the development team will have the required skills and will be the most familiar with the interfaces of the system. The need for test apparatus is frequently an afterthought for projects and becomes an unplanned burden for the development team. Hopefully, this need is identified early enough in your project that it can be accommodated in a planned and coordinated way. By documenting your apparatus requirements in your non-functional test strategy, you are communicating your needs to the development team.

You will also need to decide where any additional test apparatus will be hosted. Generally, you have two choices. You can host the software on the system infrastructure itself or on additional infrastructure designated for this purpose. Since your test apparatus is standing in for components that are outside your system boundary, it is preferable that they be hosted on dedicated infrastructure. Unfortunately, dedicated infrastructure means additional cost. If required, this infrastructure should have been planned for in your project initiation. In many cases, there will be an opportunity to co-host loading software and test apparatus on the same hardware so long as it has been sized with sufficient capacity during project initiation.

Test Beds

Your test bed is comprised of two elements: data required for load scenarios, and data that is already seeded in the software system to represent data populated by historical, previously-executed transactions.

Test-Case Data

Your load scenarios will determine what test-case data is required. An important feature of the test data is the amount of variation required. Let's consider a securities trading solution that coordinates settlement instructions on behalf of financial institutions. For such a system, there might be seven distinct types of request message types. Each request type may involve a security ID that identifies the unique security that is involved in the request. If the security IDs are referenced against a database and/or influence the complexity of processing, it will be important for the security IDs used in the load scenario to be varied and representative of the real world.

In assembling your test bed you will need to work with business resources to identify the range of security IDs that will be subjected to the system in order to do accurate testing. On the other hand, other pieces of data in the request may not be important. Price information may be effectively "pass through" in this system. In other words, there is no special processing for price information. Price information may be logged to a database table and the performance characteristics are not impacted by variations in the data.

These types of decisions can only be made in the course of reviewing test cases with technical project participants. Omitting natural, real-world variation in your data may be a time-saving simplification, but it also introduces marginal risk. Technical resources may not correctly anticipate the effect that variation in your test bed will have on the system. As a result, it is always preferable to make your test bed as similar to the expected production inputs as possible.

Test Environments

Your test environment should have been defined during the initiation and planning phase for your project. Projects that fail to allocate infrastructure for hardware during this phase can experience serious delays as time is wasted waiting to procure additional environments. Your environment will need to support the software system itself, load testing tools, and any additional test apparatus that you have identified.

In planning your test environment you will need to define the level of isolation you will achieve, the change management procedures you will follow, and the scale of your test environment as a proportion of the target production environment.

Isolation

At a minimum, you should strive for isolation of the software system from all other software components, including the load testing solution and any supporting test apparatus. The part of the system that you are isolating is, of course, all components that you have identified that are within your system boundary. As we will see in the next chapter, it can be difficult to achieve repeatable test results even in well isolated environments.

Many organizations have reluctantly conceded that the only way to reliably test mission-critical systems is to introduce a production-scale environment that is dedicated to non-functional testing. Such environments are commonly referred to as *staging*, *pre-production*, *performance*, and *certification* environments. In addition to supporting non-functional activities, these environments are useful for rehearsing production deployments. Attractive as this option is, if you do not have budget or time for a production-scale, dedicated testing environment then you may consider one of the following alternatives:

1. **Reduced-scale Dedicated Test Environment:** If the capital cost of a production-scale environment is prohibitive, you may consider a smaller-scale, but dedicated, environment to support non-functional testing. This approach requires you to make compromises and accept some additional risk as you must extrapolate test results to the target production environment.

2. **Re-purpose production hardware:** If you are building a new system for which there is currently no production environment, you may be able to test using the target production infrastructure itself. Of course, this strategy means that you will lose your test environment once the production system is commissioned. More specifically, this means that you will not have a non-production environment in which you can regression-test changes or reproduce load-related issues. For mission-critical systems, neither of these consequences are acceptable.

3. **Time-shift existing hardware:** With some coordination, you can dedicate your existing functional testing hardware for performance testing during specific intervals. For example, non-functional testing can be scheduled on evenings and weekends. You should recognize that this type of arrangement is usually not an efficient use of resources, nor does it provide for much contingency if any of the activities on the shared infrastructure begin to track behind schedule.

4. **Create logical instances:** If neither of the previous two options are realistic, you should at least configure your system as its own logical instance. For example, a single database server can often support many development and QA instances of an application. For your non-functional testing you should strive to isolate your test system on its own instance. This will mitigate outside influences, and is more representative of the target production environment.

5. **Cross-purpose the Disaster Recovery (DR) environment.** Increasingly, software systems are a core part of every large business operation. Consequently, in the event of a large-scale disaster, it is unacceptable for the business to be completely deprived of its software systems. As a result, large organizations commonly make an investment in a geographically separate computing facility that can host critical software systems in the event of a disaster. Such a facility is referred to as a DR site. A DR site must have equivalent hardware capacity to the primary facility that it supports in order for it to be effective in the event of a disaster. Since this hardware is not utilized unless a disaster is declared, it is common and cost-effective to cross-purpose this infrastructure as a non-functional testing environment. If your software solution is supported by a disaster recovery site, you are strongly encouraged to consider leveraging this site for your non-functional testing.

In designating your test environment, you need to inventory all of the hardware required by the system. This includes servers, network components, and storage devices. Many organizations provide network and storage services from a central pool of resources. Be sure that you understand what the SLA is for these components and whether or not it is consistent with the target production environment. You should also be aware of whether or not unrelated activities within your organization can exert influence on your testing with respect to these shared resources.

Capacity

Hardware costs for some systems can be exorbitant. The prospect of duplicating this cost for the non-functional test environment(s) can be a menacing thought for many executives. For mission-critical systems expected to be in operation for many years, an investment in a proper non-functional test environment is a necessary cost of doing business.

The cost of unscheduled downtime that could have been avoided with proper testing usually makes the hardware cost of the test environment seem justifiable. However, there will be situations in which a scaled-down version of the production environment is suitable for most non-functional testing. A scaled-down version of the production environment is designed with a reduction in some or all of the following resources: servers, memory, CPUs, storage and network devices. The cost of a system one-half the size of the production system may actually be one-tenth the expense. In such cases, the cost savings justify the risk. If you are going to proceed with a reduced version of production for your non-functional testing, you should review the following list of considerations:

1. **Operability Testing:** Operability testing is usually not impacted by a scaled-down non-functional testing environment. Failover, fault-tolerance, and boundary testing are typically unrelated to hardware capacity.
2. **Performance Testing:** Hardware resources like CPU and memory are readily seen as commodities that can be scaled linearly. In other words, doubling the load should correspond to twice the amount of CPU and memory requirements. However, there is no guarantee of this relationship. Further, resources specific to your application may not scale linearly. If you are unable to test peak load for your system in your test environment because of hardware limitations, you are taking a considerable risk.
3. **Capacity Testing:** If your system is not big enough to support peak load, you are relying on extrapolation for capacity planning and measurement. For many systems, this is an acceptable measure, but it is not entirely without risk.

Change Management

An important question to answer during your test planning is who will have access to the non-functional testing environment. Specifically, which individuals can deploy the system into the environment and/or make changes to the system during testing?

An ideal process is one in which the same resources and procedure that are used for deploying the production system should be used for deploying into your non-functional testing environment. This ideal assures us that the configuration in your test environment will be identical to production. Once your system is deployed, there will be an ongoing need to make subtle changes to the system. We have already discussed the need to load transaction volume—perhaps artificially. Additionally, we know that we may be introducing test apparatus into the environment that may require configuration changes to the system.

Non-functional testing, when executed by technical resources, can be intrusive. Technical resources executing non-functional tests need the flexibility to make tuning and configuration changes in order for testing to succeed. For example, operability tests often require testing resources to purposefully configure the system "wrong" to observe the outcome. Requirements to change the system can be met in two ways: the same resources responsible for the deployment can make all changes to the system on a by-request basis, or the non-functional test team can make these changes themselves.

In either case, it is imperative that a log be maintained for all changes that are made to the environment. The non-functional test team must be confident that when acceptance testing is executed, the configuration and state of the system in the test environment is aligned with the intended production configuration. Towards the end of your test cycles, changes that have been made for tuning/optimization purposes should be communicated to the deployment team, who should then re-deploy the system into your environment for final acceptance. Following this approach ensures that only changes that are in the production package are deployed to the test environment at the time that acceptance testing is executed.

The detailed specification for your non-functional testing environment should be a documented part of your testing strategy. If you are making compromises in the capacity, isolation, or change-management processes for your environment, then these risks should be documented in your test strategy so that management is aware of them.

Historical Data

Many systems accumulate data over time; such data is referred to as *transactional data*. The accumulation of transactional data may influence the performance characteristics of your system and, as a result, should be modeled and included in your testing.

Business volumes can be derived from the business usage model constructed during the requirements phase of your project. Let's revisit the example we used in the requirements chapter. For each of the transactions in Table 6.1 we have included the average daily volume for four key coarse inputs.

In consultation with the development team, we have learned that login and account inquiries do not create transactional data on the system. In other words, any number of logins and account inquiries will leave the system unchanged. As a result, we can ignore these coarse inputs.

Bill payments and funds transfers, however, do create transactional data on the system as they are completed. A technical resource has provided the information shown in Table 6.2 with respect to the database.

Operationally, transactional data is preserved for up to one year in the production system. When the system is running at steady-state, there will be one year's worth of business volumes in each transactional table. Combining the record counts and business volumes, we can forecast transactional table volumes shown in Table 6.3.

Before we begin testing, each of the tables must be loaded up to the corresponding record counts. There are two ways that this can be achieved: volumes can be generated by running load scenarios themselves or by authoring custom data-loading scripts that populate data directly into the system. It can be time-consuming to generate table volumes by running load scenarios. Also, if development for the system is still underway, sometimes this approach isn't even an option until much later in the project lifecycle. Time spent authoring scripts for generating volumes artificially is often a good investment. It gives you the flexibility to run the scripts on demand against multiple systems without impacting your timelines. However, you will need to weigh this against the risk of there being defects or omissions in the script you are using to populate data.

Table 6.1 Example Business Usage: Online Banking System

Usage Attribute	Requirement
Busiest Interval	12:00 noon to 1:00 PM, Friday 30% of the heaviest day's business volumes
Login	2,309,039
Account Inquiry	1,209,049
Bill Payment	529,143
Funds Transfer	210,985

Table 6.2   Example Coarse Inputs: Online Banking System

Coarse Input	Table	Number of Records
Bill Payment	Transaction	1
	Payment information	1
	Transaction fulfillment	2
Funds Transfer	Transaction	1
	Transfer information	1
	Transaction fulfillment	2

Table 6.3   Transactional Table Volumes

Coarse Input	Table	Number of Records/ Coarse Input	Number of Records/ Coarse Input	Total Number of Records After One Year
Bill Payment	Transaction	1	529,143	529,143
	Payment information	1		529,143
	Transaction fulfillment	2		1,058,286
Transfer Funds	Transaction	1	210,985	210,985
	Transfer information	1		210,985
	Transaction fulfillment	2		421,970

Summary

The choices you make during your test planning will determine the efficacy and the ease with which your test execution is completed. A non-functional test strategy is a critical planning deliverable that should be completed prior to any test execution. The non-functional test strategy enumerates the key factors and assumptions in preparing your detailed test plan including the definition of system boundaries, your performance and operability test scope, load testing software, additional test apparatus, test environments, and test data.

It is usually impossible to test every mode of failure with every load scenario for your system. This reality requires you to use informed judgment in the determination of your test scope. Systems that must interact with software systems outside of your control may require the introduction of additional software apparatus that mimics the interaction of external systems. The test environment in which you execute your tests may be a full-scale replica of the target production environment or a logically separate instance that is defined on the same infrastructure as your functional test environment.

The choices you make for your test environment will reflect a cost-benefit analysis based on your risk tolerance. Finally, the test data that is used for your test execution requires careful forethought. Non-functional testing is only as good as the likeness of historical and test case data used in the execution. In Chapter 7 we will delve deeply into the next topic in the software lifecycle: test case preparation and execution.

Chapter 7

Test Preparation and Execution

During the test planning phase of your project, you would have defined the high-level scope of the test execution. You would also have identified specific data requirements, characteristics of your test bed, and any additional test apparatus like injectors, reflectors, or simulators that would be needed to efficiently execute tests. Seeking out data, authoring data load scripts, and developing your test apparatus are all activities that will be completed during the test preparation and execution phase of the project. It is during this phase that you will bring each of these concepts together and actually commence the testing initiative.

In this chapter, we will review test preparation and execution activities, including common challenges that are faced and general considerations for reporting test results to project stakeholders.

Preparation Activities

The test cases that are defined in your project scope during the planning phase include most of the details that are needed for execution such as required data, execution steps, success criteria. Unfortunately, there is usually considerable work to be done before actual testing activities can begin once the development team has declared that the application is available for testing. Prior to commencing testing activities you will need to attend to the following details:

159

1. **Script Development:** If you are using load testing software, you will need to develop scripts that implement the load scenarios contained in your test plan.
2. **Validating the Test Environment:** When the system is deployed into the test environment, you will need to validate that your performance scripts execute as expected.
3. **Seeding the Test Bed:** If you are using custom data loading scripts, these will need to be executed against the test environment.
4. **Establishing Mixed Load:** Mixed load is a combination of test cases that best characterize application usage. Mixed load is the default load profile that you should use whenever you execute operability, failover, sustainability, and capacity testing. The mixed load should include test cases that generate load in proportion to the actual business usage. Because the mixed load provides broad functional coverage for the application, it is useful for verifying new deployments in your testing environment.
5. **Tuning the Load:** When you begin to subject the application to load, you will need to make adjustments to parameters in the load testing software. This is achieved through trial and error.

Script Development

The load testing software that you plan to use must support the development of test scripts that create the virtual load needed for testing. The amount of development required depends on the software package and the number and complexity of your test scenarios. You should try to retain the following characteristics for your test scripts as much as possible:

1. **Resilient to changes in the user interface:** Software systems will change over time, especially the user interface. Business users are likely to refine the user experience as a system is integrated into business operations, and they begin to see the impact of their original ideas. In order to reduce rework in your load testing scripts, you should try to avoid validation and control logic that is heavily dependent on details in the user interface.
2. **Self-sustaining:** A load testing scenario may incorporate business logic that expects the system to be in a certain state or to have transactional data pre-populated. Where possible, it is always preferable for scripts to be self-sustaining. This means that the scripts themselves create all data and preconditions that they require. Consider the example of a load testing script for a sales-force automation application. A load scenario may require a user to login and view prospect information created by a different user. One way to implement this in a self-sustaining way is to build a single script login as one user creates the prospect information. This is followed by a second step in which a

second user logs in to view the prospect information. The drawback of pairing activities like this is that they may make it more difficult to achieve your target transaction rate for coarse inputs in the right proportions. Later in this chapter we will look at sustainability testing where a load is applied for a long period of time. This activity will be complex to execute if a test operator must intervene and reset conditions following each test iteration.

3. **Leaves system in a state where tests can be repeated:** Wherever reasonably possible, use your load scripts to leave the system in a state that does not interfere with testing should you choose to resume or repeat testing at a future date. This may seem obvious, but in some cases it can be difficult to achieve. Many scripts that emulate human usage are required to login to the application as a prerequisite step for all tests. However, many applications are designed such that a user can only have one concurrent authenticated session. Trivially, this means that each one of our scripts needs to logout at completion in order to ensure that they can be executed again without error. However, we must also consider the case in which our scripts stop executing abruptly before they have the opportunity to logout. There are lots of failures that can bring this scenario about, including the following: the load testing software could fail midway through the test, a critical component in the application may start failing, or a functional defect could impact the ability of a subset of scripts to complete. In each of these cases the system will be left in a state that blocks us from repeating our testing. In such situations we may have to rely on restarting the system to reset the system state. If this is too time-consuming—or worse, doesn't work—we may need to build a custom solution in order to intervene and artificially reset the system state.

4. **Achieve target coarse inputs with an optimal number of scripts:** The business usage defined in your requirements describes the types and transaction rates for coarse inputs. In implementing load testing scripts, you should try to minimize the number and complexity of scripts while achieving the target transaction rate for your coarse inputs. The remainder of this section elaborates on this topic.

If we revisit the human inputs from our online banking example in Chapter 3, we see the following targets for coarse inputs. Our challenge now is to translate these coarse inputs (as shown in Table 7.1) into detailed load testing scripts that create the inputs in the right proportions.

Because our system requires authentication, each of our scripts require login as the first execution step. If we take a simple approach and write a separate script for each coarse input, we will run into a problem.

In order to achieve a target transaction rate of 2.17 TPS for the account inquiry operations, we will indirectly achieve a transaction rate of 2.17 TPS for login also. That is, we will overstate the transaction rate for login by a considerable margin. To make matters worse, the bill payment and funds transfer operations will also

Table 7.1 Inputs

Input	Input Type	Schedule
Login	Human	Continuous at 1.06 XXXX (TPS)
Account Inquiry: Less than five accounts	Human	Continuous at 1.87 TPS
Account Inquiry: Five accounts or more	Human	Continuous at 0.30 TPS
Bill Payment	Human	Continuous at 0.94 TPS
Transfer Funds	Human	Continuous at 0.71 TPS

introduce logins at their transaction rates. Our login transaction rate will end up being the sum of all transaction rates (i.e., 3.82 TPS). This is nearly four times the required transaction rate. If we were to follow this approach, and login performance does not meet our requirements, how will we know if we would have the same problem if the transaction rate was 1.06 TPS? Or worse, perhaps the login operation is so taxing that it is compromising performance of the other business operations also? We are going to have to plan our script development more creatively.

We note that the ratio of account inquiries to logins is approximately 2-to-1. In other words, for each login, there must be at least two account inquiries if we are to achieve the target transaction rate for account inquiry. We can also see that for each login there is a little less than one bill payment. For every four logins, there appear to be about three transfers. We can accommodate these proportions if we implement our test scripts as shown in Table 7.2.

This is a fairly simple example, and we were able to arrive at reasonable proportions through a trial-and-error strategy. The approach we have taken in this example involves creating two scripts that observe the 2-to-1 relationship between account inquiries and logins.

We consider the login transaction rate to anchor the transaction rate for the other operations in the script. For script 1, if our login TPS is 0.45 operations per second, this means that, necessarily, each discrete step in the test script must also be achieving this TPS. If we manually distribute the load between each of the two scripts, we can make adjustments until we achieve something very close to the target transaction rates in the business usage. When we go to tune our load, we will have the opportunity to make additional adjustments to our load scenario. For now this seems like a reasonable approach for us to use in developing our test scripts for our human coarse inputs.

Table 7.2 Test-Script Implementation

Test Script	Input Type	Script TPS	Login	Account Inquiry	Bill Payment	Funds Transfer
	Login	0.45	0.45			
	Perform account inquiry	0.45		0.45		
Bill Payment Script	Perform bill payment 1	0.45			0.45	
	Perform account inquiry	0.45		0.45		
	Perform bill payment 2	0.45			0.45	
	Login	0.68	0.68			
	Perform account inquiry	0.68		0.68		
Funds Transfer Script	Perform funds transfer	0.68				0.68
	Perform account inquiry	0.68		0.68		
Totals:		1.12	1.13	2.26	0.9	0.68
Target:		*1.06*	*1.06*	*2.17*	*0.94*	*0.71*

In Chapter 3 we also looked at business usage from the perspective of concurrent users. In our usage model, we established that up to 5,100 users were concurrently logged in to the system during the peak interval between noon and 1:00 PM on Fridays.

Now that we have derived a set of scripts that will create transactions in the correct proportions, we can use "think time" and virtual user load to gradually increase load and achieve the target transaction rate. We will see this process in action later in this chapter.

Validating the Test Environment

You *should* expect problems the first time you attempt to run load scenarios in your environment: custom test apparatus, a new software deployment, and newly crafted load testing scripts are being brought together for the first time. You will likely require a break-in period where you make adjustments to the testing environment. This activity is sometimes referred to as *shaking down the environment*. In many test plans, an environment validation and shakedown period is included and referred to as *cycle zero*.

If the non-functional testing environment is similar in scale and configuration to production, don't be surprised if you discover new application issues. For example, if your application is clustered across multiple servers, the non-functional test environment may be the first environment in which two or more physical servers are introduced into the configuration. You will need to work through issues like this with the development team.

In validating the environment your primary objective should be to ensure the end-to-end execution of the load test scenarios. However, you should also contrast the system response time against the documented requirements. If specific test cases are consistently failing to meet performance requirements under light or moderate load scenarios, your results are unlikely to improve with increasing loads. For these cases, you should document the failures as critical defects and escalate them to the development team for investigation.

Establishing Mixed Load

During performance testing, your goal is to re-create conditions that are representative of the production environment. If your load scenarios represent scenarios that will execute relative to each other in the production environment, then they should test the same scenarios in the test environment.

A *mixed load* is a set of test cases that execute together and are representative of a given time interval. For some systems, a single mixed load may be sufficient for all of your activities. For more complex systems, you may require a series of mixed loads for different conditions.

Standardized mixed load scenarios can be used for many purposes, as described below:

1. **Performance Certification:** Running the mixed load at peak transaction rates is usually the best condition under which to conduct performance certification.
2. **Performance Regression:** A mixed load is an efficient way to conduct performance testing. It is a single test in which you run load and compare results against the baseline from the most recent previous test.
3. **Operability Testing:** A mixed load is the most useful test scenario with which to execute operability tests. The mixed load should include broad coverage for different application functions. By using the same mixed load for each of your operability tests, you standardize the load and simplify the activities of the test operators.
4. **Sustainability Testing:** The sustainability test requires a sustained, representative load. When the mixed load is applied for a long interval, this requirement is met.
5. **Capacity Testing:** When the mixed load is run at the peak expected volumes, the environment becomes suitable for taking capacity measurements. Later in this book, we will see how this translates to capacity planning activities.

Let's revisit the online banking example from Chapter 3 again and look at assembling a suitable mixed load. For human usage, the metrics shown in Table 7.3 were defined for coarse inputs.

Earlier in this chapter we revealed how we could achieve these coarse inputs through the introduction of two load testing scripts executed at specific transaction rates. In terms of machine inputs, there were three separate interfaces (as shown in Table 7.4).

Table 7.3   Transactions

Transaction	Classification	Target Transaction Rate
Login	Light	1.06 TPS
Account Inquiry: Less than five accounts	Light	1.87 TPS
Account Inquiry: Five accounts or more	Medium	0.30 TPS
Bill Payment	Medium	0.94 TPS
Funds Transfer	Medium	0.71 TPS

Table 7.4 Machine Input

Machine Input	Input Type	Operations Window
Customer Marketing Messages	Continuous	7:00 AM to 10:00 PM, Monday to Friday 12:00 noon to 1:00 PM, Friday: 30% of heaviest day's business volumes
Bill Payment Fulfillment	Batch	Must start after 6:00 PM and complete successfully before 10:00 PM, Monday to Sunday
Business Reporting	Batch	2:00 AM, Monday to Sunday

In this example, only one of the machine inputs runs concurrently with the peak online usage. Human inputs dominate the load profile for this application, so we are most interested in the behavior of the system during the business day—that is, from 7:00 AM to 10:00 PM.

Theoretically, busy evening online volumes could coincide with execution of the bill payment fulfillment job. Since complexity is still manageable with the addition of the bill payment fulfillment job into the mixed load, we will include it. The business reporting job, however, runs off-hours. We will indeed test it in our scope, but we will not include it in the mixed load that we use as the basis for performance regression, sustainability testing, and failover.

In light of the decisions we have made, our mixed load scenario looks like that represented in Table 7.5.

Note that all of the human inputs are modeled using two load testing scripts running continuously at the specified transaction rate. The customer marketing messages are a continuous machine input. The transaction rate for marketing messages is tied to the login rate, as we saw in Chapter 3. The bill payment fulfillment is scheduled to run every six hours in cognizance of the fact that this scenario is a compressed business day, i.e. this scenario runs constantly at peak load.

In this example the mixed load scenario that we have defined is simpler than you would expect for a critical, multifunction system like a national online banking system. For enterprise systems, the mixed load may include a few dozen up to a few hundred scripts.

Table 7.5   Inputs (Mixed Load Scenario)

Input	Input Type	Transaction Rate / Schedule
Bill Payment Script	Human	Continuous at 0.45 TPS
Funds Transfer Script	Human	Continuous at 0.68 TPS
Customer Marketing Messages	Machine	Continuous
Bill Payment Fulfillment	Machine	Run once every 6 hours

Seeding the Test Bed

If your system requires historical volumes of data, you should load this data into the environment as soon as the application has been deployed and validated. In Chapter 6 we discussed two approaches for loading historical volumes into the test bed.

Irrespective of the method you are leveraging, if you are using a database it is a good idea to export the database image with the augmented volumes. In this way you can restore the database image to reset the test environment back to the original transactional volumes.

Your load scenarios may add transactional volumes beyond the required amount, or the scenarios may functionally invalidate the database through the course of script verification. A software system that is running at high capacity for a sustained period of time can subtly change the characteristics of your application. For example, most relational databases maintain internal statistics for determining the optimal execution plan for retrieving data. Over time, statistics in your database can deviate from their original values and significantly change the behavior of your system.

A database import resets statistics as well as data. If your load scenarios require frequent update, insertion, or deletion operations to be performed on the database, consider that this can impact the efficiency with which data is stored on disk. If you have the option to re-import the database, the state of the database will be consistent in terms of how contiguously data is stored on persistent storage.

Tuning the Load

Assuming you have completed the scripting of test cases and validation of your environment, you will need to run load using your load testing software and finalize configuration settings. The following tuning parameters need to be defined during this activity for each load scenario in your mixed load.

1. **Number of virtual users:** "Virtual users" is an industry term for the number of concurrent threads executing load against your application. For load scenarios that emulate human usage, the term "users" is appropriate because the load testing software is emulating actual human users.

2. **Ramp-up:** Ramp-up refers to the rate at which load is increased over the duration of the test. You can begin the test with the maximum number of users, or you can step up the number of virtual users over an interval at the beginning of the test.

3. **Think time:** "Think time" is another industry term that refers to the interval between execution steps for each script. Think time is a pause in the script execution that emulates the time a human user spends processing the output of the previous step.

4. **Test duration:** For your application, you will also need to designate the length of the load test. For example, is it enough to demonstrate acceptable performance for 30 minutes, 60 minutes, 120 minutes, or longer?

In Chapter 3 we saw that for human inputs, the number of concurrent users is an important characteristic of the overall business usage. However, the fact that you have 500 concurrent users logged on does not help you to assign virtual users across load scenarios in your test suite. For example, how many virtual users should be assigned to bill payment versus funds transfer? To get to this level of detail, you will need to make an educated guess and then refine your parameters as you observe the system.

Let's continue to work with the online banking mixed load example from earlier in this chapter. When we go to execute these scripts against the test environment, we may find that the duration for the bill payment script is 40 seconds while the funds transfer script executes in only 15 seconds. This is shown in Table 7.6.

The difference in execution time is explainable, as the bill payment script includes a number of steps that are not actually measured for performance, i.e. the script has many more steps than the funds transfer script. We know from Chapter 3 that the number of concurrent users expected to be on the system during the peak interval is 5,100. If we assign 2,550 virtual users to each of our two load testing scripts, we

Table 7.6 Script Duration

Input	Transaction Rate/Schedule	Script Duration
Bill Payment Script	Continuous at 0.45 TPS	40 s
Funds Transfer Script	Continuous at 0.68 TPS	15 s

are unlikely to achieve our target transaction rate. In order to compensate for the long execution time of the bill payment script, we will need to compensate with a higher number of users. We make an educated estimate for virtual user distribution to establish a starting point (as shown in Table 7.7).

When we allocate virtual users in the ratio above, we find that we are still not meeting our target transaction rate for the bill payment script. We are also running at significantly higher loads than required for the funds transfer script. We can try to compensate again by shifting an additional 200 virtual users to the bill payment script (as shown in Table 7.8).

By shifting an additional 200 users to the bill payment script, we have achieved our target TPS for bill payments. Unfortunately, we are still executing far too many funds transfers based on our requirements.

At this point we don't want to subtract users from either test script because our target for the total number of users is still 5,100. Ideally, we would like to slow down the funds transfer script. Fortunately, there is a mechanism for us to do so in our load testing software.

Think time is a common industry term for a pause between executions of steps in a load testing script. Think emulates time that a user spends processing the results of their previous action. The load testing software we are using injects a

Table 7.7   Virtual Users

Input	Transaction Rate/Schedule	Virtual Users	Actual TPS
Bill Payment Script	Continuous at 0.45 TPS	3,300	0.30 TPS
Funds Transfer Script	Continuous at 0.68 TPS	1,800	1.41 TPS

Table 7.8   Shifting Users

Input	Transaction Rate/Schedule	Virtual Users	Actual TPS
Bill Payment Script	Continuous at 0.45 TPS	3,500	0.44 TPS
Funds Transfer Script	Continuous at 0.68 TPS	1,600	0.98 TPS

default think time of 4 seconds between steps in the execution. We can slow down the entire script execution by increasing the think time. If we adjust the think time for the funds transfer script to 6 seconds, our results will show a decrease in the transaction rate for this script (as shown in Table 7.9).

In this example, adding an additional 2 seconds between execution steps has dramatically decreased the transaction rate for this script. As a secondary effect, the transaction rate for the bill payment script has actually increased. By slowing down funds transfer script, we have created some slack in the system that has allowed the bill payment script to execute slightly faster.

Many load testing packages also support a parameter called *delay between iterations*, which is an interval of time that the software package will wait before re-executing the load script. This parameter can also be used to adjust the load of a specific script. You should be careful in using the parameter, however. By introducing a delay between iterations, you will create periods of time in which there are less than 5,100 concurrent users on the system. Alternately, if you increase the think time, you can be assured that there are still 5,100 active users on the application at any point in time.

Before we move on we also need to discuss the concept of *ramp-up*. In the loading scenario we discussed a moment ago, if all 5,100 virtual users logged in simultaneously and proceeded to execute, how do you suppose the system would react? 200 instantaneous logins is an interesting operability test for any system, but it is not representative of the actual production environment.

A more likely scenario is that user activities are randomized. At any point in time, there are blocks of users executing different functions. Some users are finishing a bill payment at the same instance that another user is just logging in. In order to create this distribution, load testing software allows you to configure the ramp-up parameters for your load. The most common ramp-up parameter is the number and interval over which virtual users should be added to the load. If our target load is 1,600 virtual users, one ramp-up scenario would be as shown in Table 7.10.

In this configuration, an additional ten users will be added to the load every 8 seconds. As a result, it will take $(1,600/10) \times 8 = 1,280$ seconds = ~21 minutes to reach the target number of virtual users.

Table 7.9 Funds Transfer

Input	Transaction Rate/Schedule	Virtual Users	Actual TPS
Bill Payment Script	Continuous at 0.45 TPS	3,500	0.48 TPS
Funds Transfer Script	Continuous at 0.68 TPS	1,600	0.61 TPS

Table 7.10　The Ramp-Up Scenario

Parameter	Value
Target Virtual Users	1,600
Ramp-up Interval	8 seconds
Ramp-up Users	10 users

Another advantage of incorporating a gradual ramp-up for your system is that you can observe error rate and response time during ramp-up to ensure that the system is healthy. If the error rate is high or response time is poor, you can abort the test before too many resources have been committed.

The last thing you need to consider in tuning your load is the length of time over which you need to run the load. For most systems, you should apply a load for at least 30 or 60 minutes. As a general rule, the higher the transaction rate, the shorter the required duration for your test. In order for your performance results to be reliable, you need your test to be long enough to capture an adequate example of data points. You will need to consider the ramp-up time in your test duration also. Since the load is initiated in a staggered fashion at the beginning of the test, your load will also exhibit a *ramp-down* period (as shown in Figure 7.1).

Load testing software will calculate statistics for the full duration of the test, including the ramp-up and ramp-down intervals. Your test length should be long enough so that the peak load interval dominates the statistics that are collected. For example, the load profile shown in Figure 7.2 would satisfy the calculated transaction rate but would not be a very good indication of system response at this rate:

Performance Testing

Business users tend to wait for performance test results with the most anticipation. Fortunately, your test execution strategy should prioritize performance testing towards the front of your execution schedule. Many of the operability tests that you will need to conduct can only be executed under load. If your application has not been certified for performance, you are very likely to have difficulty achieving the required load for your operability testing. In this section, we will look various aspects of performance testing including priming effects, stress testing, regression and reporting of results.

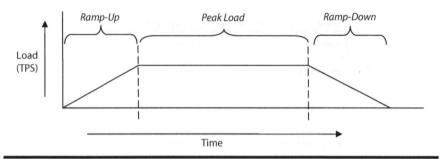

Figure 7.1   The ramp-up period.

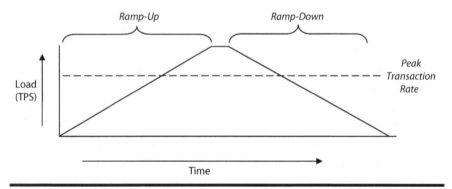

Figure 7.2   Peak transaction rates.

Priming Effects

Depending on the nature of the system you are testing, priming effects can exert considerable influence on your performance test results. Priming effects manifest themselves through degraded performance when a system is first started. There are a number of causes for priming effects, among them:

■ Preprocessing or compilation of application code
■ Loading application components into memory
■ Initializing application caches from persistent store
■ Initializing pools of application resources
■ Establishing connections to external resources or between components

If you see degraded performance following application start-up, you should continue to run load to ensure that you are not observing a priming effect. It is important to note priming effects in your test results. If there is no expectation that your system will be restarted frequently, your performance testing should be based on a "warm" system. A warm system is one that has already been subjected to load in order to eliminate priming effects.

Performance Acceptance

Performance acceptance is the process by which new applications go through testing processes focused on validating performance and also getting certified against non-functional requirements. Assuming that you have completed all of the necessary planning and preparation activities, performance acceptance is a matter of applying load and reporting response times.

A typical performance report from a load testing application for a 60-minute performance test will look like the one shown in Table 7.11.

In assessing the value of the performance results, you will need to determine if the transaction rate is accurate and also if the error rate is acceptable. The transaction rate is easy to calculate in this example for both the bill payment and the fund transfer scripts. We use the number of successful iterations in each of our calculations.

The transaction rate for the bill payment script is calculated as

$$Transaction\ Rate = \frac{Transactions}{Interval} = \frac{1,728}{3600s} = 0.48TPS$$.

The transaction rate for the fund transfer script is calculated as

$$Transaction\ Rate = \frac{Transactions}{Interval} = \frac{2,351}{3600s} = 0.65TPS$$.

Both of these transaction rates are very close to our targets of 0.48 TPS and 0.61 TPS, respectively.

Our next task is to evaluate the error rate for this test. If the error rate is too high, it is unlikely that we will achieve the target transaction rate. If the application is exhibiting a high error rate, this can also have an unknown effect on your performance results. Even if you are hitting your target transaction rate, if the error rate is higher than 5%, it is recommended that you resolve the errors before reporting performance results. For some applications, you may decide on a more- or less-forgiving error rate.

We calculate the error rate for this performance test as follows:

The error rate for the bill payment script is calculated as:

Table 7.11 The Performance Report

Scenario	Iterations	Errors	Minimum	Average	Maximum	90% Percentile	Standard Deviation
Bill Payment Script	1728	10	35.326	40.007	52.065	43.965	5.608
Login	1738	5	0.886	1.132	2.132	1.390	0.128
Account Inquiry	1733	2	1.001	1.452	2.875	1.875	0.304
Bill Payment 1	1731	1	2.309	2.675	3.925	2.871	0.560
Account Inquiry 2	1730	2	1.131	1.345	2.665	1.785	0.313
Bill Payment 2	1728	0	2.004	2.435	4.059	2.917	0.604
Logout	1728	0	0.230	0.564	1.047	0.645	0.035
Funds Transfer Script	2351	8	11.084	18.492	23.475	19.273	2.384
Login	2358	3	0.784	1.231	2.400	1.333	0.09
Account Inquiry	2355	1	0.998	1.311	2.770	1.605	0.405
Funds Transfer	2354	1	0.923	1.342	2.386	1.352	0.392
Account Inquiry	2353	2	1.015	1.441	2.806	1.911	0.430
Logout	2351	1	0.207	0.501	1.198	0.622	0.031

$$Error\ Rate = \frac{Transactions_{Errors}}{Transactions_{Total}} = \frac{10}{1,728} \times 100 = 0.57\%$$

The error rate for the funds transfer script is calculated as:

$$Error\ Rate = \frac{Transactions_{Errors}}{Transactions_{Total}} = \frac{8}{2,351} \times 100 = 0.34\%$$

The error rate is very low for both of our scripts. Fortunately, this means that we can report these test results against our non-functional requirements. If our error rate had been much higher, further investigation would have been required. Errors in your script execution can come from a variety of sources. The load testing software itself may encounter an error for a specific thread of execution.

A subset of the data in your test bed may be bad, i.e. does not meet validation criteria for the application. It is also possible that the application begins to encounter errors under load. The most common such error is a timeout, in which no response is received within the configured timeout for the load testing software. Timeouts are common as a result of priming effects, i.e. right after a system has been started. If the error rate is consistently high for your application, some recommended actions are:

1. **Repeat the test at lower load:** If the error rate goes away at a more moderate load, then your problem is likely load related. If the error rate is being caused by a high number of timeouts, you should see poor performance response times in your results. If response time is good for passing iterations, then you are probably not looking for timeout scenarios.
2. **Run scripts individually:** You may also find it useful to run each script under load individually. This will rule out interplay between different business operations as a source of problems.
3. **Look for application errors in the log:** If the software system has followed the logging best practices described earlier in this book, there should be descriptive information in the application logs.
4. **Ensure you have sufficient capacity:** You should look at the load profile on the hardware. If you are maximizing resources like the CPU (central processing unit) or memory, it should be no surprise that the error rate is high.

Before we move on, we will comment briefly on standard deviation. Many load testing packages report standard deviations in your performance results. The standard deviation is a statistical description of how distributed your data is between the minimum and maximum values. A very low standard distribution means that your data is clustered around the arithmetic average for the data set.

With respect to performance results, the smaller the standard deviation, the more reliable the average is as a projection of system response time. Assuming that your data is normally distributed about the mean, another interpretation of the standard deviation is that two-thirds of your data is within one standard deviation of the mean.

Reporting Performance Results

By now you should appreciate that obtaining meaningful performance test results is not always easy. There is a sequence of important steps required starting with assessing the original business requirements and culminating in the execution of your tests.

Before you report test results, the authors recommend that you verify that your performance results are repeatable. A good standard for repeatability is three consecutive trials. If three consecutive tests yield similar response time, you should feel comfortable reporting your results. A performance test report, as shown in Tables 7.12–7.14, includes the best summary information expected by business users in order to evaluate results

In this test report we have eliminated some of the supplementary statistical attributes from the data including minimum, maximum, and standard deviation. It is helpful to have this data available if anyone should request it, but it does not need to complicate the test report that will be shown to business users.

Note that we have also calculated the actual transaction rate for business operations as derived from the original business requirements. For clarity, we have included an additional column with the title *Calculations* that shows how the transaction rates were derived from the scripts used in the load. Note that we have also shown statistics for each test case in duplicate when it exists in multiple test scenarios. If you would prefer, you can collapse these statistics into single line items. In our experience, this requires additional effort and users are usually comfortable scrutinizing results in the original expanded format.

This simple example has focused on a very limited number of test cases. If you are supporting dozens or hundreds of test cases, you will benefit from automating the creation of test reports from the raw data that is collected from your load testing software. Some software packages support the generation of customizable reports. Other packages export the data in a raw format that can be processed into a report that meets your requirements. The authors have found that Microsoft Excel extended with VBA (visual basic script) is an efficient way of automating creation of custom reports suitable for business acceptance.

Table 7.12   Example Performance Summary Information

Performance Test Report

Test Date:	Monday, July 24, 2006
Test Duration	16:04:00 – 17:32:00
Total Virtual Users	1200
Test Operator(s):	Ido Gileadi, Mike Moerman

Table 7.13   Example Performance Report: Transaction Rates

Transaction Rates	Target Transaction Rate	Calculations	Actual Transaction Rate
Login	1.06 TPS	(0.48 + 0.65)	1.13 TPS
Account Inquiry – (Less than five accounts)	1.87 TPS	(0.48 * 2) + (0.65 * 2)	2.26 TPS
Account Inquiry – (Five accounts or more)	0.30 TPS		2.26 TPS
Bill Payment	0.94 TPS	(0.48 * 2)	0.96 TPS
Transfer Funds	0.71 TPS	(0.65 * 1)	0.65 TPS

Performance Regression: Baselining

Once a software system is established in a production environment, there is good reason to conduct performance regression testing whenever changes are introduced into the environment. The mixed load scenarios that were defined earlier in this chapter are particularly useful in the context of performance regression.

A mixed load performance regression subjects the software system to a wide variety of operations in a single test. The performance results from the regression test can be compared against the most recent previous results. The most current performance results for a system are usually referred to as a *baseline*. The baseline is the expected performance of the system in production. A confirmation of the

Table 7.14 Example Performance Report: Response Times

Scenario	Iterations	Errors	Average	90% Percentile	Requirement	Test Result
Bill Payment Script	1728	10	40.007	43.965	n/a	n/a
Login	1738	5	1.132	1.390	3	Pass
Account Inquiry	1733	2	1.452	1.875	3	Pass
Bill Payment 1	1731	1	2.675	2.871	3	Pass
Account Inquiry 2	1730	2	1.345	1.785	3	Pass
Bill Payment 2	1728	0	2.435	2.917	3	Pass
Logout	1728	0	0.564	0.645	n/a	n/a
Funds Transfer Script	2351	8	18.492	19.273	n/a	n/a
Login	2358	3	1.231	1.333	3	Pass
Account Inquiry	2355	1	1.311	1.605	3	Pass
Funds Transfer	2354	1	1.342	1.352	3	Pass
Account Inquiry	2353	2	1.441	1.911	3	Pass
Logout	2351	1	0.501	0.622	n/a	n/a

integrity of your testing would show consistency between actual production performance and the baseline that you recorded prior to introducing the system into production.

A performance regression report as shown in Table 7.15–7.17 will compare performance results against the original requirements *and* the most recent baseline for the system. In a regression test, we assume the same load as was used in previous tests.

By including the previous baseline, you get a view of how you are affecting performance as a result of the change under consideration. The new results may still meet the requirements, but users will not react favorably if performance degrades by, say a full second, across all the business operations.

Table 7.15   Example Performance Regression Report: Summary Information

Performance Test Report	
Test Date:	Monday, July 31, 2006
Test Duration	11:32:00 – 13:05:21
Total Virtual Users	1200
Test Operator(s):	Ido Gileadi, Mike Moerman

Table 7.16   Example Performance Regression Report: Transaction Rates

Transaction Rates	Target Transaction Rate	Calculations	Actual Transaction Rate
Login	1.06 TPS	(0.48 + 0.65)	1.13 TPS
Account Inquiry – (Less than five accounts)	1.87 TPS	(0.48 * 2) + (0.65 * 2)	2.26 TPS
Account Inquiry – (Five accounts or more)	0.30 TPS		2.26 TPS
Bill Payment	0.94 TPS	(0.48 * 2)	0.96 TPS
Transfer Funds	0.71 TPS	(0.65 * 1)	0.65 TPS

Table 7.17 Example Regression Report: Response Times

Scenario	Iterations	Errors	Average	90% Percentile	Average (baseline)	90% Percentile (baseline)	Requirement	Test Result
Bill Payment Script	1728	10	40.007	47.965	40.007	43.965	n/a	n/a
Login	1738	5	2.132	2.390	1.132	1.390	3	Pass
Account Inquiry	1733	2	2.452	2.875	1.452	1.875	3	Pass
Bill Payment 1	1731	1	3.675	3.871	2.675	2.871	3	Pass
Account Inquiry 2	1730	2	2.345	2.785	1.345	1.785	3	Pass
Bill Payment 2	1728	0	3.435	3.917	2.435	2.917	3	Pass
Logout	1728	0	1.564	1.645	0.564	0.645	n/a	n/a
Funds Transfer Script	2351	8	22.492	24.273	18.492	19.273	n/a	n/a
Login	2358	3	2.231	2.333	1.231	1.333	3	Pass
Account Inquiry	2355	1	1.311	1.643	1.311	1.605	3	Pass
Funds Transfer	2354	1	2.342	2.382	1.342	1.352	3	Pass
Account Inquiry	2353	2	1.434	1.942	1.441	1.911	3	Pass
Logout	2351	1	1.501	0.622	0.501	0.622	n/a	n/a

Stress Testing

Formally, your project has met its commitments if performance testing shows that response times are satisfied under peak transaction rates. However, it is informative to tell the business what transaction rate causes the system to miss its response time targets. In other words, how much more load can the business apply and still expect satisfactory performance? For some applications, this is useful information for business planning purposes.

Executives with technology portfolios will sometimes ask for this test to improve their sense of comfort with new applications. This test can also indicate the margin of error you are working with in the production environment with respect to business usage. If your business requirements for usage are way off the mark, the stress test informs you how much contingency you have in the business usage.

The performance profile for most systems looks like that shown in Figure 7.3.

As load increases, response time gradually increases until you hit a *knee* in the curve where response time increases dramatically. At this point it is futile to apply additional load. The stress test establishes at what load system response time will no longer meet performance requirements.

In Figure 7.4, L_1 indicates the level of load at which performance is certified. For L_1, response time is well below the stated performance requirements of the application. L_2 indicates the level of load at which the system response time is equivalent to the performance requirements. This is the *breaking point* for the system. In this example, we would state that the system is certified for L_1 but it is rated up to L_2. There are no guarantees of system behavior beyond L_2.

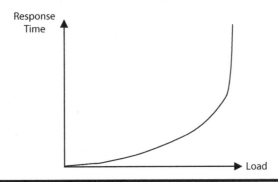

Figure 7.3   The performance profile.

Operability Testing

Operability testing is a broad category of testing that encompasses everything in the non-functional domain that is not performance testing. In this section, we will decompose operability tests into more specific categories and discuss approaches for testing each one of them.

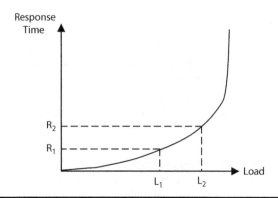

Figure 7.4 Dramatic response time increases.

Boundary Condition Testing

Boundary condition tests exercise a software system at its limits to ensure that the system is resilient. Boundary condition tests are executed as part of the functional test scope for many applications.

Consider an application used by consultants for tracking billable hours to clients on a weekly basis. For this application, consultants are asked to email an Excel spreadsheet, having a specific format to an email address that is set up to accept them.

The timekeeping application processes the attachments in the emails and responds with a status email indicating that the hours have been accepted or rejected. In the functional specification for the application, it is stated that the time tracking application can process up to five attachments on a single email. If there are six or more attachments, the email is rejected. We should expect a functional tester to design a test case in which an email is sent with six attachments to confirm this functionality.

But what happens if the consultant accidentally sends the wrong spreadsheet—perhaps a spreadsheet having tens of thousands of lines of input? Or worse, what happens if a consultant accidentally attaches a 400 MB multimedia file to the email and sends it to the time-tracking application? Both of these examples have the potential to be destructive in nature. Because they are destructive, most systems do not have written requirements detailing how the application should respond under these circumstances.

What is obvious is that we do not want exotic inputs such as these to interfere with the availability of the application. In other words, the application should discard or reject these requests with an error status. Since these inputs have the potential to crash the time-tracking application, it is preferable that these tests be executed under the umbrella of non-functional operability testing. Boundary tests are usually not difficult to execute. Often, the scope of your boundary condition tests will not become apparent until the technical design and implementation of the application are complete.

In accepting the application into the test environment, you should scrutinize each of the system interfaces and devise additional test conditions as needed.

Boundary condition test cases are not difficult to document and generally do not require a load testing solution. These tests can often be introduced into the test schedule during downtime, i.e., time during which you are waiting for other activities like deployments, script development, etc. Table 7.18 is an example of two documented boundary condition test cases.

Failover Testing

High availability is achieved using high-quality infrastructure and software components combined with redundancy. When there is redundancy in your environment, failover testing confirms that your system will take advantage of the redundancy

Table 7.18   Boundary Condition Test Cases

Test Name	Test Description	Expected Result	Actual Result	Test Result
Email Interface Boundary Test 1	Formulate a time-tracking email and send with an Excel attachment having 60,000 lines of numeric input.	Application should reject email with status message back to sender. Application should not use disproportionate system resources to process message. Availability should not be impacted.	Email took 2 minutes to process on server. Used approximately 8% of CPU during processing. No unusual spikes in memory or other resources observed.	Pass
Email Interface Boundary Test 2	Formulate a time-tracking email and send with a multimedia attachment 400 MB in size.	Application should reject email with status message back to sender. Application should not use disproportionate system resources to process message. Availability should not be impacted.	Email took 10 minutes to process on server before server crashed. Used approximately 8% of CPU during processing. Memory footprint grew rapidly. Suspect memory exhaustion caused server to crash.	Fail

to maintain availability. In the course of executing failover tests, you will need to address the following topics:

1. **What is the mode of failure for the failover test?** There are many modes of failure for most software components. A process can stop responding or the network cable can be unplugged from the server itself. You will need to decide on the mode of failover for your testing. In some cases, you may elect to test multiple modes of failure.

2. **Which software components are being tested for failover?** This question should be answered in the solution architecture, i.e., which components were intended as redundant.

3. **What load is suitable for failover testing?** Ideally, you want to identify a broad and representative mix of business functionality that can be executed during a single test. The mixed load that we established during preparation activities is usually appropriate (if not a good starting point).

4. **What are the performance requirements during failover?** Assuming the failover is successful, is there sufficient capacity in the infrastructure to accommodate peak load on the surviving components? Is there a requirement to support the performance requirements in the event of a failover?

5. **Does the system require fail-back capability?** Will the failed component be resumed automatically or manually? In either case, is the system required to fail back under load? Some systems do not support fail-back, meaning that the system must be brought offline in order to restore service the original service level.

6. **What functional expectations are there for in-flight processing?** What error rate is tolerable during failover (if any)? Most systems should expect some degree of exceptions during a failover scenario.

Let's look at an example test case definition that addresses each of these topics. In this example, we will consider a failover scenario for a clustered Web Services interface on the IBM WebSphere application server platform. The Web Service supports address lookup and validation. This is an enterprise service that supports a number of different mission critical applications. The service architecture is shown in Figure 7.5.

Incoming hypertext transfer protocol traffic (HTTP) is addressed to a VIP (virtual Internet provider) address on a Content Switching Service (CSS). The CSS load balances requests across the WebSphere cluster as shown in the diagram. In evaluating this architecture, we have two tiers of redundancy. We have redundant AIX servers managed by Veritas.

At the level of the application server, we have four clustered WebSphere processes that provide the enterprise Web Service. In this example, the address lookup service is stateless. For purposes of this illustration, the Web Service tier supports only a single request type. Let's look at how we would define failover test cases for each level of redundancy (as shown in Table 7.19 and 7.20).

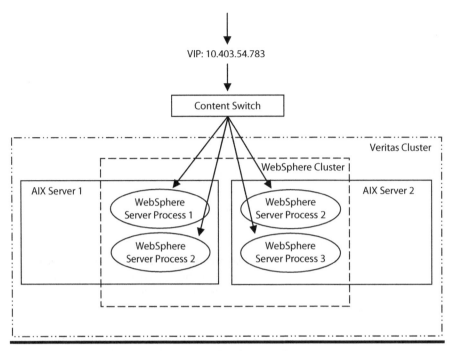

Figure 7.5   Example clustering and redundancy scheme.

Table 7.19   Test Case 1: WebSphere Cluster Failover

Failure Mode	Under load, kill one of the four WebSphere processes at the UNIX level
Software Components Failing Over	WebSphere cluster
Load During Failover	Peak transaction rate (6.5 TPS)
Performance Requirements	Must meet service level agreement (SLA) of 2 seconds response time
Error Tolerance	Transient errors are acceptable for up to 30 seconds
Fail-Back Required?	Yes; when the failed process is restarted, it should resume load

Table 7.20 Test Case 2: Veritas AIX Cluster Failover

Failure Mode	Kernel panic on AIX server
Software Components Failing Over	AIX server
Load During Failover	Peak transaction rate (6.5 TPS)
Performance Requirements	Must meet SLA of 2 seconds response time
Error Tolerance	Transient errors are acceptable for up to 30 seconds
Fail-Back Required?	No; an AIX server would only be introduced back into the Veritas cluster manually during a scheduled maintenance window

For each level of redundancy we have identified a likely failure mode. We have also identified the specific clustered components that are participating in the failover. Since component failures are random, unplanned incidents, we assume that component failure can occur under peak load times.

The maximum load forecasted for the service is 6.5 TPS. Since this service supports multiple enterprise applications, downtime is unacceptable. The system can only tolerate errors for up to 30 seconds, after which service must be restored to the two-second response time specified in the original requirements and SLA published to users of this service.

There is a shepherd process on both AIX boxes that attempts to start failed WebSphere processes. In fact, we will rely on this service to restart the WebSphere process that we will terminate during out test. The Veritas failover will not support a failback scenario. Reintroducing an AIX server into the production infrastructure under load is perceived as a high and unnecessary risk.

Fault Tolerance Testing

During a failover test, the objective is to cripple a redundant service and observe the level of service. In the case of a fault tolerance test, the objective is to fully disable a service and observe how the application responds.

In Chapter 3 we cited a common non-functional operability requirement as: "if an infrastructure component is unavailable, services provided by dependent components should only be impacted insofar as they depend on the unavailable component."

To help with our understanding, let's assume that the address validation service described in the previous section supports a reservation system for a global hotelier. Addresses are validated whenever customers provide a billing address in the course of making reservations. The reservations system services a large suite of functionality, including the ability to look up room availability, quote rate information, and create or cancel existing reservations. The address validation service is used only for validating billing addresses for new customer reservations.

As you may already have guessed, the purpose of a fault tolerance test in this case would be to prove that if the address validation Web Service is not available, a user's abilities to access the nondependent business functionality are not compromised. Test case definition for fault tolerance scenarios is very similar to failover test-case definition, including the fail-back attribute (as shown in Table 7.21).

Request timeouts can be a very destructive scenario for many software systems. If timeouts are not supported or configured, a software system can quickly become bottlenecked and begin to deny service to all clients. In the fault tolerance test case described above, some creativity may be required in simulating this failure scenario. One possibility would be to purposefully misconfigure the address validation URL (uniform resource locator) for the Web Service to an IP (Inter-

Table 7.21   Test Case 1: Address Validation Fault Tolerance

Failure Mode	Network timeout on application requests
Software Components Failing Over	Address validation service
Load During Failover	Peak transaction rate (2.4 TPS)
Performance Requirements	All non-new reservations operations expected to meet original performance requirements
Error Tolerance	Errors are tolerated for the new reservations billing as long as the address validation service is unavailable
Fail-Back Required?	Yes; when the address validation service is restored, associated error rate should go to zero without any operator intervention

net protocol) address that is not on the network. This would subject all requests to the TCP (transmission control protocol) timeout which can be as high as 15 minutes.

Sustainability Testing

The aim of sustainability testing is to prove that there is no performance degradation or risk to availability over long term usage of the system. It is not uncommon for an application to slowly bleed resources until it abruptly fails. Sustainability testing is also referred to as *soak testing* in some circles.

The most difficult challenge in executing a sustainability test is the sheer length of time it can take to complete. As a result, it is important to select a reasonable duration that maximizes the utility of the test while minimizing your efforts.

As a starting point you should ensure that your system is operable for at least as long as your longest operations window. For example, if your application must provide service for an 18-hour business window 5 days a week, your sustainability test should, at a minimum, run for 18 hours. Should your application fail in the 19th hour, this scheme means that you would need to restart the application 5 times a week. This is hardly a characteristic of a highly available, operable system.

A better suggestion would be to run your sustainability test for 5 consecutive days, or 90 hours. If your system fails in the 91st hour, your operations team has a much longer maintenance window in which to restart the application, not to mention that they are doing so less frequently. Of course, if we could run the application for much longer—say, 4 weeks—this would improve our confidence level in the application even further.

Unfortunately, what we are considering is a time-consuming endeavor. As we have discussed previously, well designed tests are tests that can be run repeatedly and conveniently. A 90-hour test will take almost 4 days to run, assuming we have the resources to operate the test on a 24-hour basis. If we are running the test on a 10-hour workday, the test will still take 9 working days to complete. To make matters worse, if the test fails on the eighth day, perhaps because of a software failure, we must restart the test.

Few organizations have the luxury of weeks of resource and environment availability in which to complete this type of testing. We can approach this difficulty by changing the criteria for the test. Instead of planning our test based on elapsed time, we can plan our test based on elapsed business volumes. For most software systems, an idle system is not a very interesting specimen. In the 90-hour test we have been considering, the system is idle or at least not very busy a large fraction of the time.

In fact, the system may do 25% of its processing in a 1-hour window. Let's consider a content management application for a pharmaceuticals company. Employees of the company use the content management system to look up documentation on drugs that the company manufactures. A large number of employees actually update and create new documentation in the system also.

The business usage for this system is normally distributed around two peaks at 11:30 AM and 3:30 PM. It appears that employees strive to finish documentation tasks prior to lunch and again at the end of the day. The business usage for the system has been documented as shown in Table 7.22.

In looking at the usage, it is clear that 60% of the transaction volumes are expected within 2 two-hour windows. When we go to calculate the transaction rate for these intervals, these will be our peak periods of usage. Next we look at the operations window for the system and see that it is fairly generous. The system is available from 7:00 AM until 6:00 PM, seven days a week (as shown in Table 23).

Our objective is to prove that the system is sustainable for a four-week period. Instead of elapsed time, let's calculate how long it would take to drive our weeks of business volumes based on the peak transaction rate for the system. We do this in the calculation shown in Table 7.24.

In the previous calculation we see that we can drive four weeks of business volumes in a little less than four days. Based on our schedule, it will be difficult to accommodate a full four days of testing of this type. We have one week in which to complete sustainability testing. Four days is less than the one week we have allotted, but there is little margin for error.

If we need to repeat or restart the test, we will immediately overrun our activity. As a result, we compromise on 14 days' sustainability and will run load for two days. We will compensate for the abbreviated test duration with close attention to system metrics while the system is under load. Our next point of business is to discuss system monitoring during sustainability testing.

Table 7.22   Example Content Management System: Coarse Inputs

Usage Attribute	Requirement
Busiest Interval(s)	11:00 AM–12:00 noon (30% of volume) 3:00 PM–16:00 PM (30% of volume)
Document Retrieval	5,600
Document Search	9,800
Document Update	1,300
Document Creation	650

Table 7.23   Example Content Management System: Users and Operations Window

Usage Attribute	Requirement
Operations Window	07:00 AM to 6:00 PM Monday to Sunday
Number of Users By Class	Supervisors – 55 Documentation – 75 Engineering – 35 Legal – 10 Quality – 60
Number of Users by Class (1 year)	Assume 5% annual compound growth
Number of Users by Class (5 years)	Assume 5% annual compound growth

Table 7.24   System Sustainability

Coarse Input	Daily Volume	Peak Transaction Rate (operations/hour)		Time Required for One Day's Volumes	Time Required for 28 Days' Volumes	
Document Retrieval	5,600	5,600 x 30%	1,680	3.3 h	93.3 h	3.9 d
Document Search	9,800	9,800 x 30%	2,940	3.3 h	93.3 h	3.9 d
Document Update	1,300	1,300 x 30%	390	3.3 h	93.3 h	3.9 d
Document Creation	650	650 x 30%	195	3.3 h	93.3 h	3.9 d

The most common mode of failure in sustainability testing is the exhaustion of a finite resource such as memory. It is also common to exhaust a pooled resource like connections. If you are exhausting a finite resource, there are two possible explanations:

1. **Resource Leak:** You have a resource leak in your application. That is, the system is creating or requesting resources and then losing track of them. The system continues to create or request resources until the requests cannot be fulfilled. For lower-level programming languages like C/C++, it is entirely possible to allocate physical memory and then obliterate all references to this memory. This is a true memory leak in which the memory can never be recovered. If this pattern continues, your process will reach the maximum process size for the operating system and be terminated or exhaust the physical memory available on the server. On other platforms, including Java, memory is managed by the execution environment (JRE), so it is not possible to truly leak memory. However, if your application allocates memory into an unbounded collection and never destroys references to this data, the effect is the same: an increasing memory footprint that will eventually exhaust all memory.

2. **Resource Sizing:** You have sized a configurable resource in your system too large or too small. For example, if your system has a hard limit of 250 MB of available memory, and you configure an in-memory cache to contain 10,000 objects (each object being 25 kB or more), you will exhaust the memory you have allocated. This problem is easily resolved by shrinking the number of objects permitted in the in-memory cache. Of course, this may impact performance, so configuration changes in this category will require performance regression. A good illustration of where this type of sizing can be problematic is in the area of sizing Enterprise Java Bean (EJB) cache sizes for the J2EE platform. J2EE containers manage cached and pooled bean instances on your behalf. The number of objects that can be pooled is set in XML deployment descriptors, which can be configured on a per-environment basis. If these parameters are not sized properly, it is easy for the cache sizes to overrun the physical limitations of the runtime environment and cause memory exhaustion.

For you to be confident that your sustainability test is successful, it is not enough to observe performance over the duration of the test and conclude that your test has passed. It is equally valuable to monitor the system behavior throughout the test and ensure that the system has reached a steady-state in which there is no unbounded resource growth. The following metrics merit close attention during sustainability testing:

1. **Memory:** As discussed earlier, unbounded memory growth surely spells the demise of your application. Some platforms allocate physical memory to the process and then manage this memory internally. The Java platform can be configured to work in this way. The Java heap can be allocated once at system

start-up. In order to have a view of the Java heap internally, you can configure verbose memory logging for the JRE. For cases like this, be certain that you measure the memory footprint at the OS level and internal to the process.

2. **CPU.** You should monitor CPU during the course of your test. If the amount of CPU that is required for the application is steadily increasing while load remains constant, you may have a *CPU leak*. A CPU leak will eventually exhaust the available processing power on your platform and cause your application to fail.

3. **File System Growth:** You should monitor the file system to ensure that the application is using disk at a sustainable rate. In the production environment, you will need to allocate sufficient storage for log files and transactional files that are generated within the required retention period for the application.

4. **Internal Caches and Pools:** Depending on your platform, you may be able to monitor standard containers, caches and pools. For example, on J2EE-based applications, most pooled resources for connections and EJB caches are exposed through the Java Monitoring and Management API (JMX). There is a growing population of monitoring tools that support this standard and allow you to monitor your system over the duration of the test.

5. **Performance:** The easiest way to measure performance for degradation is to run a performance regression on your system at the conclusion of your sustainability test. If you certified the application using a one-hour peak load, then run this same test and compare the performance results against the original baseline.

Sustainability testing is among the most important tests in your repertoire as a non-functional expert. Sustainability testing can expose subtle defects that are hard to detect in a production environment where you may not have the flexibility of your test environment and the benefit of intrusive monitoring capabilities. You should be satisfied with your efforts once you have demonstrated consistent performance for a period at least as long as your longest operations window. At the same time, you can improve your confidence level by carefully monitoring system metrics and showing stable and predictable resource usage for your application at steady-date.

Challenges

Test execution can be a trying activity fraught with system restarts, database imports, data loading, and script warm-up, amongst other time-consuming events. Before we move on to the next chapter, we would like to share some wisdom on the challenges you may face during your test execution.

Repeatable Results

A great deal of coordination and planning is sometimes necessary to execute non-functional tests. It can be a major inconvenience to repeat all of this effort in your quest to achieve consistent, repeatable results. By now, you should know that you can't trust your results until they are repeatable. If your results are not consistent, you should look to the following possible explanations:

1. **Isolation:** If your test environment is not isolated from other activities, it is possible that external influences are impacting your test results. The only way to mitigate this is to discover who is impacting your environment and try to schedule your tests during periods when they are inactive.
2. **Variable Load:** If your test results are not consistent, you should verify that you are running the same test. It is not difficult for a test operator to configure the load with different scripts, or different parameters such as ramp-up or think time. If response time is radically degraded, make sure the number of virtual users hasn't been increased.
3. **Example Size:** If your results are not consistent, make sure your sample size is large enough. You can also extend the duration of your test, if need be. A statistical average will not be consistent if there aren't enough data points in the calculation.
4. **Rollback the Application:** If you are seeing dramatically different results for a new version of the application, you should try to execute an equivalent test on the previous version of the application. This may indicate whether the problem is in the application or the environment. If you've followed the advice in Chapter 4 on test planning, you should have a logical instance of the previous version in your environment already.

Limitations

Werner Heisenberg, a founding scientist in the field of quantum mechanics, is best known for the uncertainty principle, which states that it is impossible to measure the precise position and momentum of a particle at the same time. The basis for the theory is that your measurement of position compromises measurement of momentum. To put it more simply, it is impossible to measure an attribute of the particle without exerting an effect on the particle that invalidates the other measurement.

The complexity of non-functional testing is not exactly on par with quantum theory, but, interestingly, we consistently face the same challenge. When a phenomenon of the system occurs under load, it is often very difficult to conduct analysis of the behavior without changing the phenomenon itself.

For example, a performance problem may arise once load has crossed a certain threshold and we need to determine what is causing the degradation. Two strategies come to mind: we could introduce custom instrumentation code (performance logging; see Chapter 3) or, if our platform supports it, we could run the load with profiling software attached. Unfortunately, in both cases the additional load imposed by these alternatives will certainly change the performance characteristics of the system. In fact, the specific performance degradation may not arise at all when we run in this configuration. Perhaps more likely, we may not be able to achieve the production load because of the additional overhead of our measurement. If we are lucky, we may see a similar performance degradation and if we are luckier still, our instrumentation may point to the source of the problem. All things said, it is important that you understand that intrusive efforts to measure and understand your system have the capacity to also influence system behavior.

Summary

The mechanics of test case preparation and execution take time and experience to master. This chapter has equipped you with the tools you need to approach each set of activities with confidence. By now, you should be comfortable with each of the tasks that are prerequisite for your test execution. You should be familiar with performance testing itself, including stress and regression tests. In devising test scripts, we explored strategies for combining execution steps in scripts to achieve target transaction rates. This chapter introduced two important concepts: *mixed load* and *performance baselines*. A mixed load is a representative combination of test scripts that can be leveraged for a variety of operability tests; a performance baseline is the most recent successful performance test result that is used to contrast with new test results. In this chapter, we also reviewed a number of categories of operability testing including boundary conditions, failover, fault tolerance, and sustainability. Based on our experience, we also discussed common frustrations including the difficulty of achieving repeatable test results and in intrusively measuring system behavior. In the next chapter we assume that your test activities have executed successfully and move on to a discussion of deployment strategies that mitigate risk and improve your chances of delivering successful projects.

Chapter 8

Deployment Strategies

We have spent most of this book describing how to build and test software systems. In this chapter, we shift our focus and begin to look at considerations for *deploying* critical software into a production infrastructure.

Failed deployments are a nightmare for everyone. Your project team has spent months building and testing your application only for it to fail business verification when it is deployed. The ensuing weeks will be a scrambled, unplanned effort to correct the issue and prepare for another deployment. Generally speaking, there are two varieties of failed deployments, and this chapter provides you with tools to mitigate the likelihood of either of them.

A deployment can fail because the deployment procedure itself is bungled. This can happen for many reasons, the simplest of which is that the procedure itself can be wrong. Alternately, an operator executing the procedure can make a mistake. Or, an important set of configuration parameters may not be correct for the production environment. Basically, the software itself may be fine, but the procedure to implement it is not. For software systems that are large, complex, or both, the deployment procedure can be equally large and complex.

A deployment can also fail because the new software itself does not anticipate the production environment correctly. Rigorous functional testing does not always ensure compatibility with the production environment. This is common for scenarios where your system must interact with complex legacy systems that do not have well-defined behavior. In these cases, your functional testing may have relied on a test system that is woefully out of synch with the production environment.

For new systems, you may also face a situation in which projected business usage falls well short of reality. The result being that your application must cope with volumes that were not part of your non-functional test scope. In this chapter we will look at deployment strategies that help mitigate your risk in these types of circumstances.

Procedure Characteristics

Risk management is an important theme throughout this book. A good deployment process is focused heavily on minimizing risk. Deployment strategies that manage risk effectively have the following characteristics:

1. **Minimal:** There is always the potential for error in a software deployment. By minimizing the number of components that you are changing, you are likely to shorten and simplify the deployment procedure. As we will see in this chapter, structuring your applications in loosely coupled component architectures helps to position you for future deployments with a minimal footprint.

2. **Automated:** There are two key reasons why you should strive for automated deployment procedures. Firstly, manual processes are executed by human operators who are prone to error. Secondly, automated procedures deploy the application in the same way in every environment. A human operator may follow a deployment procedure and introduce subtle differences across different environments. The objective of a deployment is to propagate the exact same system that was tested and verified in non-production environments into the production environment. Automated deployments also tend to complete more quickly and efficiently than manual deployments. This efficiency gives you more time to verify the deployment and reverse the deployment if necessary.

3. **Auditable:** Each step in the deployment should be auditable. This means that a person looking at the production environment should be able to reverse-engineer the deployment procedure from the production environment and the outputs of the deployment. Many automated deployment procedures generate a deployment log that can be used for this purpose.

4. **Reversible:** Given that there is always risk that a deployment will introduce serious problems in a production environment, it is always recommended to have a back-out, rollback, or contingency procedure that resurrects the state of the software system prior to your deployment. Of course, each of the characteristics mentioned in this list should also apply to your back-out procedure that reverses the deployment.

5. **Tested:** If you have invested design and development effort in your deployment process, you need to ensure that it is fully tested and exercised. This means that you should use it consistently to build all of your test environments. If possible, you should encourage the development team and individual developers to use your process for building environments in their own activities.

The approach you take to achieving an auditable, reversible, automated deployment will depend on your software platform. There are dozens of scripting languages and technologies that can be used to automate deployment procedures for common enterprise platforms like UNIX and Windows.

Packaging

Packaging refers to the way in which your application code is bundled into deployable units. Your packaging options will depend in large part on the software platform with which you are developing. Many software platforms like J2EE and .NET are designed to encourage and support component architectures.

Component architectures consist of a family of components that interoperate in order to implement the overall software system. Individual components can be upgraded (or downgraded) independently. In order for such a scheme to work, you need to ensure that the combination of components you are deploying has been *certified* to work together in your testing. Development activities also scale better for component architectures; as developers can be aligned to work on different components in parallel.

Component architectures are also efficient at supporting code reuse; individual components can be shared among different applications.

In component architectures, you can group features and application code into components that are likely to change together. For example, you may have a complex set of application code that implements some industry-specific business logic. Since business logic is more likely to change than structural and utility functions in your application, you would be well advised to package all of the business logic into a dedicated component. In minor releases that alter business logic, only the component encapsulating business logic need be upgraded as part of the deployment.

The alternative to component architectures tends to be a monolithic application that forces you to re-deploy the entire application every time you need to make a single change. Re-deploying the entire application increases your testing obligations to confirm that nothing unexpected has been somehow introduced into the deployment. The deployment procedure itself is likely to include many more steps, increasing the number of opportunities for error.

Configuration

Technologies like XML and Spring for Java-based applications have made it increasingly attractive for developers to make software systems highly configurable through text files. Among other things, text file configuration is commonly used to enable and disable business functions, size software resources (e.g., cache size), and parameterize business logic.

The advantage of flat-file configurations is that they are highly transparent. It is easy for a third-party to audit text file changes and be confident that a deployment includes no more than the stated changes in configuration. Database-based configurations offer a similar advantage as configurations are manipulated using SQL (structured query language), which is also quite readable in plain text.

From a packaging perspective, it is always attractive when configuration can be database- or file-based and packaged separately from application code. When a component that includes application code undergoes a change, it is more difficult for the testing organization to determine what to test. Also, it is more difficult for a third-party to audit the change itself.

Text files can also be supported by version management strategies applied to other project documentation (e.g., CVS [concurrent versions system]).

Deployment Rehearsal

In Chapter 6 we discussed the advantages associated with a production-scale test environment used to support non-functional testing activities. A production-scale environment is also advantageous for rehearsing your production deployment.

The rehearsal process ensures that your deployment is compatible with all of the infrastructure nuances of the production environment. It is a test where the emphasis is not on the application itself, but rather on the mechanism by which it is deployed.

Deployment rehearsals also create a familiarity with the deployment team so that when the system is deployed to production there is reduced risk in human execution. A deployment rehearsal is also often referred to as a *dry run*. Ideally, a deployment rehearsal should also exercise the verification and back-out procedures of the deployment.

Rollout Strategies

The deployment of your application is often only the first step in making new or upgraded functionality available to end users. Once the software is deployed, you can choose from different strategies for actually rolling out new features to users. This section will look at common rollout strategies.

The Pilot Strategy

A pilot rollout strategy is one in which a new or changed application is introduced to a small community of users prior to introduction to the entire user community. Feedback is gathered from the pilot user group that may result in changes to the system before rollout to all users. Pilots are common and often involve internal users or preferred customers.

In many cases, for existing systems, pilot functionality is available at the same time as the original system. If users have a negative experience with the pilot system, they can always revert to the original system.

This is a good strategy for mitigating the reaction of sensitive end users to major changes in an existing application. If the pilot system is hosted outside the production system, this is also a good rehearsal for the deployment procedure itself.

The Phased Rollout Strategy

In a phased rollout, deploying new or changed functionality to end users is a two-part process. First, the software itself is deployed into the production infrastructure. Second, a series of configuration changes is made to gradually introduce functionality to users.

Consider an ordering system for a manufacturing parts supplier. If a major upgrade is applied to the production system, the business is at considerable risk if none of the business' suppliers are able to use the new system. However, if the system is rolled out to customers one at a time, the business is able to manage the risk incrementally.

This type of rollout strategy can be managed in two ways. In some cases you may be able to run both systems in parallel and segment and transition users from the old system to the new system through communications only. In other cases the development team will need to build functionality into the system that exposes new functionality to segments of users based on configuration.

If a phased rollout strategy is appropriate for your application, make sure that you engage the development team and specify business requirements in the same way as you would for any other feature.

A phased rollout is also a good way to mitigate risk when you lack confidence in your non-functional testing efforts. As you gradually introduce users onto the new system, you can monitor performance and capacity to ensure that the system behavior is acceptable.

The Big Bang Strategy

As you might expect, *big bang* rollout refers to a scenario in which all users are suddenly cut over to the new system. Obviously, this type of rollout does little to mitigate risk. However, this strategy is acceptable for systems with a good release track record and comprehensive non-functional testing.

Sometimes big-bang rollouts are foisted upon otherwise reluctant project teams by management eager to see the conclusion of the project. In these cases you need to help management understand that the project may take much longer if a big-bang deployment is a failure and needs to be repeated.

The Leapfrog Strategy

Some systems reside in such a complex and heterogeneous production environment that it is impossible to reliably back up the existing system and the new system onto the same infrastructure within the allowable window. For these situations, you may have no recourse other than to make a costly investment in a duplicate set of infrastructure that will assume the production identity as part of the deployment.

Under this strategy, the back-out procedure is to revert users to the existing production environment and leave the failed deployment intact on the leapfrog infrastructure. The term leapfrog is used because the new production environment (R^{N+1}) "leapfrogs" over the current production environment (R^N).

Upon subsequent releases, the previous production environment is upgraded and it leapfrogs over the R^{N+1} environment to become R^{N+2}. For most organizations, this strategy is undesirable because of the cost associated with maintaining a twin set of production infrastructure. In some cases, the leapfrog environment can also be leveraged as the production-scale non-functional test environment.

As discussed in Chapter 6, the disadvantage of this approach is that you forgo your non-functional test environment as soon as the new system is commissioned. The authors do not recommend this approach unless it is impossible to safely compress your deployment procedure into the allowed change window.

Case Study: Online Banking

An interesting case study that combines many of the concepts in this chapter comes from the financial services industry. An institution with more than 250,000 online users was in the process of totally replatforming their online banking offering. Web-based banking was a core channel for this bank; during typical busy periods, there were over 3,000 customers using the system concurrently. The system upgrade included a totally rewritten software interface, a new vendor platform, new hardware, and a new hosting partner to handle all operational aspects of the new system. Thousands of customers depended on the existing system, and there was virtually zero tolerance for any disruption in their abilities to conduct banking activities. Customers depended on the system as a critical service that was well entrenched in their everyday lives.

Once the new system had been tested, the bank elected to combine a pilot and phased rollout strategy. In the first step, the bank deployed the new system to the new infrastructure and made it available as a pilot to internal users (as shown in Figure 8.1).

In this pilot scheme, external customers continued to use the legacy system. The bank's internal employees and partners participated in a limited pilot by accessing the new online banking system directly. This strategy allowed business users to

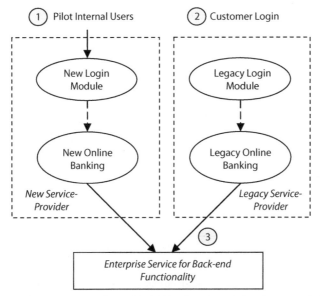

① Pilot Internal Users ② Customer Login

New Login Module

Legacy Login Module

New Online Banking

Legacy Online Banking

New Service-Provider

Legacy Service-Provider

③

Enterprise Service for Back-end Functionality

① Internal Pilot users access the new online banking system directly using a dedicated pilot URL. Access to the new system is un-published to external customers.

② Customers access the Online Banking site through the original, legacy login form.

③ The new and legacy banking systems are both connected to the bank's back-end systems through a common services tier. Technically, customers can conduct banking from either the new or the legacy site.

Figure 8.1   The banking pilot.

confirm application functionality in the production environment with full connectivity to the bank's back office.

Once the internal pilot had completed, the next step was to begin gradually rolling out the new system to external customers. A big-bang rollout was considered too risky for a core channel like online banking; management opted for a phased rollout instead.

The total customer population was split into phases that could be incrementally transitioned to the new system. Despite an intense performance and capacity testing effort, this approach also mitigated any outstanding risk in terms from a non-functional perspective. The visual architecture for the phased rollout strategy is shown in Figure 8.2.

Once all external customer segments had been transitioned to the new system, the legacy system could be fully decommissioned. The bank successfully executed this strategy in replatforming a strategic and critical customer-facing system.

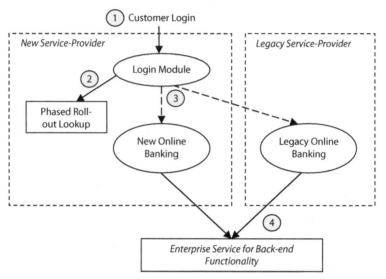

① Customers access the Online Banking site through a single login form. The login form is rendered by the new banking system login module as shown in the diagram.

② Customers supply user information to the login module. The login module does a determination based on user information whether the user should be redirected to the new or legacy online banking system.

③ The login module redirects the customer to the new or legacy online banking system as appropriate.

④ The new and legacy banking systems are both connected to the bank's back-end systems through a common services tier. Technically, customers can conduct banking from either the new or the legacy site.

Figure 8.2   Visual architectural representation.

Case Study: The Banking Front Office

A second case study demonstrates a much simpler implementation of a phased roll-out strategy. The investment division of a major financial institution invested in a multiyear effort to improve and optimize back-office operations using a new software system.

A key factor in the success of this effort was the workflow integration of front-office personnel, interacting directly with customers with back-office personnel responsible for taking action on customer requests. Both front- and back-office staff had access to a single workflow system.

The back-office employees using the new system were a small group who were actively supervised and managed by people intimately involved in the creation of the new system. The front-office user population was a much larger and unwieldy group of 4,000 individuals.

As new features were introduced, the institution needed a strategy for gradually rolling out new business functionality to the front office in increments. Immediately following a release, the institution did not want all 4,000 front-office users simultaneously attempting to access the same new feature.

Unfortunately, the front-office group could not be trusted to comply with a phased rollout strategy, i.e., if you added additional capabilities to their current interface, they would use those capabilities, irrespective of what had been communicated to them. Front-office users were located at retail branches across the country. Each branch would have between 5 and 200 front-office users. A good solution would have been to allow users to have access to new features based on their associated branch. Branches could be added incrementally to the rollout.

The solution to this problem was solved programmatically in the application itself by building an additional layer into the security model for the system.

The development team imposed a branch lookup prior to building the menu of available options for front-office users. In this way, a list of branches could be configured to have access to a given new feature, as shown in Figure 8.3. The branch list was implemented in a database that could be altered via simple administrative interface. This simple feature gave the transition team the control needed to implement a phased rollout strategy.

In the screen schematics above, you can see how the Transfer Securities menu item is only available to users who are associated with branches that are included in the rollout.

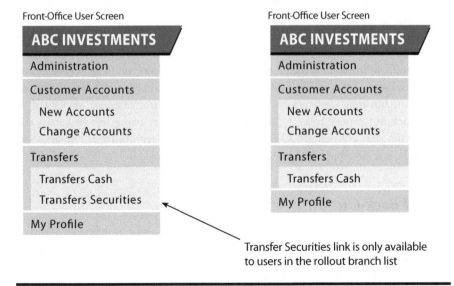

Figure 8.3   Functionality is selectively available to pilot users.

Back-Out Strategies

A back-out is usually what follows a failed deployment; it is required when a deployment fails and puts an existing business critical system into a state that is unusable to end users. Backing out an application is itself a risk, but when you decide to back out you are already in a situation where the production system is broken.

A deployment procedure for an enterprise application should always include a back-out procedure. The back-out procedure needs to be tested with the same rigor as the deployment process itself. Backing out an application is an embarrassing and undesirable scenario for any project.

Complete Back-Out

A back-out procedure can follow one of two strategies. The most conservative approach to back-out removes all traces of the new deployment from the production environment. This approach reverts the production system to a state identical to the pre-deployment state of the infrastructure. Your deployment plan should always include a complete back-out procedure.

Partial Back-Out

As you might expect, a partial back-out removes a subset of the deployed changes from the production general. In general, partial back-outs are heavily discouraged for enterprise systems because it is too difficult to test and anticipate all of the possible combinations of partial back-out procedures.

Partial back-outs also have difficulty meeting our requirement that deployments be fully auditable as it isn't clear in the documentation which back-out procedures were actually followed and which procedures weren't. However, in some situations, partial back-outs are a manageable way to mitigate the impact of a failed deployment. Your business verification should outline which test cases are associated to which back-out procedures. If the components that are being left in versus the components that are being backed out are sufficiently remote from one another, this can be a reasonable strategy.

Logical Back-Out

An alternative back-out procedure leaves the deployed application intact, but disables the new or changed functionality. This type of back-out is quicker to apply, but usually requires built-in support from the application. For this case, toggles can be built into the database or text file configuration to enable and disable specific business functions.

This approach to back-out leaves the door open to re-enable the new business function—if for example, a required external dependency is met post-deployment. Your deployment procedure will need to include technical and business verification steps that also indicate the conditions for when a partial or complete back-out is acceptable.

Summary

Any seasoned technologist will tell you that risk accompanies any change you make in a production environment. You mitigate this risk in your deployment procedure by ensuring that your deployments are minimal, automated, auditable, and reversible.

Once you have deployed software into your environment, you can choose from one of several rollout strategies including piloting, multiple and short phases, and a big-bang implementation, depending on your risk tolerance. A rollout strategy is a good way to compensate for shortfalls in your non-functional test coverage. Finally, in the event that your deployment is unsuccessful, you will need to follow a pre-determined back-out strategy.

In this chapter we have reviewed complete, partial, and logical back-outs as alternatives if you are in this undesirable situation. In the next chapter we will look at operations considerations including important topics like monitoring, trending, and reporting.

Chapter 9

Resisting Pressure from the Functional Requirements Stream

Non-functional requirements make a system usable, while functional requirements make the system itself. This distinction lies at the core of the challenges that are faced when trying to balance project resources so that both requirement streams can be successfully completed.

Functional and non-functional requirements must both be satisfied before a nontrivial system can be built to run in the real world. However, in the real world, the pressure to get the functional requirements stream completed often dominates and results in neglect of the latter due to resource and time contentions. Actually, the situation is even more complex, perhaps even insidious, as will be discussed shortly.

The resources subject matter experts (SMEs), for example, need to construct requirements are generally in short supply in most organizations. The knowledge, experience, and ability of SMEs is required to support the operations of a company, so just getting them focused on a project can be a challenge. There is usually unrelenting pressure from the business to get their services back to meet operational obligations.

During periods when a business SME team can focus on project requirements, there is going to be competition for their time from both the functional and non-functional requirement streams. The former will almost always get the undivided attention of the business team. There are several reasons for this, including the following:

1. Defining functionality is challenging and can become all-consuming in time and effort. SMEs feel the need to focus all their efforts and energy to get the functional requirements absolutely right.
2. Non-functional requirements are considered important, but until the functional requirements are clearly known, there is believed to be little point in spending time on them.
3. SMEs, due to their background, will focus on what they know best—driving out the functional requirements, while viewing non-functional requirements as being a technical issue only.
4. Functional requirements are generally on the critical path on most project plans.
5. Businesses do not pay for a system that is very fast, very secure, and highly usable. They pay for functionality that is all of these things.

The importance and criticality of functional requirements cannot be reasonably debated. This is what the business is buying; this is the reason the project exists in the first place. Very few business resources would deny the importance of security, availability, performance, and ease of use. This is where the insidious challenges creep into the picture. Despite everyone's best intentions and recognition of the importance of non-functional requirements, this stream is still usually neglected, incomplete, or incorrect. This is true even when the non-functional requirements stream is launched at the same time as the functional stream.

On a continuum of focus, even when non-functional requirements are underway, when push comes to shove, the functional requirements stream will win the competition for resources. The demands from the functional stream can insidiously creep up and draw attention and resources away from the non-functional stream. There clearly needs to be a balance in the pursuit of both functional and non-functional requirements.

This chapter focuses on defining a framework that allows a project team to resist continued and unrelenting pressure from the functional requirements stream to draw resources and attention away from the non-functional stream despite everyone's best intentions to the contrary. Non-functional requirements require attention, but the key is to maintain that attention for the duration of the project, regardless of the pressure being felt to complete the functional requirements.

A Question of Degree

Functional requirements tend to be business-domain-specific, while non-functional requirements tend to have several components. They are generic in the sense that performance, throughput, and security requirements are universal. This implies that non-functional requirements can be gathered and documented without continuous subject matter expertise. However, this is not enough.

Generic non-functional requirements must be customized to suit the specific requirements of an application. Consider this example: both a banking application and a video download application require a user/permission administration function. The former however, requires significantly more controls and audit trails than the latter. Making these requirements equivalent might be considered to be overengineered in the latter application.

Non-functional requirements are clearly dependent on specific functional cases. This means that they cannot be completed by themselves in isolation. This is both the strength and the weakness that must be addressed to successfully implement an application.

Table 9.1 describes the different approaches that are commonly used for tackling this set of activities. Some are completely undesirable, but unfortunately not altogether uncommon; others are commendable, but ultimately futile; while the last one on the list is recommended.

These options show how non-functional requirements are viewed in different organizations, beginning with neglect and moving toward a mature view of their mandatory importance to the eventual success of the project.

Approach 5, parallel start and parallel completion, offers the most balanced and optimal approach for consolidating functional and non-functional requirements. Dependencies between the streams are considered and included in the project plan. For example, the performance requirements for a specific user-input screen may not be defined until the screen is mocked up to gauge its input complexity. Another example consists of defining security requirements without getting a deep understanding of the potential application users and their profiles. This option requires both requirement phases to be initiated and concluded based on mutual dependencies and priorities—instead of as an afterthought. Some of the resources will be shared between the streams, but there will also be additional experts: SMEs on the functional side, architects and designers on the non-functional side.

Pressures from the Functional Requirements Stream

Given real-world experience, it is not surprising that Table 9.1 only shows one desirable approach (approach 5) for handling both functional and non-functional requirements. Approach 1 is sadly a reality in some instances, but the fact is that very few organizations place little or no importance on non-functional requirements. This is refreshing, but only a starting point.

Most real-world situations start with the best of intentions by driving out non-functional requirements early in the project, in conjunction with the application functionality. These situations are covered by approaches 2, 3, 4, and 5. However, approaches 2, 3, and 4, while starting strongly, end up competing for resources

Table 9.1 Approaches for Dealing with Non-functional Requirements

Approach	Description	Considerations	Impact
1	Completely neglected	Non-functional requirements are not included in the core requirements gathering phase.	Inadequate architecture, design, and coding. Could potentially result in project failure.
2	Completed separately	Non-functional requirements are built without input from the SMEs.	Misalignment between the requirement needs of the business and those believed by the technical team. Will result in over- or underengineering, and additional time to align the needs.
3	Parallel start, but abandoned	Both streams are started according to plan; however, the non-functional stream begins to lose resources to the functional stream over time.	Dealing with this situation is a subject of this chapter.
4	Parallel start, ad-hoc support	Both streams are started according to plan; however, non-functional resources are continuously used to compensate for work peaks in the functional stream.	This situation is better than approach 3, but will still have negative impacts on the project schedule. (This is a subject of this chapter.)
5	Parallel start and parallel completion	Addresses dependencies between the two requirement streams.	Requires additional attention by the SME team; may delay the functional specifications delivery, but will produce a better product in an overall faster timeframe.

with the non-functional stream and drawing them away to meet their own schedule at the expense of the project as a whole. The situation is insidious because it happens slowly and innocently. The project team believes they are doing the right thing, not realizing that they are postponing some of the most difficult requirements into the time crunch that typically happens at the end of a project lifecycle.

The process starts simply enough. A project plan is constructed that shows, among many other things, how functional and non-functional requirements are going to be accommodated. More than likely, activities representing the start of the functional requirements stream will be reflected in the project plan with earlier start dates than their non-functional counterparts. The latter will also likely reach completion sometime following the former's end date. This is shown in Figure 9.1. Note that there is likely to be some degree of iteration and reworking in the process.

Figure 9.1 also shows several points of dependency between the two streams. The non-functional requirements stream can be initiated, but it requires input or answers from the functional team at specific points. The figure shows a collection of generic non-functional requirement categories that include the following:

- Business Usage/System Availability
- Performance
- Operability
- Maintainability
- Expandability
- Throughput
- Hardware
- Software/Licenses

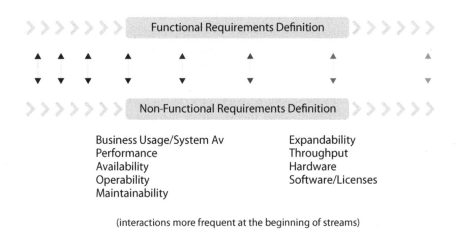

Figure 9.1 Linking the requirements streams.

Figure 9.1 also shows that the functional requirements stream can be dependent on the non-functional requirements stream. This may sound like a novel idea to some purists, while others might be confused at this statement, believing it to be completely obvious. The principle behind this is to produce a stronger return on investment by aligning technical/non-functional capabilities with the objectives sought by the business. It is possible for the business to modify their requirements in response to technical feasibility rather than to spend the extra money (e.g., on hardware) to completely satisfy their wish list. This type of alignment is only possible if the two requirement streams are jointly conducted and are equally respected.

The two-way dependency between the phases results in resource contention on project resources. The two streams can begin as per plan. As time progresses, however, we tend to start seeing a magnetlike attraction for resources in various areas, including the following:

1. Attention
2. Human Resources
3. Hardware Resources
4. Software Resources
5. Issue Resolution

These are described further in the following subsections.

Attention

This really refers to the areas that are getting the attention of the project team and stakeholders. While everyone is interested in non-functional requirements, the level of detail in the functional stream—business rules, input screen layouts, reports, interface dialogue—are the immediate artifacts for user signoff. These then get the attention until signoff is achieved. In most projects, the complexity of the functional requirements stream needs continued SME and business attention to get the level of detail and accuracy to warrant user signoff.

Coupled with the architecture, modeling, and design teams to ensure that the functional requirements are supported, a good portion of the extended project team is involved in the activity. If—and this is usually the case—there are challenges in getting signoff due to missing, incomplete or incompatible functional requirements, overlapping team members will delay involvement in the non-functional stream.

Human Resources

This is the greatest point of contention in completing both the functional and non-functional requirement streams per a project plan. The resources that are required in both streams can include: SMEs, business analysts, architects, designers, users, project sponsors, and modelers. Increasing complexity on the functional side requires more attention from these resources, with a corresponding decrease in attention to the non-functional requirements. These are discussed in further detail later in this chapter.

Hardware Resources

Hardware for non-functional requirements such as stress testing, throughput verification, and end-to-end security is often neglected due to the high cost of acquisition, setup, and maintenance. This pushes these activities well into the project lifecycle and may delay them to a point where they cannot be completed in time to meet the project deadline. This leads to a choice of delaying the project or implementing the application without a full understanding of how it will behave in a production environment.

Software Resources

This deals with the type of software and the number of licenses required by the application. The focus of most project teams tends to be on the tools required for designing, modeling, and building the application. Tools for non-functional requirements are left until later or entirely written out of the budget. This also tends to be a first point of reduction when the budget needs to be cut back. It is difficult to see the impact of a delay here during development, while a missing development tool is visible immediately.

Issue Resolution

As development progresses, many issues are identified by different members of the project team. These are typically categorized, prioritized, and logged. As the pressure to sign off on the functional requirements increases, related issues tend to have a higher prioritization and an earlier resolution date. Non-functional issues tend to be given lower priorities or longer resolution dates, which again removes urgency and attention away from them to the point that there again may not be enough time for resolution.

Defining Success

The definition of project success in the industry is fairly standard, and based upon whether the project is completed on time and on budget. This also assumes delivery of a mandatory set of functions that are within the project scope. The functions themselves are governed by a set of non-functional specifications that drive out how well and completely the functions behave. Consider the following examples:

- A claim entry screen that requires more than one second to save or update a claim is unusable
- A funds transfer in a banking application that adds funds to one account but breaks before subtracting them from the other is a complete disaster
- A reporting application that needs information that is current to the hour otherwise meaningful executive decisions cannot be made needs several non-functional design solutions

Each of these examples begins with a business requirement that provides further definition to the non-functional requirements stream. The project's success depends on both parts of the statement requirement being met. Without paying full attention to non-functional business requirements, and maintaining that attention, the project cannot be successful. Completing either the functional stream or the non-functional stream alone is not enough.

Setting the Stage for Success

A successful non-functional requirements stream involves three provisions that will be discussed in this section:

1. Identification of non-functional requirements.
2. Alignment with the functional requirements.
3. Avoidance of negative impact from the functional requirements stream.

Non-functional business requirements must go through the standard project development lifecycle (as shown in Figure 9.2), which is generally used to satisfy the functional requirements stream. Non-functional requirements cannot be an afterthought only; clearly, lead time and planning is required to accommodate them into the solution.

Specific milestones within the phase shown in Figure 9.2 are as follows:

Figure 9.2 The standard project development lifecycle.

- Plan
  - Non-functional resource estimates complete
  - Budget secured for hardware/software needed
- Architecture and Design
  - Non-functional test environment defined
  - Software testing tools defined
- Develop
  - Non-functional requirements completed
  - Development completed with attention to performance/operability
- Test
  - Deployment to non-functional test environment completed
  - Development for automation and load testing completed
  - Performance testing completed
  - Failover and operability testing completed
  - Sustainability testing completed
- Deploy
  - Capacity model and plan completed

Successful inclusion of non-functional business requirements into the mainstream of the project requires specific attention, and, more importantly, commitment by the project team. Left alone, chances are that non-functional activities will be the first to be shifted over time, in favor of protecting the timelines of the functional stream. This section provides a set of principles for protecting the interests of the non-functional requirements stream, described under the following categories:

1. Framework
2. Roles and Responsibilities
3. Raw Resources Required by the Non-functional Requirements Stream
4. Performance Metrics
5. Setting Expectations
6. Controls
7. Impact of Not Acting

Framework

The best way to protect non-functional requirements against the pressures of the functional requirements stream is to build the activities directly into the standard project-development lifecycle and to align delivery to the performance metrics of the resources on the project team. Figure 9.3 shows a number of non-functional threads that should be incorporated as a set of activities across the project lifecycle.

The non-functional requirements thread stretches across the entire framework. It is not an afterthought. It has as much importance as the project management thread. This should be complemented by a set of milestone deliverables in the project

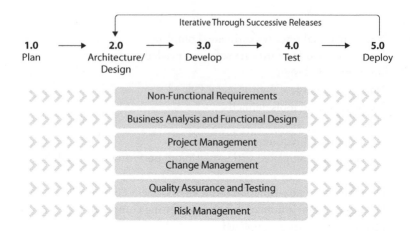

Figure 9.3 Project threads.

plan (as shown in Table 9.2). The milestone deliverables can be further subdivided. For example, Hardware requirements can be subdivided into development server, stress testing server, testing server, development desktop, and external user acceptance area.

Roles and Responsibilities

The mandate to complete a full set of non-functional requirements on a project is clearly in the mandate of the project manager. Table 9.3 identifies the other critical roles and responsibilities needed to ensure this is done correctly. Out of these, responsibility for delivery rests with the project manager and the project sponsor.

Raw Resources Required by the Non-Functional Requirements Stream

In addition to the roles and responsibilities defined in the previous section, this section collects the other raw materials needed to ensure a proper handling of the non-functional requirements stream.

The Core Project Team

A basic core team of a team lead, architect, business analyst, and technical resources should be allocated to drive out the known or industry best practices around non-functional requirements. The business analyst and team lead coordinate with the project manager to work along the dependencies with the core team.

Table 9.2   Non-functional Requirement Milestones

Milestone Deliverable	Draft Availability Date	Review Date 1	Review Date 2	Signoff Date
System Availability Defined	[dd/mm/yyyy]	[dd/mm/yyyy]	[dd/mm/yyyy]	[dd/mm/yyyy]
Performance Expectations	[dd/mm/yyyy]	[dd/mm/yyyy]	[dd/mm/yyyy]	[dd/mm/yyyy]
Interoperability Requirements	[dd/mm/yyyy]	[dd/mm/yyyy]	[dd/mm/yyyy]	[dd/mm/yyyy]
Security Requirements	[dd/mm/yyyy]	[dd/mm/yyyy]	[dd/mm/yyyy]	[dd/mm/yyyy]
Maintainability Requirements	[dd/mm/yyyy]	[dd/mm/yyyy]	[dd/mm/yyyy]	[dd/mm/yyyy]
Expandability Requirements	[dd/mm/yyyy]	[dd/mm/yyyy]	[dd/mm/yyyy]	[dd/mm/yyyy]
Throughput Requirements	[dd/mm/yyyy]	[dd/mm/yyyy]	[dd/mm/yyyy]	[dd/mm/yyyy]
Hardware Requirements	[dd/mm/yyyy]	[dd/mm/yyyy]	[dd/mm/yyyy]	[dd/mm/yyyy]
Software/Licenses Requirements	[dd/mm/yyyy]	[dd/mm/yyyy]	[dd/mm/yyyy]	[dd/mm/yyyy]

Extending the Project Framework

The non-functional requirements framework can be further defined with the following major activities that fit into the generic project lifecycle shown in Figure 9.3.

- Fast-Track Definition: This involves identification of the categories (e.g., as shown in Figure 9.1) and basic requirements, as known within Industry best practices.
- Requirements Gathering: This involves working with the SMEs to elaborate on the specifics of each Functional Requirement by Category.

Table 9.3   Roles and Responsibilities

Role	Responsibility	Comments
Project Manager	Project planning, controls, and successful delivery of the application.	Cannot be successful if any of the critical project requirements are not met.
Subject Matter Expert	Provides input into the non-functional requirements. Should also sign off on the documented requirements.	
Project Lead	Managing the work stream for the non-functional requirements.	
Project Sponsor	Removing obstacles and supporting the non-functional stream.	Can provide substantial support when there is pressure to focus only on the functional requirements.
Project Stakeholders	Providing additional SMEs where required to meet the demands of the project.	May need to adjust operational needs to meet increasing demands of a project.
Technical Architect	Defining the overall technical environment of the application.	Should include timeframes and lead times.
Data Architect	Possibly the owner of the data and the database. Must lead efficiency of the data architecture.	Works closely with the data modeler and the database administrator.
Application Architect	Defining the overall application environment.	
Business Analysts	Coordinating the collection and documentation of the functional and non-functional requirements.	

Table 9.3 (*continued*)

Developers	Sounding the alarm when non-functional requirements are not being identified or addressed.	
Technical Resources	Including setup and execution of hardware and software tools.	Includes systems administration, networking, and tuning skills.
Testers	Specializing test team.	Needs to be able to repeat and regress large series of tests.

- Architecture and Design: These need to align the functional requirements with specific metrics e.g., what performance level (average, slowest, and best) is required by the business when a user hits enter on the claim screen.
- Testing: This generally involves different flavors of stress and throughput testing. A separate test team may be required to test for the specifics of Non-functional Requirements as a lot of environment setup may be required.

The other project development lifecycle activities apply around these specific ones. In constructing a framework for dealing with non-functional requirements, consider these objectives:

- get specific requirements and measurements for each non-functional requirement in a system
- get broad agreement on system metrics or service level agreements
- incorporate non-functional requirements into a master project plan
- deal with the requirements from the beginning of the lifecycle
- architect and design with these in mind
- dedicate specific resources
- measure the performance of resources against the defined performance metrics

Technology and Tools

The major issue for technology and tools revolves around the industry-strength nature of what is required by the non-functional requirements stream. We need to support requests such as the following:

- Major increases in concurrent users
- Major increases in data transfer and date updates
- Administration functions
- Stress testing
- Throughput testing
- Single Sign-on
- Sub-second performance
- Regular maintenance releases

Requirements such as these may require additional technology and tools to build and test. The architecture and design should be built upfront assuming the worst-case, expected, and best-case scenarios.

Some types of requirements end up falling into the non-functional category by omission. For example, screen usability might be considered a functional requirement if the business users are discussing specific dropdown lists, entry codes, search criteria, and colors. But they might not consider the overall framework, navigation, metaphor, and fast links. Other areas that could fall into this category include the following:

- Usability
- Documentation
- System Help
- Call Center
- Ease of Future Enhancements
- Audit Reports
- Ad-hoc Reports

Project Sponsorship

While the project manager has the ultimate responsibility to deliver the successful application, the project sponsors play a key role. As the ultimate source of problem resolution on the project, they must ensure that non-functional requirements are not ignored if deadlines begin to slip or resources begin to get drawn in different directions. They can also work with other stakeholders to bring additional resources onto the project to ensure that the project plan continues to be met.

Ideally, a business and a technical sponsor will jointly have access to all the other resources in the organization required to complete the project. While these resources may be involved in operational activities, the combined sponsor team can work with senior management to affect other priorities in the organization.

Performance Metrics

We have discussed the importance of non-functional requirements and ensuring that they are included in the project plan. We have also discussed the fact that the project manager and the project sponsors have the ultimate responsibility for ensuring that resources are in place to adequately address these. However, members of the project team must have the incentive and initiative to also play a key role in the fulfillment of these.

In an ideal stiuation, all the members of the project team would share in the prioritization of non-functional requirements. However, many different priorities emerge in the project trenches. The real-world situation is generally far from ideal, and so we need a vehicle to share the responsibility. Neither the project manager nor the stakeholders can be successful only by themselves. It is also difficult for them to ascertain the truth or ambiguity of statements they will undoubtedly hear from project team members that satisfying both requirement streams is impossible due to time considerations or other reasons.

Performance metrics need to be extended to the key project team members that are needed to adequately address the non-functional stream. Working on the functional stream should not be enough to give them an excellent performance review. Signoff of the non-functional requirements, per the key milestone deliverable list, should be included in their success criteria. This should be regularly revisited with the project team members until the dependencies have all been met.

With the performance metrics in everyone's mind, a regular (e.g., weekly) status report should track each of the non-functional requirements so that progress is clearly visible.

Escalation Procedures

With the other tools in place, the non-functional requirements stream should be positioned to resist pressure from the functional side. However, feedback from different members of the project team may still identify risks, future or immediate, that need to be processed. The feedback may also show that the non-functional stream is starting to be neglected or is falling behind.

A published escalation procedure is needed from the start of the project to deal with issues where this stream is still being neglected. This should include a process for establishing project responsibilities above stream responsibilities. This could mean that a specific function may actually not get the resources that are needed to work on backup and recovery capabilities, for example.

The escalation procedures should go through the project manager into a regularly occurring meeting with business users, stakeholders, and the project sponsors. Lack of resolution may lead to an executive steering committee that has the authority to provide any of the following:

- Additional funding for resources, tools, and technology to deal with competing requests
- Ability to divert knowledgeable resources from operational responsibilities
- Ability to divert knowledgeable resources from other projects to provide relief
- Ability to modify the scope or timeline of the project

Setting Expectations

Clarity at the outset of a project around risk management, problems that may occur, and what is expected to resolve them from anyone involved in the project is the only way to ensure that there is the will and ability to deliver both requirements streams within the constraints of the project. Expectations need to be established in the following areas:

- Resolving conflicting requests
- Resolving conflicting demands on resources
- Change Management and prioritizing
- Conditions under which funding, time, or scope will change
- Any critical requests

These should be written and shared with the project sponsors at the start of a project. With their agreement, the expectations should be shared with the team leads and then the rest of the project team. They should also be communicated to executive management.

Controls

Controls are needed to ensure that the functional stream does not encroach on the non-functional stream. Indeed, they are also needed to ensure that the converse does not occur, either. Projects that are driven by the business tend to be the former; projects that are dominated by the IT (information technology) team can easily slant toward the latter. The following controls offer balance to a project:

- Regular Team Status Reports
- Executive Dashboard
- Risk Assessment
- Issues Log
- Change Request log
- Project Plan

The Impact of Not Acting

It is useful to document impacts on the project of not acting on non-functional specifications. This documentation can form a core part of the risk assessment, which can be included in the project charter. The worst-case impact of not acting is clearly project failure. However, in the thrall of an intense project, the team may not believe that this is a likely outcome. And it may not be. The project plan is the best document to demonstrate the impact on what matters most to the project sponsors. This includes the delay in the project schedule when non-functional requirements are neglected. The following list identifies additional likely impacts of not acting when the functional stream begins to take resources to meet their own deadlines:

- Higher overall project cost
- Higher maintenance costs
- Increased risk of application failure in production
- Delayed project implementation
- Lower team morale
- Missing functionality

Summary

Businesses do not make money by constructing systems that are defined by typical non-functional requirements such as fast response time, being highly secure, or being immensely scalable. Businesses spend money and time to get systems that satisfy specific functions. However, many of these are complex and time-consuming to define, design, and build. Most times these functions are at odds with non-functional requirements.

There are many factors that drive tight—but usually competitive—relationships between meeting functional and non-functional requirement streams. There will be pressure on dedicating resources to define, design, and build. But they generally do not get the same "mind space" of a project team. Nobody is going to say that response time or security is unimportant. But do project teams make the investments of time, money, and other resources commensurate with the importance of response time? The answer is generally *no*. In the subset of cases where this level of attention if made, does it remain? Again, the answer is generally *no*. The reasons for this are complex, and not due to any planned negativity.

This chapter described situations where a functional requirements stream can begin to draw resources from the non-functional requirements stream, thereby putting that stream and the project as a whole at risk. This chapter also presented a framework for ensuring that this does not occur, along with suggestions on how to deal with the inevitable pressures to do so when the project timeline becomes threatened.

Chapter 10

Operations Trending and Monitoring

No amount of careful design and testing can substitute for a thorough and effective operations strategy. From an availability standpoint, monitoring and trending are critical. Eventually, things will go wrong at some point in your operations and you will be measured by how quickly you detect and respond to the failure. The organization's profitability and perhaps even survival may depend on minimizing or neutralizing the impact of any problems that occur. Setting up early warnings may make all the difference between successfully dealing with a problem, or perhaps avoiding it altogether.

Monitoring

Monitoring your system has two distinct objectives:

- Detect and alert for problems as quickly as possible
- Provide maximum diagnostic information

If you can detect problems early, you may be able to correct them before they have any end-user impact. Your ability to resolve an issue quickly depends on the quality of diagnostic information you have available at the time of the failure. Consider the difference between these two failures for a production system (Table 10.1).

Table 10.1   Error Message Comparative Examples

Bad	Users report that they are no longer receiving e-mail from the production system
Good	Tuesday, 2 January 2007: 14:14:56 ERROR <Application Alert>: Email failure Tuesday, 2 January 2007: 14:21:05 ERROR <Application Alert>: Email failure Tuesday, 2 January 2007: 14:22:33 ERROR <Application Alert>: Email failure
Better	Tuesday, 2 January 2007: 17:14:56 FATAL <Infrastructure Alert>: SMTP Server process at 10.192.14.15 not responding Tuesday, 2 January 2007: 17:14:56 FATAL <Infrastructure Alert>: SMTP Server process at 10.192.14.15 not reachable from 10.192.14.23 Tuesday, 2 January 2007: 14:14:56 ERROR <Application Alert>: Email failure for request: 456 Tuesday, 2 January 2007: 14:21:05 ERROR <Application Alert>: Email failure for request: 457 Tuesday, 2 January 2007: 14:22:33 ERROR <Application Alert>: Email failure for request: 458 Tuesday, 2 January 2007: 17:14:56 FATAL <Application Alert>: Email failure for request: 459

In the first scenario, users begin to report that they are no longer receiving e-mail from the production system. At this point, there is already a business impact. Users are likely consorting with one another, comparing experience, and complaining about the impact. They may be questioning the validity of the work they are doing on the system. This lost productivity is a financial impact that could have been avoided.

In the second scenario, a series of errors are logged by the application when individual e-mail requests are attempted and failed. Each attempt results in a generated alert. Because errors are at the level of an individual transaction, they are logged and alerted with ERROR severity. This may attract the attention of the operations team, depending on their training and the criticality of this application. It is certainly preferable to the first scenario. A proactive operations team may be able to do further investigation and discover the root cause of the failure. Unfortunately, other than reporting that the error is associated to the e-mail capability for the system, there is very little diagnostic information to help the operator.

In the third scenario, we see a much better level of service from our monitoring infrastructure. Additional monitors in the system have detected that the simple mail transfer protocol (SMTP) gateway process is actually down. Because this is such a clear mode of failure, the alert level has been correctly raised as FATAL. This is certain to command the full attention of the operations team. Furthermore, a correlating alert has been raised from the application server indicating that the SMTP gateway is not reachable on the network. This event is consistent with the fact that the SMTP server is down. This alert shows the link between the application errors and the root cause failure of the SMTP gateway. Again, this connectivity failure is logged as FATAL; if the SMTP gateway is not reachable, it is clear that e-mail services are totally compromised. Because the diagnostics are so clear and precise in this situation, the operations team is able to restore the SMTP server quickly.

The operations team does not need to escalate involvement to the infrastructure or development teams. Most importantly, the business user community may never learn that there was a temporary failure for e-mail services on the application. Of course, this would require a defensive design pattern that supports automated retry to recover failed transactions. Readers of this book will have acquired this knowledge in Chapter 4.

In the previous example, there can be no disputing how valuable a comprehensive monitoring strategy can be for high-availability applications. In this section, we will look at how to wdevelop such a strategy for your application.

Attributes of Effective Monitoring

Using the previous example of an SMTP gateway failure, let's enumerate the attributes that provide for effective monitoring solutions:

- **Redundant Monitoring:** When designing a monitoring solution, it is tempting to omit monitors because they can appear to be redundant. Redundancy is an important attribute in the application itself to support high availability. Why should monitoring be any less highly available? There is no guarantee that any one monitor will succeed for every mode of failure. In addition to providing better and more detailed information, redundant monitors are backups to one another, ensuring that no failure will go undetected.
- **Monitors that Correlate:** In the previous example, the second FATAL alert that showed that the SMTP server was not reachable from the application server appears to be redundant. Root cause was evident from the first infrastructure alert that showed the SMTP gateway process itself was down. However, the second alert was indeed valuable. It established a link between the cause (the first alert) and the effect (application errors in the logs showing that e-mail attempts were unsuccessful). If there were multiple SMTP gateways in the infrastructure, this alert will show you precisely which systems are affected by an outage for any single gateway.

■ **Detailed Alerts:** If we look at the FATAL alerts generated in the previous example, we also see that they provide detailed information on the nature and source of the failure. For example, the second infrastructure event clearly indicates a network failure, and shows the source and destination for the network communication in the alert itself. This detail minimizes the effort required from the operator. It also accelerates the process of cross-referencing alerts to one another. For the application alerts, we see that the alert has scraped the request information from the log itself; we can see that the errors correspond to consecutive requests. This type of information is useful in understanding whether the failures are affecting all or a subset of requests. Failures with consecutive request IDs likely point to a total failure.

■ **Consolidation:** As much as possible, monitors for the software system need to be consolidated and presented to operations through a single interface. If your monitors generate e-mail or alerts to a variety of monitoring platforms, your environment is overly complex and will be more difficult to manage. Your operations team will struggle to correlate events if they are being generated to multiple disparate interfaces.

Monitoring Scope

An approach that is useful in assessing your application for monitoring starts with dividing the application into layers and evaluating each layer independently. In this approach, we will also see how roles and responsibilities can be defined for each layer.

This approach begins by considering your sysem as a composition of the following elements:

■ **Infrastructure:** This refers to the hardware and software components that are part of the base platform for your application, and includes network connectivity between servers, server availability, storage devices, and network devices. Infrastructure monitors also apply to commoditized resources like the central processing unit (CPU), available disk, and memory. We will look at example monitors in this category later in this section.

■ **Container:** Container monitors are resources that are explicitly configured and installed in the infrastructure to support your application. Container resources are typically vendor software applications. Your application may use services from these components, as in the case of the SMTP gateway example from earlier in this chapter. You application may also be deployed into a container provided by a software vendor. We will also see examples of this type later in this chapter.

- **Application:** Monitors that target your application look up application-specific messages or conditions to verify application health. The most typical example is application-generated log files.
- **End User.** End-user monitors observe the application from the point of view of the end user. These types of monitors will respond and report on error conditions in the same way that a user would.

Before we discuss these types of monitors in more detail, we should first outline roles and responsibilities. Defining good monitoring interfaces requires application knowledge, so it is important to have the right people engaged. At a minimum, your project should designate one person who is responsible for the monitoring strategy as a whole. This person will need to be a liaison to infrastructure, development, and business participants. Usually a technical person is best equipped to function in this capacity. It may make sense for the monitoring task owner to also be engaged with non-functional test activities. In this way, verifying monitors can be interwoven with non-functional tests.

Your approach to building monitoring capabilities into your platform will need to follow the same guidelines as the rest of the functionality in a project lifecycle. You need to define requirements, design a strategy that meets these requirements, and then test and implement your solution. When you are solutioning a new system with high-availability requirements, it is key to designate an individual with overall responsibility for executing a plan that delivers the intended strategy.

On most projects, whether you are hosting your application or outsourcing, you will have an infrastructure lead. This person is responsible for building and maintaining the production infrastructure. This same person needs to be accountable for the quality and depth of infrastructure monitoring. Fortunately, as we will see shortly, infrastructure monitors are fairly commoditized and there are management platforms that can be purchased for this purpose. The monitoring strategy lead will challenge the infrastructure monitoring lead to ensure that the appropriate monitoring is in place.

Container monitors require a joint effort from the infrastructure and development teams. The development team will need to designate a monitoring lead for defining custom application monitors. It is recommended that this same person work in tandem with the infrastructure lead to define appropriate container monitors. Again, the monitoring strategy lead should challenge the other participants to ensure maximum coverage from custom and configured monitors.

Finally, end-user monitors require cooperation between the development and business teams. The development team is positioned to recommend a series of monitors that exercise application functionality in a way that efficiently monitors overall availability. A business participant is usually required to validate that these monitors are permissible and do not have any negative business impact. Business participants may also need to provide suitable data for end-user monitors. The business user in this case is an advisor and participant only. It is recommended that the development monitoring lead or the overall monitoring strategy lead own end-user monitoring.

We summarize the roles and responsibilities we have defined in Table 10.2. Please note that this is by no means the only way to structure your efforts, but it is a proven configuration that will work for many types of projects. For small or medium-sized projects, these roles are usually not full-time commitments.

Now that we have introduced high-level categories for monitoring, we will look at each of these categories in detail in the following sections.

Infrastructure Monitoring

Infrastructure monitors are low-level monitors that verify hardware availability and capacity. For highly available systems, Table 10.3 provides a reference for common, critical metrics for some example device types. You should consult vendor documentation for specific devices to identify additional metrics. Many of these metrics are threshold based—that is, you specify a threshold based on percentage utilization.

In setting a threshold, you need to appreciate the granularity over which you are taking measurements. For thresholds that are applied to rate, this is particularly important. In CPU measurement, the instantaneous CPU utilization may be 100% for a small fraction of a second, but the steady-state average CPU utilization based on measurement at 1s intervals may be only 30%. For CPU monitors, a suitable polling interval for CPU measurement is 1 minute.

Table 10.2   Role Owners

Role	Recommended Owner
Monitoring Strategy Lead	Technical resource (possibly designated from non-functional test team)
Infrastructure Monitor Lead	Infrastructure lead
Container Monitor Lead	Development resource
Application Monitor Lead	Development resource
End-User Monitor Lead	Monitoring strategy lead
End-User Monitor Advisor	Business analyst

Table 10.3   Metrics for Device Types

Device Type	Metric
Server	Server availability (Boolean) Available CPU (threshold) Available memory (threshold) Swap versus virtual memory (threshold) Network input/output (I/O) utilization (threshold) Disk I/O utilization (threshold)
Storage	Device available (Boolean) Free space (threshold) I/O speed (threshold)
Switch	Device available (Boolean) Available CPU (threshold) Error rate (threshold) Error count by port (threshold) Network speed (threshold)
Router	Device available (threshold) Available CPU (threshold) Error rate (threshold) Network speed (threshold)

Though it is possible to write custom software and scripts to perform infrastructure monitoring on your behalf, it is far more efficient to procure a vendor solution for this purpose. Management and monitoring software is a mature and growing industry; there is no shortage of options.

Infrastructure monitors are implemented largely with the help of the simple network management protocol (SNMP), which is a lightweight protocol originally designed for managing and monitoring network devices. The SNMP specification has been in existence since 1988 and is widely implemented, in large part because it is fairly simple. Figure 10.1 shows an overview of an example SNMP apparatus.

A central management interface, referred to as a *network management system* (NMS), captures monitoring and management information and consolidates it for an administrative user. Network nodes that are under management of the NMS are referred to as managed devices. A managed device can further have agents installed on it that communicate with the NMS using the SNMP protocol. The agent software responds to SNMP requests and also maintains a local database of monitoring and management information. The SNMP protocol itself is also simple. It supports the following commands:

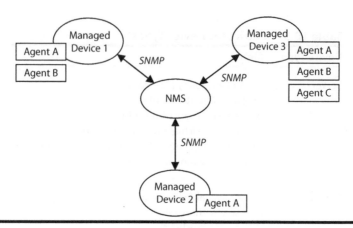

Figure 10.1   SNMP specification overview.

- **Read:** The NMS can interrogate a managed device to collect data on device health.
- **Write:** The NMS can also issue configuration commands to devices to control them. This is less interesting to us from a monitoring standpoint.
- **Trap:** Managed devices can also asynchronously send messages to the NMS. These events are called *traps*.
- **Traversal:** Traversal operations are used by the NMS to determine supported variables on the managed device.

Monitoring and management information on a managed device is organized into the management information base (MIB). The highest level of information exposed to the NMS by an SNMP agent is an MIB. An MIB is a hierarchical collection of managed objects. Each managed object is further comprised of object instances. Individual object instances contain data that describes the state and configuration of the device. Ultimately, object instance data is the "variable" data that is reported back to the NMS via read operations. This data can be compared to a threshold value and then used to trigger alerts when appropriate.

Many enterprise monitoring and management vendor solutions also include their own proprietary distributed agent architecture. For these systems, a custom agent is typically installed on each device under management. This custom agent may or may not support SNMP itself. Any enterprise solution will also support SNMP at the level of the NMS.

At the time of this writing, the most widely used enterprise management and monitoring solution by far is the Hewlett Packard OpenView platform. HP and software vendors partnered with HP provide over 300 OpenView-based programs that provide application-specific monitoring capabilities. HP OpenView is readily configurable to support all of the infrastructure metrics we have looked at in the chapter. As software solutions become an increasingly integral part of most business operations, monitoring and management software is an industry that is growing quickly. BMC Software and NetIQ are also significant players in the system management and monitoring business who offer products with rich monitoring capabilities. There are dozens of competing solutions, many of which are very cost-effective—if not free—alternatives to HP OpenView.

Container Monitoring

Container monitoring refers to the installed vendor software in your infrastructure and its attributes. This category of monitoring can be further broken down into the following types:

- **Availability Monitoring:** This is the most basic level of monitoring for software containers and services. Basically, this type of monitoring determines if the software itself is available. In the SMTP gateway example from earlier in this chapter, the monitor for SMTP availability is clearly an example in this category. Some vendor software supports a "ping" capability that can be used to ensure that it is responding normally. This type of capability may be exposed via SNMP or through a custom plug-in for a well-penetrated vendor solution like HP OpenView. In the absence of anything else, you can always configure a vendor monitoring solution to detect processes at the operating system level. If you are running an application server, you may expect four processes with a specific footprint to be running at all times and this can easily be configured.
- **Dependency Monitoring:** If the vendor software you are running is dependent on specific services in the infrastructure (e.g. an SMTP gateway), you should consider introducing additional monitors that will create alerts when this dependency is broken. For example, for Oracle to run efficiently, you may decide that no tablespace configured on physical storage should ever exceed 60% capacity. This is a finer-grained monitor than the available disk storage that would be part of infrastructure monitoring. This Oracle-specific monitor is a type of container monitor.
- **Vendor Messages:** Most vendor software applications will report errors to an exception log. As part of your container-monitoring strategy you should ensure that you are monitoring and alerting on these errors. Vendor software may also be capable of generating SNMP traps that can be caught and alerted for using your management and monitoring solution.
- **Container Resource Monitoring:** Container resources are specific resources configured in the container to support your application. These resources can be heavily impacted by the runtime behavior of your application and require the most sensitivity when applying monitors. Resource monitors are the most interesting aspect of container monitoring, and we will spend the rest of this section on them.

In this book we have intentionally tried to engineer examples that will appeal to a broad audience and are not vendor- or technology-specific. However, container monitors are by definition vendor-specific, so much of the discussion in the following example will revolve around the BEA Application Server. Fortunately, BEA exposes its monitoring interfaces using the Java management extensions (JMX) standard. All of BEA's competitors, including JBoss and WebSphere, have chosen the same direction conceptually; thus, everything we discuss in this example will apply to you if you are writing software applications that are deployed to J2EE-based containers.

Resource monitors are really the meeting point between development and infrastructure team responsibilities. Resource monitors need to be implemented in a standardized way. This inclines us to involve the infrastructure team, which can equip the infrastructure with generic monitoring capabilities for the containers in the environment. On the other hand, the development team is specifying and sizing the resources that are important to the application. Consequently, only a joint effort between teams is effective in specifying and implementing a proper container monitoring solution.

The BEA example we will look at next is ideal because it includes resources that are widely used by applications. For our purposes, let's revisit an example from Chapter 4. The example shown in Figure 10.2 is a conceptual architecture for a fulfillment service that includes a retry capability and a software valve. (You may wish to revisit Chapter 4 to familiarize yourself with this example if you have not done so already.)

As our first step, let's recast this example using J2EE constructs (as shown in Figure 10.3). We will then look at the example from the perspective of how we would monitor container resources within the application server.

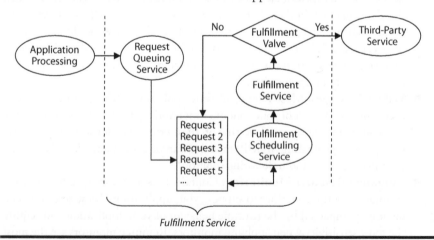

Figure 10.2 Conceptual architecture for a fulfillment service.

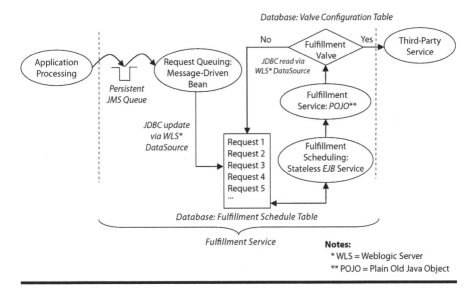

Figure 10.3 J2EE implementation of a fulfillment service.

Our fulfillment service implementation now includes two types of enterprise Java beans (EJBs). It is also dependent on Weblogic data sources for database updates. The initial fulfillment request arrives via a persistent Weblogic Java message service (JMS) queue as well. There are also two additional characteristics of our design that cannot be reflected in the diagram. First of all, we have configured the EJBs in the fulfillment service to run on a dedicated execute queue. (Execute queues are basically Weblogic thread pools). We have done this to ensure that the fulfillment service does not compete with the online service for execute threads. Second, the fulfillment service has been packaged as an Enterprise Application Resource (EAR). This allows us to deploy and update the fulfillment service as an independent component. As you should expect, we have container resource monitoring options for each of these references and constructs. Before we describe these in detail, we first need to discuss a technology highly relevant to this example: JMX.

JMX (*Java Management Extensions*) is a specification for building monitoring and management capabilities into Java-based applications. Like SNMP, the JMX architecture is not complex. At the time of this writing, it is also not complete. In particular, it is not yet a distributed architecture, as noted in Figure 10.4.

Individual Java applications are able to implement the JMX specification, but the specification itself does not require remote lookup and management. A distributed connector architecture is a planned future addition to the JMX specification. The basic architecture is hierarchical with a collection of managed objects, called *MBeans*, belonging to an MBeanServer. Individual MBeans have attributes that can be referenced as purely read-only objects for monitoring or can be set with con-

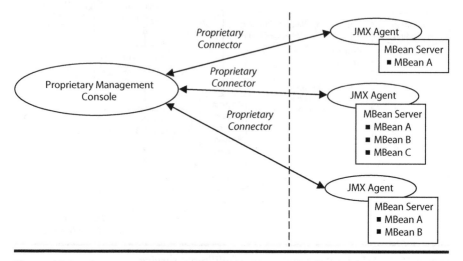

Figure 10.4   Java management extensions.

figuration values for control purposes. For our immediate use, application server vendors like BEA have implemented their own connector architecture that can be used to expose JMX MBeans to monitoring software. This means we can use JMX to interrogate and monitor J2EE components in the infrastructure. You will find that many enterprise monitoring solutions have built-in capabilities for looking up JMX-exposed objects and attributes on J2EE application servers.

Let's now look at the JMX attributes that apply to our example. They are as follows:

- **Enterprise Application Resource (EAR):** As our first point of business, we should ensure that the application component is deployed in the environment as expected. Following a system upgrade, this component could fail to deploy. It is also possible that an operator could mistakenly compromise the configuration and take it out of the active cluster. Alternately, the application could fail to deploy following a server restart. The deployed status of the EAR can be easily verified using JMX-based application programming interfaces (APIs) on the application server.

- **Execute Queues:** In Weblogic, execute queues are also exposed as JMX MBeans. From a monitoring perspective, we can monitor that there is always at least one idle thread available on this execute queue. In our design, we should have sized the thread pool to easily accommodate the expected load. An exhausted thread pool is symptomatic of blocking behavior, which is a problem that warrants immediate investigation. Fortunately, the number of idle threads is a JMX-exposed attribute on the execute queue and can also be easily monitored in the container.

■ **Message-Driven Beans (MDBs) and Stateless Enterprise Java Beans (EJBs):** The EJBs in our design are also exposed as JMX MBeans. We can use APIs provided by the application server to ensure that both of the EJBs in our fulfillment service are deployed at all times.

■ **Data Sources and Connection Pools:** Both the connection pool and the data source abstraction that gates application access to the connection pool can also be monitored through JMX APIs. In our case, we should monitor that both of these resources are deployed and that the number of available connections is always one or greater. This ensures that there is always a database connection available for a thread if it needs it.

■ **JMS Queue:** Lastly, the JMS queue is the asynchronous messaging interface between the rest of the application and the fulfillment service. We expect messages to be consumed from this queue immediately after they are deposited from the requesting application. Consequently, we can verify that the queue is deployed and that the message depth in the queue never exceeds a threshold value that is reasonable based on the expected business usage.

In this exercise, we have introduced seven container-based monitors for our fulfillment service. None of these monitors require any custom application development, but they each provide detailed diagnostic and alerting information that will be helpful in a troubleshooting situation. We summarize the new container monitors in Table 10.4.

Table 10.4   Resource Monitors

Resource	Monitoring Capabilities
EAR File	Verify component is deployed
Execute Queue	Verify idle threads exceeds 1
Message and Stateless EJBs	Verify components are deployed
Data Source and Connection Pool	Verify components are deployed Verify idle connections exceeds 1
JMS Queue	Verify queue is configured and deployed Verify that queue message depth does not exceed threshold

In summary, container monitors are an important category of monitoring, but they cannot be implemented by the infrastructure team without clear input from the development team. Our next section will introduce application-specific monitors where responsibility lies primarily with the development team.

Application Monitoring

In our discussion thus far, application monitors can be described as monitors that are custom built or rely on custom application outputs. Container and infrastructure monitors tend to be supported through configuration of vendor monitoring solutions. Application monitors require a little more work, but we are rewarded for our efforts with improved diagnostic information.

For most software systems, application alerts are derived from application errors logs. Software packages like HP OpenView include capabilities for monitoring application log files and generating alerts based on text-based pattern matching. This is a powerful and flexible mechanism but it requires careful thought and consideration.

If you have adopted a universal logging severity level in your software implementation, you will be well-positioned to take advantage of log-file monitoring. This will enable you to establish policies like *for every log message with a FATAL severity, generate an alert with FATAL severity*. Further, you can include the full text of the error message and an excerpt of the surrounding log file with the alert that is generated.

If you are monitoring a log file for messages that do not include severity, or—worse—your log file includes severities that are not dependable, then you will need to inventory error messages that can be generated from your application, assess them for criticality, and then configure your log file monitoring solution to watch for these messages. This is error-prone, unreliable, and time-consuming. You are highly recommended to adopt and enforce a universal log severity strategy to avoid this manual effort if at all possible.

If your development team has been strict in applying correct log levels to application logs, then you are well positioned for FATAL events. You will also want to consider ERROR events. A common pattern is to assign ERROR severity to errors that the application believes are specific to a transaction or request. FATAL errors are reserved for exceptions that indicate a common component or service is down or unavailable. Failures in the FATAL category indicate that service is totally disrupted.

What if you application begins to generate hundreds or thousands of logged events with ERROR severity? Does it make sense to ignore them if there is no corresponding FATAL event? Probably not. To address this scenario, you are recommended to implement frequency-based monitoring for log events with ERROR-based severity. You would implement such a rule with the logic, *If there are more than 100 errors in a sliding 10 minute window, raise a single FATAL alert*. You may wish to implement this additional logic for specific types of error messages or as a general rule. This decision will depend on your application.

In addition to log-file-based application monitoring, there are many other types of monitors that we encourage you to consider. Most of these monitors are easy to script and/or are supported by vendor monitoring platforms.

- **File system condition-based monitors:** It is common for software systems to exchange data with each other using files. File-based processing can be ad hoc or scheduled. For scheduled processing, you should consider monitors that ensure file creation or receipt at expected times. For example, if your system must meet a service level agreement (SLA) that expects a file to be generated and available for pick-up via secure file transfer protocol (SFTP) by another system at 5:00 PM each day, then you should implement a monitor that verifies that the file exists prior to 5:00 PM. File-system based monitors can also be used to sweep the file system for undesirable file outputs like process dumps (e.g., a core file on a UNIX-based file system)
- **Database monitors:** Databases will often express the state of your software system and can be used to evaluate its overall health. There are scenarios in which an SQL (structured query language)–based database monitor is an effective monitor. If records in a transaction table are expected to be marked with a success status, you can implement a database monitor to calculate the error rate and generate alerts when it exceeds a threshold value.
- **Log file growth monitors:** You should understand the expected growth patterns for the log files that your application generates before your application is deployed to production. If the log file experiences a sudden surge in volume, this is indicative of a problem. A common exception pattern causes infinite loops that generate an infinite number of exceptions. This can overflow the log file and, ultimately, the file system.

Application monitors rely on intimate knowledge of the application design to function. Since they are devised by the development team, there is really no limit to what can be implemented and we encourage you to be thorough and creative in your efforts. As you walk through your application design, ask yourselves what metrics are reliable indicators of application health. For each of these metrics, consider ways of exposing these metrics to the monitoring infrastructure by implementing a custom application alert.

End-User Monitoring

If you are resource-constrained and have very little capacity to implement a monitoring strategy, you should implement end-user monitors. End-user monitors generally do not require technical expertise, and they can usually be implemented without deploying additional software into the production environment itself. End-user monitors exercise the application in the same way as users and, consequently, are a very reliable measure of application health. The most typical example of an end-user monitor is an automated service that exercises a user interface. Such a service may login to the application, execute some read-only operations, and then logout. End-user monitors are not limited to user-interface driven systems. If your system has a transactional SLA that is file- or message-based, you are well-advised to implement monitors based on these transactions. In many circles, these types of operations are referred to as *artificial transactions*. Artificial transactions may not exercise the full breadth of system functionality, but if they are carefully planned, can provide you with a wealth of information.

Firstly, end-user monitors are also very helpful for correlating with other alerts in your infrastructure. If you receive a sudden deluge of container-based alerts, but you do not receive any end-user alerts, then you can assume that the issue is not user-facing.

You can also implement multiple end-user monitors, designed to align with technical dependencies. If you are designing monitors for an online reporting system that supports reports drawn from three underlying databases, you would be prudent to implement three end-user monitors that create a report from one of each of the three databases. If only one of the three end-user monitors fails on any given occasion, you may prioritize verification of the database used by the failing end-user monitor.

Monitors that operate from the end-user perspective are very useful in tracking system performance against the requirements that were originally committed to the user community. End-user monitors can also be used to verify quality of service from different geographic locations. Many monitoring solutions allow you to inject artificial transactions from remote sites based on the installation of a piece of agent software. This capability can be very useful in assessing the performance impact of network latency. We will come back to this topic in the next section. For the moment, our focus is on monitoring for incidents that compromise availability.

Lastly, end-user monitors are also critical because they are the most reliable monitor in your infrastructure. End-user monitors see the application as a black box. Success is measured at the level of the business operation. End-user monitors may not tell you *what* is wrong, but they are unlikely to fail to alert when your system is experiencing problems.

For many systems, there are limitations to what you can achieve in a production system with respect to end-user monitoring. Many systems limit you to read-only operations in the production environment. For some systems, providing a generic, authenticated user that can be used for monitoring is an insurmountable challenge. Privacy and security issues can factor heavily in the decision to implement end-user monitoring. In your discussions with business users, you may need to make a forceful case for the need for end-user monitoring, as it will require their cooperation to implement.

Trending and Reporting

Monitoring is an important activity for detecting problems that have already happened. Trending is about identifying potential problems before they happen. In this section, we will look at categories of problems that foreshadow their own occurrence with warning symptoms. We will also look at reports that require regular review and analysis in order to ensure smooth long-term operation of your system.

Historical Reporting

As we will see in Chapter 11, when a problem arises it is extremely valuable to have a historical view of your system. Information that has been recorded by your monitoring solution will give technical resources information on system state in the period leading up to the failure. If a resource is exhausted, data logged by your monitors will show the depletion of the resource over time. Further, logged metrics can often answer the important question, *When did this problem first start to happen?* Finally, historical information for your system is also critical from a tuning, sizing, and capacity-planning standpoint. We will come back to this topic later in this chapter.

Performance Trending

As systems mature, performance can gradually change over time. From an operations perspective, it is in your best interests to monitor your system and detect this before it is reported to you by your users. Responding to an issue in its infancy will give you time to plan a suitable resolution. If you wait until the problem is perceptible to your users, you will find yourself referencing the materials in Chapter 11 on crisis management.

Fortunately, performance trending is readily supported by a host of vendor software solutions. Earlier in this chapter we discussed artificial transactions as a technique for end-user monitoring. In order to perform trending against artificial transactions, you need to ensure that the software package you are using is capable of storing historical data over a sustained period (i.e., years). Trends are easily identified graphically. If your software package supports long-term reporting, it is also likely to support graphing. If you graph response against time, your graph is likely to resemble one of the examples shown in Figure 10.5.

In example A of Figure 10.5, we see steady-state response over time. Example A is what you should expect from a properly designed and tested system, assuming constant business usage. In example B we see a more worrisome scenario. Response appears to be gradually increasing over time. From looking at example B, we have no way of knowing if response time will ultimately plateau to a value within the stated requirements for the system. Example C is also a problematic scenario; in it we see a dramatic spike in response over time. The increase in response time seems

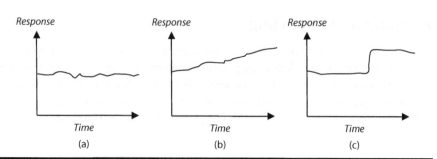

Figure 10.5   **Graphical views of system performance over time.**

to have been a one-time event, but performance has not returned to its original level. Let's now look at a list of frequent explanations for the patterns we see in these examples.

- **Increased or Changing Business Usage:** The smoother your system operates, the more likely it is that your business users will take it for granted. A consequence of this is that they may make sudden changes in business volumes or usage schedule without informing the operations team responsible for the technology. Business volumes may also increase naturally as the business itself expands. Hopefully, your non-functional requirements have anticipated the impact of either of these events and your system is resilient under the new volumes. Despite your best efforts, there is never a guarantee that your non-functional requirements or testing is 100% reliable. If you see a sudden or gentle degradation in performance, your first step should be to try to correlate this to changing business usage.
- **Diminishing Capacity:** If your application is running in a shared infrastructure or depends on services that support other applications, performance may be affected by diminishing capacity in this infrastructure or for these services. You should be able to correlate your observations of response time to trends for other infrastructure metrics like CPU and network performance.
- **Accumulating Business Volumes:** As business volumes accumulate in your system, performance can steadily degrade. The most frequent culprit is the database where business data is usually stored. Today's databases do an excellent job of storing and retrieving data efficiently, but they require some guidance from the application development team. Your development team should be well aware of the need to create indexes to allow the database to optimize access paths to find data. However, for some tables, the need for indexes may only become obvious once a critical mass has been reached in terms of record count. Database performance can also be impacted by more subtle configuration changes once accumulated data has reached a certain threshold. For example, your production DBA (database administrator) should be monitoring the cache hit ratio for the database on an ongoing basis. As the

volume of data increases, the proportion of that data that can be accommodated in memory will steadily decrease. Degraded performance is not only
associated with database behavior. In the shorter term, your application may
traverse data structures or caches that have steadily increased in size, causing
a gradual impact to system performance.

■ **System Changes.** In example (c) of Figure 10.5, we see a sudden, drastic
impact to performance. Depending on the sensitivity of your end users, this
may or may not be reported. Following any system change, you should contrast the new system performance against response time prior to the change.
If you have worsened performance as a result of an application or infrastructure change, you will need to determine the explanation, evaluate the impact,
and then take action if necessary.

Error Reporting

Large, complex, and especially new enterprise software systems will create errors.
If your system processes thousands or millions of records every day, your application may log hundreds or thousands of errors. It is non-tractable for an individual
or support team to manually assess application log files and evaluate which errors
merit investigation. As a further complication, it is not uncommon for systems
to have many known errors that can be safely ignored by the operations and support teams. The development team may have gone so far as to request that alerts
be suppressed for specific error events. There can be no disputing that fixing real
errors and erroneously logged error messages alike is an important priority for the
development team. However, cluttered log files are a reality for many systems and
it may take some time before a new system has settled and is no longer generating
large volumes of error-log output.

An effective strategy for managing error output is to process it into a summary
format as part of an automated daily routine. This summary report categorizes
error using text-match patterns for severity and uniqueness. This is easier to illustrate with an example than it is to describe; see Figure 10.6.

In this example, errors have been force-ranked by severity and frequency. There
are some significant advantages to having information in this format. First of all,
the support team can more readily identify *new* errors in the log output. If an existing error suddenly shows a higher incidence rate or loses its position to a new error,
the support organization can hone in on this particular error. In the next chapter,
application log output is an important input to your troubleshooting efforts.

When you are investigating a production issue, you will find it useful to consult
this report to look for changes over time. This report is also a useful mechanism
for setting priorities for the development team. Obviously FATAL events and high-
incident ERROR log events should be addressed by the development team. As your
application matures, your objective should be to drive your application logs to zero

```
Date:      10/07/2006 19:00:34
Source:    app_error.20060802.log

FATAL

Count              Description
--------------------------------------------------------------------
2                          Tue Jul 10, 2006 09:08:22 -- FATAL --
                   QuoteHelper.java:67 "InvalidQuoteRequest exception being thrown
                   for request:
1                          Tue Jul 10, 2006 13:14:01 -- FATAL --
                   QuoteHelper.java:67 "InvalidQuoteRequest exception being thrown
                   for request:

ERROR

Count              Description
--------------------------------------------------------------------
97                         Tue Jul 10, 2006 10:12:06 -- ERROR --
                   QuoteHelper.java:67 "InvalidQuoteRequest exception being thrown
```

Figure 10.6   Summary report generated from application log file.

length. This strategy can still be applied to systems for which there are no standardized log severities. As you would imagine, all of the log events will be force-ranked in a single category.

The script that generated this report used a raw application log file as input and outputted this result. You may want to configure such a script to e-mail the error report to the support team on a daily basis. As an alternative, you could also have the script deposit the report to the document root of a Web server.

Reconciliation

Reconciliation is another category of reporting that is an important check for many types of applications. Reconciliations balance business inputs with application outputs to ensure that no records have been omitted from processing. Some reconciliation reports are simple counts that match the number of inputs with the number of outputs. You may also have reconciliation reports for your application that applies business logic to calculate expected values for a given set of inputs. More sophisticated reconciliation and balancing is common in the financial services industry. In Chapter 4 we outlined the circumstances under which a reconciliation process is recommended. We mention reconciliation again in this chapter because it is an important safety net for detecting failed processing. You should consider automating your reconciliation if possible and generating alerts when the reconciliation fails.

Business Usage Reporting

In our earlier discussion on the topic of performance trending, we mentioned the importance of being able to trend business usage against system response. For transactional systems, business usage reports can frequently be driven by the database. You may be able to count business operations based on transaction volumes as they accumulate in database tables. For Web-based systems, there are a number of software packages that monitor detailed usage patterns in the application. At time of writing, the dominant software product in this space is WebTrends. The requirements for this category of monitoring will often come from the business community itself. Business usage is input to marketing, business strategy, and operations decisions and planning. If your system does not have requirements for business analytics, you should think about how you can use the database and/or application logs to derive the approximate business usage. This will be useful information for troubleshooting and capacity planning alike.

Capacity Planning

There are entire books on the topic of capacity planning, and many of these books are academic and theoretical in their approach. Capacity planning is an essential part of operating an enterprise software system and we would be remiss if we did not address it in this book. Capacity planning is the exercise of determining the required hardware for a given software system. This includes CPU, memory, network, and storage requirements. In this section we will outline some practical strategies and advice on the topic of capacity planning. Our goal is to equip you with the knowledge to develop an accurate capacity model based on the right inputs for your application. First, we will present a set of best practices and then we will illustrate the use of these recommendations using a detailed example.

Planning Inputs

A capacity model states the infrastructure requirements for your system over time. In the end, your capacity plan may simply draw the conclusion that you have adequate capacity on the existing hardware for the foreseeable future. Alternately, your capacity model may point to an impending problem unless additional hardware is provisioned in the very near future. In either case, your capacity plan will be based on an analysis performed using a capacity model. A capacity model is a theoretical view of your system that considers load requirements over time mapped against required physical resources in the infrastructure. Once you have established an accurate capacity model, you will be equipped to define your capacity plan, which will specify exactly what hardware purchases and upgrades are required to maintain your system over time. As we will see, most of your efforts will be expended in building a capacity model in which you are confident.

Capacity planning and modeling starts before a software system is commissioned and is ongoing over the lifetime of the system. This activity is at its most challenging before your system is in production. For many endeavors you are required to order hardware before your application has even been built in order to meet timelines. At this point, capacity planning is best described as a mixture of art and science. Hardware sizing is based on a combination of inputs, including:

1. **Vendor recommendations:** If you are able to quantify your business usage, many software vendors are willing to provide recommendations for your hardware configuration. These recommendations can be a good source of input, as the software vendor may have broad experience working with clients who have similar needs to your own. On the other hand, vendors often license their product based on hardware configuration, so they may have a stake in sizing your system towards the high end. And of course, your hardware vendors may have input to your sizing efforts but their objectivity is even more questionable for obvious reasons.

2. **Equivalence estimates to existing, similar systems:** If the system you are building is similar in terms of technology and business usage, you may be able to draw comparisons to existing systems. If you do not have existing systems suitable for basing estimates, you may want to involve consultants who can make this expertise available to you.

3. **Growth and business criticality of the system:** You may also wish to apply some subjective factors to your decision making. If your software system is considered strategic and business-critical, then additional cost may be a good trade-off to ensure a wider margin for error. Also, if your system is expected to experience rapid growth that has not been well quantified by the business you may want to provide more capacity rather than less.

4. **Technology platform:** The technology platform that has been selected for your architecture will influence your hardware options. Some software is not supported or runs better on specific hardware platforms. This could easily mean the difference between a large farm of Windows-based x86 servers and a single multiprocessor reduced instruction set computer (RISC)-based server.

In your sizing decisions, you will likely have the option to purchase hardware that provides varying levels of flexibility for future expansion. It may be more cost-effective to purchase a fully loaded entry-level server, but you will soon strand this investment if you grow outside of its capacity. You may elect for a more expensive midrange server that is not fully configured with CPUs and memory to provide for future growth. Hardware costing is complex, and vendor strategies are designed to try to maximize your expenditure. Beyond this brief introduction, there is little advice we can offer you to make this decision any easier.

A more preferable circumstance is one in which you have time to test your system under load before making procurement decisions for your infrastructure. In your non-functional test cycles, you will have prepared load scenarios that are representative of the forecasted business usage. In Chapter 7 we described strategies for execution of sustainability testing. We proposed that you run your mixed load of performance scenarios at peak transaction rate to perform the required number of business operations in the shortest amount of time. If you record system metrics during execution of a similar test in which you run your application mixed load at peak, these metrics are good predictors of the required capacity you will need in the production environment. It is important to note that these measurements are based on a model that approximates the actual business usage. This is clearly superior to no measurement at all, but it can only project the required capacity within a certain degree of accuracy.

For most systems, you determine required capacity based on peak usage plus a contingency factor based on risk tolerance. Software systems do not run well on hardware that is almost fully utilized. You will usually see performance begin to degrade significantly once CPU utilization passes the 75% point on most systems. The contingency factor is there to ensure that your application runs below this threshold. The contingency factor is also there to compensate for any inaccuracy in your measurement or estimate of the system load.

A standard contingency for enterprise systems is 40% over and above the measured system load. In other words, you require 140% of the measured hardware capacity required by your mixed load at peak. A contingency factor can also be designed to account for increased load due to a failover scenario. If your application is load balanced across two application servers, you need to consider the effect of failover. If a single server fails, and the second application server is overwhelmed by the additional load, then you may as well have not bothered to implement failover for your application. For your application, you may decide on a higher or lower contingency factor; this is not written in stone, but 40% is a good value for most systems.

The accuracy of your capacity plan will depend on the quality of the capacity model you are able to devise based on available inputs. You may have no choice but to estimate your system load if your application is yet to be built. If your application can be tested, you can measure system load based on the business usage model that you constructed from the non-functional requirements. However, neither of these inputs is superior to actually measuring system capacity for a production system. As a result, once your application is rolled out to production users, you should measure the actual capacity and feed this back into your capacity model to ensure it is accurate.

Once you have real production measurements, there is no need to rely on hypothetical or experimental values in your capacity model. If you are completing a capacity plan to determine hardware requirements based on increased business usage, then you may be able to use exclusively production measurements in your model. Later in this chapter we will look at an example that employs this strategy as part of building a complete model.

Best Practice

Let's review the key points from the preceding discussion. The following list enumerates our view on best practice in the area of capacity planning.

1. The accuracy of your model will depend on the accuracy of your inputs. Use production measurements, test measurements, and estimates based on equivalent systems in that order. Some capacity models will require a combination of these three inputs.
2. Your planned capacity should be based on a mixed, representative business load running at peak volume.
3. You should decide on a contingency factor and apply this on top of the estimated or measured needs of the application; 40% of the required system load is a standard contingency. Do not add contingency to each input as you build the model. You should use the most accurate, yet conservative, estimate available and apply contingency once when the capacity model is nearing completion.
4. When possible, use measurements based on the full application load. If logistics do not permit for this, you should assume that hardware capacity is a linear commodity, i.e., you can stack application load and the required capacity will sum together.
5. Express all present and future capacity as a percentage of your existing hardware platform.

The remainder of this chapter will illustrate the application of these best practices in a detailed example.

Case Study: Online Dating

Example is the best teacher, so let's look at a specific case and apply some of what we have discussed so far. For our example, we'll consider an online dating service with a large presence in Canada and the United States. Based on the success of the service in North America, the business plans to expand operations to the United Kingdom at the beginning of the next fiscal year, approximately one year away. We have been asked to assess the required hardware capacity for this expansion. The release to the United Kingdom will include all of the standard North American functionality. However, the release will also include two new features that are not currently supported. These two new features will be available to all users in North America and the United Kingdom. The first feature allows customers to make third-party introductions between online users or between an online user and an external person. For introductions to nonusers, the introduction is made via e-mail, with the goal being to draw additional users onto the network. Normally, customers contact other customers directly, so the notion of third-party introductions is a significant enhancement. We will refer to this feature as *introductions* in the rest of this example. The second new feature allows customers to post recommendations for date venues to a bulletin board. The bulletin board is accessed by online users who are looking for ideas on where to go for dates. In a future release, the business would like people to actually initiate dates based on mutual interest in different date venues. This feature is referred to as *date venues*.

As a simplification, we will focus our example on the application server tier for the online dating service. For a software system like this we would normally need to consider multiple software tiers, including Web, application, and database. The logic we will follow is identical for each component in the infrastructure; we do not want to clutter our example, so we will focus on a single tier.

We start by looking at the current and forecasted business usage for the online dating service. The current service has over 250,000 customers in North America. This number is expected to grow at the established rate of 15% per year for at least the next five years. The total UK market is estimated at 150,000. In the first year, marketing anticipates 10,000 users. The number of users is expected to double in each of the first three years and then grow at a rate of 15%. These statistics are shown in Table 10.5.

It is reasonable to assume that the number of business operations will vary directly with the number of users on the system. The best quality information we have for this system is the actual business usage and production utilization for the current system. A graph for CPU utilization of the current system is shown in Figure 10.7.

Table 10.5   Usage Attributes and Requirements

Usage Attribute	Requirement
Operations Window	12:00 midnight to 11:59 PM, Monday to Sunday
Number of Users by Class	North America: 250,000 United Kingdom: 0
Number of Users by Class (after 1 year)	North America: 287,500 United Kingdom: 25,000
Number of Users by Class (after 5 years)	North America: 502,839 United Kingdom: 132,250

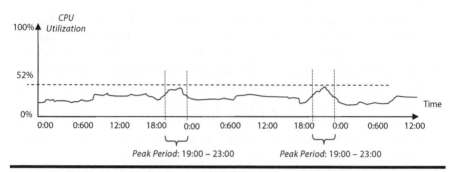

Figure 10.7   Online dating example: current capacity model.

In this graph we clearly see an evening peak-usage period starting at 7:00 PM and lasting four hours until approximately 11:00 PM. This busy interval is fairly wide because it spans all North American time zones. Let's start by trying to antici-pate the additional required CPU based on the 15% increase in North American usage. Again, if we assume that 15% more users will execute 15% more business operations, we are able to simply apply a factor of 15% to our CPU requirement. Let's see what this looks like on our graph (shown in Figure 10.8).

Adding 15% to our volumes has moved our peak CPU to almost 60% utili-zation of our current infrastructure. If we add our 40% contingency factor, the required hardware capacity is 83.7%. We are already starting to tax our existing infrastructure heavily and we have not added UK volumes or increased usage based on the new features that are being added. Our assumption here is that the CPU requirements for the system will scale linearly with increased user volumes. This is acceptable for purposes of our capacity model, but this does not substitute for the need to actually perform testing in a non-functional environment to validate the assumption.

Our next step is to add the additional volumes from the United Kingdom. The business has given us no reason to believe that the usage profile in the United Kingdom will be any different from usage in North America. The United Kingdom

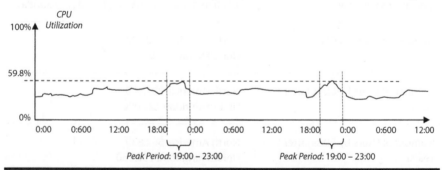

Figure 10.8   Online dating example: capacity mode with additional U.S. usage.

spans fewer time zones, so our spikes will probably be somewhat more compressed. One year from now, the UK market as a percentage of the North American market will be

$$\frac{25,000}{287,500} = 8.6\%.$$

To apply the additional UK usage, we can inflate our model by 9%. We must also time shift this usage to account for the time zone difference between North America and the UK. Time shifting in this case works in our favor as it distributes our peaks and smooths our CPU usage, as shown in Figure 10.9.

Our next step is to sum the time-shifted UK contribution to the required CPU with the forecasted North American CPU requirements. When we do this, our graph of the outcome is a smoother utilization as predicted (see Figure 10.10).

The North American and UK evening peaks do not overlap. The UK non-peak usage does contribute to the original North American peak, shifting it up slightly to 61.6%. Management will be happy to learn that in the first year of operation, the UK expansion makes more efficient use of the existing hardware capacity without introducing the need for additional expenditure. Remember, we still haven't looked at the impact of the additional features that are being introduced, nor have we considered the five-year outlook for this system.

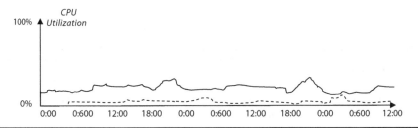

Figure 10.9   Online dating example: capacity model for additional UK usage only.

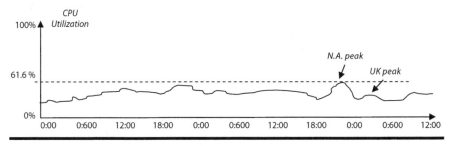

Figure 10.10   Online dating example: capacity model for combined UK and U.S. usage.

Let's complete our one-year outlook before we generate a five-year forecast. All of the inputs to the model have been based on the one-year forecasted business volumes, so all that is remaining is to add the business usage for the two new features that are being bundled with the release. We start by looking at the business usage in Table 10.6 as it is defined for the North American user community. (A similar table would exist to describe the UK usage, but it is omitted for brevity.)

Table 10.6 is taken from the updated non-functional requirements for the online dating service. We see that the busiest period for site activity is between 7:30 PM and 9:30 PM, which aligns with our production CPU measurements. The business feels that for every two individual contacts that are made on the site, approximately one introduction is likely.

Posting date venues is forecasted to be far less common than browsing data venues. In fact, the marketing team plans to supplement postings if take-up is not high among users. Finally, for every ten personal profiles that are viewed marketing feels that there will be at least one data venue that is also browsed. The business has posted the expected one- and five-year business volumes based on the projected increase in usage.

Business volumes for this online data service are not seasonal, nor is there much weekly variation in online usage. (This may or may not be true. Feel free to write to us should you have information that contradicts this assumption.) As a result, we need to calculate what the incremental peak load is expected to be for the system and then add it to our current model in order to determine the new hardware capacity.

Table 10.6   Business Usage in North America

Usage Attribute	Requirement		
Busiest Interval	7:30 PM to 9:30 PM, weekday evenings (40% of average day's business volume)		
Search Personals	38,500	48,125	97,790
View Personal Profile	52,300	65,375	132,842
Contact Individual	1,800	2,250	4,572
Make Introduction	900	1,125	2,286
Post-Date Venue	200	250	508
Browse Date Venues	5,230	6,538	13,284

Fortunately for us, the non-functional testing team had previously identified that the North American and UK peak loads do not intersect one another. Accordingly, they have devised two mixed load scenarios, one for each of the North American and UK peaks. As you may have guessed, they are actually the same mixed-load scenarios run at different transaction rates. For the two new features, the non-functional test team added additional load scenarios to the original mixed load for the dating service.

The transaction rates for the three coarse inputs defined by the business were calculated as follows. For these volumes, rates are calculated in transactions per minute (TPM). We assume 40% of business operations will be completed in the two-hour window indicated. Remember, the calculations below describe North American usage only; an equivalent set of calculations would be required for the UK usage to derive the UK transaction rates.

$$Transaction\ Rate_{Introduction} = \frac{Transactions}{Interval} = \frac{900x0.4}{120m} = 3.75TPM$$

$$Transaction\ Rate_{PostVenue} = \frac{Transactions}{Interval} = \frac{250x0.4}{120m} = 0.83TPM$$

$$Transaction\ Rate_{BrowseVenue} = \frac{Transactions}{Interval} = \frac{6538x0.4}{120m} = 21.79TPM$$

In order to complete our model, we ask the non-functional test team to execute two sets of performance trials in which they run load for the incremental scenarios that exercise the new business features in which we are interested. The performance team fulfills our request and provides two numbers that reflect peak CPU usage under both the North American and UK transaction rates (as shown in Table 10.7).

Before we can incorporate these inputs into our model, we need to convert them into our standard units of measurement. Our capacity model is currently expressed in terms of *percentage of current capacity*. The non-functional test environment is actually half the size of the production infrastructure. The application server has half the number of CPUs as its production counterpart. As a result, the numbers we need to use in our analysis are actually 6.5% and 3.5%. If we add these numbers to the two observed peaks in our capacity plan, we arrive at the conclusions shown in Table 10.8 for our one-year capacity model.

Table 10.7   Peak CPU Usage in North America and the United Kingdom

Scenario	CPU Measurement
New Feature Incremental Load—North American Transaction Rate	13%
New Feature Incremental Load—UK Transaction Rate	7%

Table 10.8   One-Year Capacity Model Conclusions

Required Capacity	Forecasted One-Year Baseline	Incremental Performance Test	System Capacity Required	Contingency	Total Capacity Required
NA Peak	61.6%	6.5%	67.1%	40%	93.9%
UK Peak	42.3%	3.5%	45.8%	40%	64.1%

At the end of the next year, the online dating service will be straining the limits of its current infrastructure based on the North American peak business usage. The advantage in building this model incrementally is that you can summarize results for management so that they can see the impact of different factors on hardware requirements. By creating an incremental view of your capacity model, you provide the visibility management needs to make more efficient business decisions. Based on the work we have done, it is clear that expansion to the United Kingdom does not impose an urgent need for increased capacity.

You should also complete this same exercise based on the five-year business volume. The one-year view of the capacity plan indicates that the business will need to make an additional investment in infrastructure very shortly. The five-year view of the capacity plan will give them a perspective on how big an infrastructure investment is required in the long term. In this example, we have seen that the impact of new features is the single largest contributor to the need for more capacity. In a real situation, we would emphasize this in reporting results to management. The five-year plan will not show the need for increased processing power based on features that will no doubt be introduced as the platform matures. Conversely, as the development team refines the application, you may see a significant drop in the capacity requirements for the system. This can only be evaluated on an ongoing basis using an approach that strongly positions current production measurements in the revised capacity plan.

Maintaining the Model

In a capacity model based on experimental results, business usage is a key factor in the accuracy of your model. If the actual production usage turns out to be double the volume you used during testing, then your capacity model is unlikely to make very accurate predictions. Another potential weakness in your capacity model can result from load scenarios that are not representative of the actual usage. Load scenarios may create coarse inputs in the quantities specified in the non-functional requirements and still seriously misstate the future system load. Users may adopt a different usage pattern than what you have modeled in your load scenarios.

Another serious gap can come from your business usage model. You may totally fail to include key user activities that require significant capacity from the infrastructure.

For all of these reasons, we recommend that you make maximal use of production business usage and CPU measurements when you are assembling a capacity model. It is tempting to think that your load scenarios are a pure representation of the production system, but there is a good likelihood that one or more of the above factors may be at play for your system. Non-functional testing is always an approximation of the actual production usage. It should never be substituted for the actual usage when the actual usage is available.

In the previous example we used an incremental approach to add the forecasted load for new features on top of the measured production load. You may have thought that this was inappropriate as there is no guarantee that the incremental load of the new features will add linearly to the baseline load; you would be correct in this suspicion. However, this risk is substantially smaller than the risk that one of the factors we have just described will have an even more serious impact on your model.

In our example, you may also remember that the non-functional test environment was not large enough to conduct a full-scale test. The one-year forecast predicted by our model showed the production infrastructure to be almost fully utilized. It would have been impossible to conduct a test under the full load of the system in an environment that is half the size. Many projects do not have the luxury of a non-functional test environment that is at least as large as the production infrastructure.

Completing a Capacity Plan

The trickiest part of any capacity exercise is in formulating the best possible capacity model. As we have seen, a capacity model is a description of the forecasted resource requirements for the system under an expected business usage. Once you have established a good model, you complete your efforts by documenting a capacity plan. A capacity plan specifies exactly how your infrastructure needs to evolve over time to meet the needs projected by your model. The capacity plan specifically addresses which hardware expenditures will be needed and when, and will make statements along the lines of *the current Sun Enterprise 10K (40 x 400MHz Ultra-SPARC II) servers will need to be upgraded to Sun Fire 6900 (16 x 1.8GHz 48GB UltraSPARC IV+) servers no later than July of next year in order to sustain performance for projected volumes.*

The capacity plan typically makes considerations as to when the best time for your organization to accommodate an upgrade would be. For example, the plan may recommend that the total upgrade be accomplished in stages over the course of 16 months. The capacity plan will also need to factor in the requirements of non-production environments (e.g., if the production environment is expanding, a cost-benefit analysis will be required for whether to expand the pre-production non-functional testing environment as well).

Since cost is a factor for every organization, it is the responsibility of the capacity plan owner to make judicious decisions about which hardware vendor and platform are appropriate for the organization. In some cases, the capacity plan may recommend retiring equipment from one production platform to be re-introduced as part of the infrastructure for another smaller, existing production system.

Summary

This chapter has covered a broad range of topics that come into play for systems that are already deployed to production environments. We have looked at application monitoring from an operations perspective spanning application, infrastructure, container, and end-user categories of monitoring. This chapter has also emphasized the importance of trending and reporting as a means of understanding system health and predicting future system failures. The second half of the chapter explored the complex topic of capacity planning based on measurement of the production system combined with test results from non-functional activities. We illustrated how to define a capacity model based on multiple inputs and how to draw conclusions and make recommendations based on that model. In Chapter 11 our focus shifts to the topic of troubleshooting and crisis management. Despite your best efforts to design, test, and operate highly available systems, you must still be prepared to respond quickly and effectively to production incidents if they occur.

Chapter 11

Troubleshooting and Crisis Management

It is with great sincerity that we hope you never have need for any of the material in this chapter. Yet, despite your best efforts to design and test for robustness in your applications, you may be required to manage and resolve unforeseen issues for your production applications. You may also have the misfortune to inherit responsibility for applications that have not been designed and tested using the expertise in this book. In either case, this chapter enumerates a list of troubleshooting strategies and outlines crisis management techniques developed by way of hard-earned experience. Much of what we describe in this chapter is common sense, but in a crisis, discipline and calm are required to work through the situation in a structured fashion. This chapter is a good reference for situations in which things are quickly going from bad to worse.

Reproducing the Issue

Reproducing the issue is critical to your success for two reasons. First, by reproducing the issue at will in a non-production environment you are validating that you understand the issue correctly. Second, once you can reproduce an issue you can develop, apply, and prove your solution. Given that you already have a serious production issue, your credibility with business users is already in a weakened condition. If you are going to persuade them to allow you to make an expedited change in order to correct the problem, you will need to demonstrate beyond reproach that your solution will fix the issue without introducing any harmful side effects. The mindset of the business may be severe, i.e. *If these guys knew what they were doing in the first place, we wouldn't be in this mess. And now they want me to authorize more tinkering in the environment?*

In earlier chapters on project initiation and test planning, we recommended that you plan for a logical environment in your non-functional test environment that is at all times synchronized with the version of your application that is in production. If you have followed this advice, you are well positioned for your efforts in reproducing a production issue. If you do not have such an environment, you will need to acquire or designate a suitable environment. This may mean repurposing an existing environment and deploying the production version of your application in there.

Reproducing the problem usually precedes your determination of root cause. In fact, once you have reproduced a problem, it doesn't tend to take long for capable technical resources to hone in on the underlying issue. In the next section, we will look at the difficult task of troubleshooting a problem, including scenarios that are not readily reproduced.

Determining Root Cause

Your efforts to resolve a production crisis are ultimately about determining root cause. Root cause will fall into one of the following categories:

1. **A software defect in your application:** A defect in your application is usually the easiest root cause to identify and to resolve, assuming the application is fully within your control and the support team has the necessary development expertise.

2. **A software defect in a vendor application:** Defects in vendor software can be more difficult to isolate and resolve. Vendors are reluctant to investigate issues until you can present convincing arguments that the issue is *not* an application issue of your own. Frequently, you will not have access to vendor code or insight into the internal design of vendor components. Vendors may also be unwilling to engage in a collaborative technical discussion if they feel that such a dialog is proprietary.

3. **An illegal input or usage for which your application was ill-equipped:** This scenario can occur in any number of ways. A common scenario is when requirements do not anticipate the actual usage of the system. Functional requirements can fail to capture all possible data inputs, causing system failure when the application must react to unrecognized inputs. Defensive design and implementation should never cause a total system failure, but a high volume of errors can be as serious as total system outages for many applications. Note that inadequate requirements can also be non-functional

in nature. Consider a case in which business volumes suddenly surge well beyond the levels described in the business usage.

4. **An illegal or mistaken procedural error by an operator:** You may impose strict controls on access to the system. You may make every effort to automate operations processes, but a potential will always remain for a user to compromise the system through human error. These problems can be difficult to pinpoint as humans will sometimes compound the original error with reluctance to admit their involvement. *It is worth mentioning that study after study has shown that operator error is responsible for the preponderance of system outages.*

5. **An infrastructure event:** Depending on the level of capacity and redundancy in your environment, there will be scenarios in which an infrastructure event causes issues for the end users of your application. This category of error includes hardware failures such as memory corruption and disk failure. Highly available applications can be designed and deployed to highly available hardware, but there are limits to what can be accomplished.

In some rare cases it is even possible that a combination of the above is the root cause of your problem. For instance, a vendor's clustering product has a bug that failed to detect an infrastructure event that should have triggered the cluster to failover the application, or an application that is ill-equipped to deal with problem situations has crashed because of a simple operator mistake.

In the following section, we will look at troubleshooting strategies that will help you to isolate the type of failure responsible for root cause. As you rule out categories of root cause, you will be able to engage resources in the most efficient way. For example, a problem that has been identified as an infrastructure event will be less dependent on input from the application support team or representatives from the end user community.

Troubleshooting Strategies

For tough problems, it can be difficult to know where to start. The strategies we discuss in this section are a reference for these types of situations. This material will also be helpful to you if you find that you are completely blocked because you believe you have exhausted all avenues of investigation.

Understanding Changes in the Environment

If a system is running trouble-free and suddenly begins to encounter difficulties, this will almost always be traceable to a *change* in application, runtime environment, or usage by the end users. This pearl of wisdom is commonly understood, and so the first question in a crisis is, *What changed?* If your organization adheres to detailed change-control procedures, you will be able to reference the system and begin to answer this question. In many cases, this exercise will yield nothing or a list of changes that have no discernable linkage to the symptoms of your failure. Consequently, you must do two things: look harder, and cast a wider net. You must capture all changes in the system, including those that are not documented in your change control process. The full list of changes that can be responsible for a sudden system failure are:

1. **Documented Changes:** These include application upgrades, bug fixes, vendor patches, scheduled maintenance tasks, and hardware migrations. If a problem arises following a significant change in the environment, it is obvious that this should be the focus of your initial investigation, as discussed above.

2. **Undocumented Changes:** In some organizations, changes are made in the production environment without the benefit of an audit trail. A well-intentioned technical resource may perform a seemingly harmless maintenance activity unrelated to your application. You should challenge the operations team to be forthcoming about any of these undocumented activities *no matter how benign or irrelevant they may seem at the time.* Remember that the operations team may be reluctant to volunteer this information if it exposes a flaw in their operations, so this may take some coaxing. In many environments, the application support team may have access to the production environment, so ensure that you clearly understand the full population of users with access to the production environment.

3. **Scheduled Jobs:** You should look at the execution schedule for batch jobs. If jobs run on an infrequent basis, there may have been a change since the last job was executed that triggered the failure. Many systems have multiple subsystems or scheduling components that can launch jobs so make sure you inventory everything including operating system (OS) schedulers (e.g., CRON, Windows Scheduling), custom application scheduling (e.g., in J2EE, Java Message Service (JMS) supports deferred message delivery. Also, the EJB 2.2 specification includes support for timed operations) and third-party scheduling software.

4. **Usage:** You should question the user community to understand how the application usage may have changed. About eight years ago, I was part of a technical team supporting the rollout of a call center application. Without any notice to the operations or support teams, the call center manager decided to triple the usage of the online system when he moved training activities into production one Monday morning, unexpectedly. This decision triggered a serious degradation of service that required immediate intervention. Unfortunately, the technical team wasn't expecting a surge in business usage and wasted considerable time looking at alternative explanations and scenarios.

5. **External Systems:** If your application interfaces with external systems, you should verify that those systems are available and ask for an inventory of recently applied changes.

6. **System Administration:** Many applications support administration interfaces that allow business users to make configuration changes in the application. In working with users you need to impress upon them the need to understand all recent changes of this type. If your system follows the design best practice described earlier in this book, all administrative actions should be audited in the application. You can cross-reference the usage that is reported by the business with the system log.

7. **Time:** If nothing else has changed, time itself has elapsed. There are a host of failures possible for systems as they age, mostly related to the accrual of data in system files, databases, or any other long-term data store. This is a special category of problem, so we will look at this as a special case later in this chapter.

The key point to understand is that computer systems are not capricious and emotional. A computer system that is functioning properly will continue to do so until something changes. If all of your inputs are telling you that nothing has changed, then you need to keep looking.

Gathering All Possible Inputs

In this activity you need to put aside any bias you have and ensure that you capture and understand all of the inputs that are available to you. The most important inputs you gather are related to changes in the production environment or the application usage. We have emphasized this category of input in the previous section. Additional inputs that will aid your investigation include:

1. **Business Usage Timeline:** At the time of the failure, what business operations were active? What scheduled jobs and automated application function can be correlated to the time of the failure? If a specific business function is only active in the evenings, and you experience a system failure at 10:00 AM, then that evening's business function is unlikely to be implicated in the problem.

2. **Error Distribution:** At the time of the failure, which business functions experienced errors and which business functions did not? Answering this question may help to establish a common dependency for applications that failed. This can refine your investigation to look more closely at the availability of specific resources. This includes looking at other unrelated systems that are hosted on the same infrastructure or that share dependencies.

3. **Application Logs:** You should gather all application logs in which error information may be deposited. Are there unfamiliar errors in these logs? Do the errors correlate to the time of the system failure? If the logs are void of errors, are there unusual or unrecognized log entries of any type? Logs that are available are usually a combination of vendor and custom application logs; make sure you are looking at both. Vendor products will often create a series of log files; make sure you are looking at *all* of them.

4. **Cross-Reference Business Inputs:** Business users are notoriously poor at describing problems. They may be angry at the system failure, and may feel frustrated that they need to participate in the problem determination. To many users, a "technology problem" is something that technologists should fix themselves once they have been told that there is a problem. Given this potential for bias, business users do not always accurately describe a problem. They may exaggerate the problem to try to escalate urgency. Encourage business users to forward information directly to you for interpretation; encourage them to *quantify* information. Business users will tend to report problems using phrases like: "the system is slow" or "there were lots of errors." Neither of these comments is very useful. You need to coach them towards statements like, "login is taking 20 seconds on every attempt—login usually takes less than 1 second" and "We have attempted 100 requests in the last hour and 50% of them experienced the error shown in the screen capture attached to this email." Don't be reluctant about asking the same question twice or involving multiple business users to improve the quality of your information.

5. **Exception Outputs:** If your system has failed completely (i.e., crashed), it is possible that it produced a core file or process dump at the time of failure. Vendor software and custom applications can both produce these types of outputs. If vendor software has created a core file or process dump, you should engage the vendor to help scrutinize the output. Software that is written defensively should never crash. If a process belonging to a vendor program has crashed, you have become the victim of a known issue or you are about to help the vendor debug and document a new issue. If your own custom process has crashed, you are most likely looking for a bug in your own software—short of a flaw in the operating system, that is.

6. **System State:** If the system is in a failed state, make sure you extract as much state information from the system as possible before restoring service. For example, J2EE systems expose a large number of runtime metrics through a JMX (Java management extensions) interface, including the active number of database connections for connection pools and the number of available execution threads on the server. For systems that are running but unresponsive, the amount of information you can capture may be limited. In previous chapters we emphasized the importance of system trending and monitoring. If your application is totally unresponsive, you will need to rely more heavily on the outputs of your monitoring. There will be pressure to restore service as quickly as possible, but you must balance this against the potential for the problem to happen again if the problem is not properly understood.

7. **Previous Failures:** You should also assemble a list of previous system failures. Ask yourself, has a similar problem happened in the past? Did we resolve that problem and if so, how? What is common about the circumstances or symptoms of this problem with recent previous problems?

By assembling information and generating discussion in an open forum that includes a spectrum of technical resources, you will catalyze analytical thinking. Be certain to encourage discussion as each input is introduced. What one person perceives to be obvious or common knowledge may be a critical new piece of information for another participant.

Approach Based on Type of Failure

In a large or complex environment, isolating the source of a problem can be difficult when there is a lot of concurrent processing. If there are hundreds of parallel threads of execution, which one is responsible for a sudden failure of the system? Your options for isolating the source of a problem will be different depending on the type of failure.

For systems that fail suddenly and fatally (i.e., a system crash), your best quality information will come from any process dump information that was generated at the moment the server crashed. Process dumps will tell you exactly what machine instruction was executing when the process died. If the process crash does not create any output (and often it will not), then the next best source for information is the log files. Log files will not give you information that is as granular as what you can expect from a process dump, but it is the next best thing. If your application logged an exception and then failed upon further processing, you may be in luck. If, however, your application processes high volumes, then it is unlikely that your logging is granular enough to inform you what the application was doing at the time of the crash. If there is no process dump information and logs are not helpful, then your only recourse is to establish the business usage at the time of the failure and attempt to reproduce the problem. If you can reproduce the problem, your next steps should include:

- **Verify the Application Configuration:** You may find that a process dump was not created because of an OS or application configuration. In one experience, we failed to capture a core dump from an Oracle database failure because the system was not configured to deposit core files onto a file system with sufficient capacity. On another occasion, a multiple virtual storage (MVS) system we were working with was not configured with the correct job control language (JCL) settings to create a detailed dump on system ABEND (abnormal ending or termination) codes.
- **Enable Additional Logging and Trace Information:** If you were attentive to the recommendations in Chapter 4, your application should include extensive debug and informational logging. You can reproduce the issue with these settings enabled to glean more insight into the problem.
- **Run Incremental Load:** Once the problem is reproduced, you should continue to try to reproduce the problem with an objective of using the mini-

mum possible business load. If you reproduce the problem with seven load scenarios, you may find that it only takes two of the seven scenarios to actually cause the failure. This allows you to focus on what distinguishes those two load scenarios from any others.

If you cannot reproduce the problem, then you should think about what additional monitoring may be helpful should the problem happen again. If you do not understand the root cause of the problem, you should assume that the problem *will* happen again. Sometimes you have no choice but to wait for another occurrence of the problem, but there is no excuse for not capturing more information on subsequent occurrences. It is tempting to conclude that the problem was a one-time glitch, especially if the problem appears to go away once the system is restarted. This is ill-advised; *if you do not understand the root cause of a problem, you should assume that it will happen again.*

Another common failure scenario is one in which the application enters a state from which it begins to experience a high number of application errors. In this situation, it is common to have to restart the application in order to restore service. For these types of incidents, it may be obvious what is causing errors. What is not clear is the event that forced the system into this state in the first place. For this type of problem, a reliable strategy is as follows:

1. **Determine the time of the last successful transaction:** You need to establish a timeline for the events that led up to the failure. The last successful transaction completed is usually a good starting point. For busy systems under constant load, the timestamp of the last good transaction will be very close to the commencement of the failure condition.
2. **Inspect application logs and outputs at that time:** From the point of the last successful transaction, look closely at logs and application outputs. If you are lucky, these inputs will provide an indication of what triggered the failure.
3. **Inspect data and system state at that time:** It is worthwhile to look at the last valid data that was processed by the system and compare it to the data of transactions that are now failing. Differences in what you see may lead you to an explanation.
4. **What was the business usage and application behavior at that time:** A sudden change in business usage or unusual inputs may have forced the system into a state that compromised future processing. There may not have been errors at the time, but the actual usage may be the cause of the errors you are seeing now.
5. **Reproduce the problem:** Using the information gathered, try to reproduce the problem by subjecting the system to the equivalent load and set of inputs.

We've looked at two template approaches for two different types of system failures. Many of the problems you face will fall into one of these two categories. In the sections following, we will look at more specific techniques and examples for troubleshooting.

Predicting Related Failures

There are times when a problem appears to have no explanation; it is not reproducible in any test or development environment. Configuration and environment have been confirmed multiple times, and the application does not produce any useful error information. The only advantage you may have is that the business usage has been isolated to a single simple test case that reliably reproduces the problem. This same scenario works as expected in every other environment, and the technical team is running out of ideas. In this type of situation, it is time to get more creative. As we discussed earlier, you need to cast a wider net and acquire more information. We know that the application fails when it is supposed to work; now let's see if the application fails when it is supposed to fail. A useful technique for extracting additional information from a problematic system is to:

■ Subject the system to negative inputs and observe how it reacts
■ Introduce failures for its dependencies and observe how it reacts

As a simple example, let's consider a backend system that processes a loan application. In this example, the development team for a financial institution has upgraded a loan application and approval system. Approximately two hours into the operations window for the new system, users are reporting that they consistently get errors when submitting new loan applications. All other aspects of the system appear to be functioning normally, and the development team is perplexed. Loan application processing was tested and verified during the system upgrade. There is no reason to expect errors.

Before we look at troubleshooting approaches to this scenario, let's understand the high-level architecture for this application. Loan applications are input by backend operations users based on handwritten applications. When the loan request is accepted, a confirmation number is returned by the application. The operator uses this number to continue with additional processing, including contacting the customer to inform them of their loan status.

The development team has asked the users for information, and they have provided a screen capture that is not helpful. It is a generic system exception that does not include any information that is useful in determining the nature of the problem. For our failure scenario, we know that the request is causing a failure, but we are not certain where or why. We do not see any data in the structured query language (SQL) Server since the error was reported. This in itself isn't helpful, because the persistence of form data to the SQL Server database is part of the same transaction as the posting of the fulfillment message. The fulfillment system has not received any loan requests since the time that the problem was reported either. This isn't helpful, because we don't know if the application is attempting to send fulfillment requests or if it is failing when it does so. For both the database and the

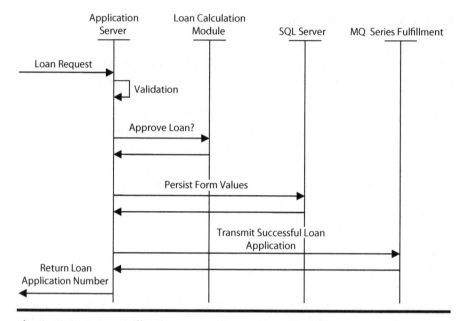

Figure 11.1   Loan application example: sequence diagram.

fulfillment service, we can't tell if the transaction is attempted and rolled back or never attempted at all. We need to get more information.

Our first approach will be to subject the application to negative inputs. This should tell us whether the form validation itself is functioning correctly. We ask the business user to submit a valid loan application, but omit a required field. The business user does this and finds that the loan application is immediately rejected. The business user attempts various combinations of illegal inputs and finds that the loan application is rejecting them all, as expected. Based on this, we conclude that it doesn't look like there is a problem with the form validation processing itself.

Our next effort is to submit a well-formed loan application that purposefully triggers a business rule that causes the loan application to be rejected. Loan applications that are rejected are not persisted to the SQL Server, nor are they posted to the IBM MQ Series for fulfillment. Again, our business user attempts multiple loan application inputs and, as expected, the bad loan applications are rejected with the correct business error, and the eligible applications produce the same error as was originally reported. Based on this evidence we conclude that the business rules engine for loan processing is working correctly.

So far our efforts seem to be pointing to an issue in either persisting or fulfilling valid loan application requests. We need to continue our efforts to isolate the problem. We ask a database administrator (DBA) to temporarily remove the insert privilege from the SQL Server table into which the record is being recorded. If we see the same error, then this is evidence to support the theory that there is a problem with the database operation. If we see a different or more informative error, then this means it is less likely that the database is implicated in our problem. The DBA accommodates our request and we repeat our testing. To our surprise, we see the *same* obtuse error message that we have been struggling with since the problem was first reported. It seems that the error handling for database operations has been poorly implemented. At this point, it would be prudent to ask a support resource to look at the application code and confirm that a SQL Server exception would result in the observed error. At the same time we decide to look closely at the insert operation and try to formulate theories that explain this behavior. Following the advice from earlier in this chapter, we ask the DBA to tell us when the last *successful* insert was made on the database. The DBA reports that inserts were made successfully today at 11:01 AM. This closely corresponds with the first reports from the field that the system was experiencing errors. We ask the DBA to forward the last 6 successful entries in the loan application table and they appear as follows (see Table 11.1).

In inspecting the data, the technical team very quickly identifies that the last successful input is suspiciously 999,999. When the data type for the primary key column is scrutinized, the team realizes that it was improperly designated as a character field instead of a numeric field. The field width was suddenly exceeded at 11:00 AM when an attempt was made to process the millionth loan application. Unfortunately, this field overflow coincided with deployment of a new version of the application. This coincidence distracted the team, causing them to focus on application changes that were introduced as part of the system upgrade.

Table 11.1   Loan Application Example: Database Records at Time of Failure

Application ID	Agent	Date and Time	Last Name	First Name	...
999994	blacksa	02/01/07 10:56:06	Tomken	Glenda	...
999995	browne	02/01/07 10:58:51	White	Barbara	...
999996	pascalti	02/01/07 10:58:57	Howard	Michael	...
999997	williamvi	02/01/07 10:59:21	Milton	David	...
999998	laderoupa	02/01/07 11:00:07	Druze	Sandy	...
999999	emondgr	02/01/07 11:00:14	Pate	Emily	...

Discouraging Bias

In a crisis situation, you cannot afford to let bias play a role in problem determination. The following list includes common sources of bias. You will need to work actively to encourage open-mindedness. As a general rule (and unlike our criminal justice system) *everything is suspect until proven otherwise.*

1. **Politics:** In many organizations, politics are an unfortunate and inescapable part of getting things done. In a crisis situation, politics can be very counterproductive. Spinning a problem as an "application problem" is a convenient way for the infrastructure or operations team to shift emphasis and responsibility in an investigation. This type of bias works in many different directions. The application team will often cite "environmental issues" as the most likely explanation even when there is little or no evidence to support this claim.

2. **Pride:** No one likes to think that they are responsible for a problem. Technologists can be fiercely proud and opinionated. However, good technologists also appreciate that anyone can make a mistake, an oversight, or a flawed assumption.

3. **Expertise:** If you have a task force comprised mostly of DBAs that are looking at a problem, then this team will do a great job of formulating theories based on their own expertise. In other words, the database may quickly become the focal point of your investigation. We often become beholden to the theories we understand best, but these are not necessarily the correct theories. In a crisis situation, you need to stretch yourself and your team to ensure that theories and speculation are grounded and supported by evidence. If you don't have sufficient technical coverage for the application, be honest about it and escalate the investigation to get the right people involved.

4. **Communication:** Don't assume that everyone knows everything that you do about the system. If you find yourself thinking, "that person should know this already," then take the time to confirm that they, in fact, do.

Pursuing Parallel Paths

Finding a solution needs to be a team effort if it is going to happen quickly. In a team environment, there is a temptation for participants to focus on or yield to the front-runner or most likely theory at any given moment. Team members will wait until the current theory is fully played out before reinvigorating efforts on alternative trains of thought. In a crisis, where there is little time to waste, your team needs to be disciplined about working on parallel tacks. If a team member identifies a promising avenue of investigation, ensure that that person is well supported and then move on and continue looking at the problem from as many different angles as possible.

Considering System Age

Once you have exhausted all possible sources of change for an application, the only remaining category is that of time itself. As systems age, they experience changes in a number of ways, including:

1. **Overflows and Exceeded Resource Limits:** Earlier in this chapter we saw an example in which an autogenerated sequence created a primary key value that overflowed the database column in which it was stored. For applications that do not consider the long term, it is possible for a sudden resource limit to become an issue and cause failures for the application. Hopefully, this type of failure causes a descriptive error message so that it can be identified quickly in your system.

2. **Performance Characteristics:** As a system accumulates transactional data over time, the performance characteristics of the system can change significantly. This should be mitigated by your approach to non-functional testing as described in Chapters 6 and 7. If you loaded transactional volumes during your testing, you should already have certified your application for the worst-case scenarios for data accumulation. If this testing was never done, it is even more critical that you follow the advice in Chapter 10 on monitoring and trending. Regularly benchmarking applications, response times, and database metrics is an important safety net for performance issues that can gradually worsen over time. If monitoring and system trending have not given you any warning of impending disaster, database statistics and analysis can usually identify performance bottlenecks quite quickly. Your challenge will be how quickly you can resolve the issue in the event that it requires application changes.

Working Around the Problem

Sometimes you don't need to fix a problem; sometimes it isn't even necessary to understand what is causing a problem. Your business users are interested in conducting business; your application enables them to complete specific functions. If there is a way to work around a problematic technology or interface, this is sometimes preferable to fixing the root cause, especially if the root cause is not readily understood or requires a high-risk fix. Vendor problems are good examples, since they are often found to be in this category. If a feature in vendor software is fragile or unreliable, then despite vendor proclamations that the component will be "better in the next version" it is often worthwhile to design around the feature rather than wait for a fix from the vendor. If you wait for a vendor fix, you are trusting that they will understand the problem fully and implement a quality solution that does not introduce any other problems. Your application and environment are unique; not all vendors deserve this level of trust.

As painful as it may be, there will be situations where a subtle design change in your application is the best way to mitigate risk and satisfy your end users.

Applying a Fix

Determining root cause for a problem is usually the hardest part of responding to a failure in a production system. Developing, testing, and applying a fix, however, may be less challenging work but just as much effort. In this section we will look at processes and considerations for introducing a fix into a production environment.

Fix versus Mitigation versus Tolerance

Introducing changes into a production system is usually and rightfully met with resistance. Mission-critical software systems achieve high availability by closely managing and limiting change. When a fix for a serious production problem becomes available, it is preferable to align this fix with the natural maintenance release schedule for your system. Aligning your change with an existing release schedule generally ensures that it will be thoroughly tested as part of a standard process.

If business reasons are such that you cannot wait for a scheduled release, you should fully explore alternatives that mitigate the problem and do not require an intrusive change to the system. In the loan application example from earlier in this chapter, it is unlikely that mitigation would be found. The loan application system was no longer capable of processing any new loan applications. For sake of our discussion, let's consider a situation in which the loan system was only rejecting loans that were for amounts over $50,000. If the business informed us that less than 5% of all loan requests are for this amount or greater, it may be preferable to process these loan requests manually until a fix can be introduced under the normal release management cycle.

Our point is that you will always need to assess problem severity in a way that weighs business impact against technical risk. The simplest imaginable application fix still entails a change to a production system. There is always room for human error to creep in and cause problems that are bigger than those you are trying to fix. If there is no non-intrusive mitigation for your issue, you may decide that the safest course of action is to simply tolerate it. As we've described it, our loan application is not a good candidate for tolerance; however, many systems are. Let's revise the problem for our loan application again. Perhaps the loan application kicks users out of the system randomly and causes them to lose any information they were in the process of inputting. This problem would be enormously frustrating, but it is a problem that your organization may decide to tolerate if the technical risk associated with the fix is considered to be high.

Assessing Level of Testing

In the previous section we introduced three ways in which you can react to a known production issue: fix, mitigate, or tolerate. In this section, we will look at considerations in determining the level of testing required for a known fix. At a minimum, fixes should be functionally verified in a UAT (user-acceptance testing) environment or a controlled production-support environment. The full spectrum of levels of verification is represented in the figure below.

Factors that should figure in your assessment of where you should be on this sliding scale are as follows:

1. **Complexity of the Fix:** If the fix itself is complex, then this warrants a higher degree of testing. It is more difficult for the development to foresee the impact of a complex fix. Any changes that alter data exchanged between your system and external system or between major subsystems are going to be complex.

2. **Business Impact:** If there is an ongoing financial impact to the business, you may decide to waive some testing and accept higher risk.

3. **Complexity of Testing:** If the complexity and duration of testing when weighed against the current business impact is overly cumbersome, then you may accept higher risk.

4. **Complexity of Deployment and Back-Out:** An important consideration in assessing the level of testing you require is how involved the deployment and rollback of the change will be in the production environment. If the change is simple to apply and can be reverted quickly and safely, then you may compromise on the level of testing you accept for an expedited change.

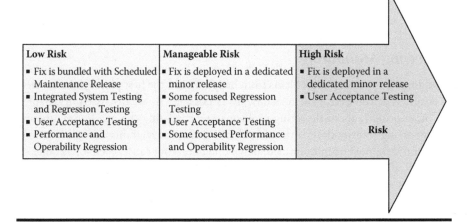

Low Risk	Manageable Risk	High Risk
■ Fix is bundled with Scheduled Maintenance Release ■ Integrated System Testing and Regression Testing ■ User Acceptance Testing ■ Performance and Operability Regression	■ Fix is deployed in a dedicated minor release ■ Some focused Regression Testing ■ User Acceptance Testing ■ Some focused Performance and Operability Regression	■ Fix is deployed in a dedicated minor release ■ User Acceptance Testing **Risk**

Figure 11.2 Applying a fix and associated levels of risk.

5. **Comfort Level Regarding Root Cause Analysis:** In many cases you may think you have found the root cause of your problem but you are not quite certain. When you are acting on a hunch or don't have undeniable proof that root cause has been found then make sure that your uncertainty is compensated by sufficient verification.

It is never a comfortable option to waive testing cycles when considering a production implementation. Ultimately, the decision to put a change in production without the benefit of testing needs to be an objective business decision that weighs business benefit against technical risk.

Post-Mortem Review

Once you have implemented a successful fix for a production incident, your last obligation in emerging from the crisis is to conduct a post-mortem review. The goal of the review is to ensure that you never wind up in a similar predicament ever again. In the review you need to look at the root cause of the problem, whether it was preventable, and whether it is theoretically possible for anything similar to happen again. You are also encouraged to review your monitoring and operations procedures and score your organization on how effectively you reacted to the crisis. We will discuss these topics next.

Reviewing the Root Cause

Your organization should ask itself different questions depending on the type of root cause that was ultimately implicated in your failure. This is best expressed in a tabular format. In Table 11.2 we refer to the types of failures that we listed earlier in this chapter.

Reviewing Monitoring

In addition to preventing problems from happening in the first place, you also need to ensure that you detect them as quickly as possible. As we discussed in Chapter 10, monitoring is about detecting problems *and* capturing the maximum amount of supporting information. If the alert that is generated contains enough information for the support team to immediately hone in on root cause, then it has done its job admirably. In reviewing your problem-detection capability, your organization should ask itself the following questions:

Table 11.2 Failure Type and Corresponding Post-Mortem Assessment

Type of Failure	Assessment
Application Defect	Has the defect been fixed? Is the fix now under source-code management? Has the application been reviewed to ensure that it is completely free of this or any similar problem? Has the root cause been communicated widely to the development team to ensure that no new code is written with this type of flaw? Has the application error handling been strengthened to ensure error messages are as descriptive as possible?
Vendor Defect	Has the vendor fixed the problem, or did we work around it? For a vendor fix, have all environments—including development environments—been upgraded to the new version? Has the vendor stated that the fix will continue to be included in future versions of their product? For a work-around, has it been communicated widely to the development team that this vendor feature is problematic?
Operator Error	Has the operator been identified and informed of the error? Has operations documentation been reviewed and updated if required?
Illegal or Unexpected Usage	For illegal inputs, has a business analyst reviewed the unexpected input and updated requirements? Has the development team reviewed the application for all other processing that may have to process a similar input? For unexpected usage, has a business analyst reviewed the observed usage and updated the business usage model including future forecasts? For unexpected inputs from other systems, have external parties been contacted to confirm the possible range of inputs from their systems? Has the development team reviewed and strengthened (if necessary) the application handling for unexpected inputs?

– continued

Table 11.2 Failure Type and Corresponding Post-Mortem Assessment

Type of Failure	Assessment
Infrastructure Failure	Did redundancy in the infrastructure compensate for the failure?
	Did we confirm our current hardware configuration with vendors, and make changes if necessary?
	Was this mode of failure tested prior to implementation, and did the production behavior confirm the test results were accurate?
Configuration Error	Have all related configurations been reviewed by the development and deployment team for correctness?
	Has the deployment team identified why this parameter was not configured or was misconfigured in the environment?
	Is there a risk that this parameter is misconfigured in other nonproduction environments or other applications under your management?

1. Through what channel was the problem first reported? *(If the answer is, "a business user called the help desk," then you have a problem.)*
2. Did the monitoring infrastructure detect the problem through multiple interfaces? If not, what additional monitors should have recognized a problem?
3. Did each monitor include as much diagnostic information as possible to aid in the technical investigation?
4. Did the monitors produce alerts with the correct severity for the urgency of the problem?
5. Did the monitors produce alerts with an appropriate frequency for an ongoing problem?
6. Did technical support resources have efficient access to data and alerts generated by the monitoring infrastructure?

Improving your monitoring and diagnostic capability is an ongoing responsibility for owners of mission-critical systems. There is an applicable expression that comes to mind: *what doesn't kill you makes you stronger.* Every application failure is an opportunity to improve your monitoring and response capability. Failures can also be canaries in the coal mine: they can alert you to more serious, imminent, problems.

Summary

We hope that this is a chapter that you will not reference very often. This chapter is an admission that we will occasionally face problems in our production environments. We have provided you with practical advice on how to minimize the impact of production incidents and optimize your efforts around troubleshooting and problem resolution. This includes properly assessing the severity, managing all stakeholders in the incident, and prioritizing mitigation activities against root-cause analysis and resolution. We have emphasized the importance of being able to reproduce issues in nonproduction environments. This approach insists that fixes are fully verified and tested prior to implementation. In this way, you are assured that you are solving the "right" problem and mitigating the risk associated with the technical change under consideration.

This chapter also introduced a series of troubleshooting strategies that you may find helpful. We discussed the need to evaluate all changes to the environment irrespective of how unrelated they may seem. When faced with a difficult problem, we recommend capturing all possible inputs and discouraging bias on the part of the technical team that is tackling the problem. We have also looked at specific examples of failures and proposed methods for poking and prodding the system into revealing more information. This chapter also discussed the criteria by which you should assess the required level of testing for a fix that is proposed for production. Finally, we have explored the post-mortem process and challenged you to review all aspects of the incident management with an emphasis on whether or not the monitoring infrastructure performed to expectations.

Chapter 12

Common Impediments to Good Design

Design is the cornerstone for supporting performance, operability, and other non-functional requirements in an application. It is the point of intersection where many different project streams converge and is the place to confirm that all the different pieces fit together. Design activities sit between the conceptual, logical view of an application and the physical one that will ultimately be deployed into the production environment.

In terms of the system lifecycle, the design phase precedes development but follows the requirement-gathering activities. Design usually follows architecture, but is often described as being the "architecture/design phase," which in itself can be a problem that we will examine later in this chapter.

Performance and operability are dependent on design. An inefficient or inappropriate design will destroy the possibility of meeting both of these non-functional requirements, as well as other functional ones. Improper design can also make it impossible to scale the application without violating these requirements. There are several common impediments to establishing good design on most nontrivial projects. This chapter looks at these and describes ways to mitigate their impact.

Design Dependencies

Design has a dependency on the requirements—functional and non-functional—and the overall architecture. Architecture is constructed to satisfy both the defined requirements and the anticipated requirements if there is enough information to

277

forecast the future needs. Architecture is constructed through a series of activities that begin at an abstract level. With the finalization of a business definition and sign-off of the business requirements and functional specifications, the architecture transitions through states that include conceptual, high level, and detailed. The latter state can be driven out further with additional levels of progressively more detailed views of the architecture.

As shown in Figure 12.1, a solution's design relies on a set of detailed views of the architecture. It also relies on other considerations, such as the business requirements, budget, and timelines. The architecture can also address a broader set of requirements than what is currently described, by anticipating future needs based on some assumptions. The architecture blueprint can be far reaching and extensive without requiring all of it to be available on day one.

Design extends architecture into a precise physical implementation of how technology, data, and the application will interoperate. Design needs to be more pragmatic than architecture, as it is the single point where all the requirements converge and must be maintainable. If the design cannot support a need, it cannot be used to support a proposed solution. The known requirements can be viewed as filters that keep the design in line with what is really needed.

Architecture is typically separated into several subcategories: technical, data, and application. Each of these architectural streams can be further extended into their design counterparts. Technical architecture becomes technical design. Data architecture becomes data design. Application architecture becomes application design. You generally go from the detailed architecture deliverables to the high-level design deliverables. Unless otherwise specified, *design* refers to all three of the technical, data, and application categories.

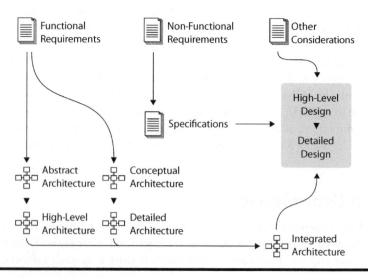

Figure 12.1   Design dependencies.

What Is the Definition of Good Design?

The answer to the question of what defines good design would be completely different if we had an infinite amount of money and time available to us. In the real world, design objectives must be more modest and affordable because of the limitations placed on both of these resources.

Agreeing on a clear definition for what can be described as good design is a problem that often confounds project sponsors, project managers, architects, and designers. The answer is not absolute and is, in fact, partly objective, partly subjective, and partly intuitive. It might be easier to start this discussion with an agreement on the objectives of design.

What Are the Objectives of Design Activities?

Design brings the documented or modeled ideas of functional and non-functional requirements together and combines these with the architectural considerations that have been defined. Design begins to show how the details of what is being asked for will fit together and work. The high-level objectives of design can be described as follows:

1. Bring together the requirements and the architectural decisions and show that they are consistent or show where they are inconsistent. This includes confirming the architecture and showing the impact of different requirements.
2. Support non-functional requirements.
3. Drive out a detailed solution that shows how the technical, data, and application streams will operate and interoperate.
4. Allow for future changes or additions to the requirements.
5. Show overall gaps in the proposed solution.

The design activities and the completed design deliverables are positioned to feed several activities that provide additional structure to the project. This includes addressing a couple of broad categories that include validation, cost, and planning. A detailed list of activities supported by design deliverables are identified in the following list:

1. Confirm the project plan or update it where additional details have changed previous assumptions.
2. Cost out the technical solution, hardware, and software, or calculate a narrower range based on a smaller number of assumptions.
3. Right-size the project team in terms of number of resources and the skills that are needed, and when they will be needed in the project lifecycle.
4. Demonstrate the physical impact of the functional and non-functional specifications that are defined for the solution (e.g., a 24/7 fault-tolerant system might add $1 million to the project capital budget).

Defining Good Design

Good design must satisfy the objectives described in the previous section. For example, a design must be capable of showing how the functional requirements will be met by the application that is being built. This needs to address all the design categories—namely, data, technology, and application. Application design is used to show how specific functions will be supported in the application. Data design shows the data elements and data stores that are used for persistence. Technology design shows everything from the software tools to the hardware that will be used to support the application and the data.

For example, consider what is required to save a user profile and use it to support workflow. Data design needs to support the related application requirements, but also the non-functional requirements (e.g., performance) as well. In this instance, the data structures must be constructed to save the elements of the user profile. They must also account for the performance requirements and be efficiently designed to support transactions such us *save*, *update*, *retrieve*, and *search*. Architecture typically would not go to this level of detail. Technical design would be extended with this requirement to show how the database will be accessed, along with the related software components, communication protocols, and the hardware that runs the solution.

Design activities need to address the known requirements, but must also define a solution that does not break down with the slightest change in the future. For example, an application may be required to support 100 concurrent users when it is launched. What happens if another 20 concurrent users are added three months after launch? How much effort will be required to support this change at the application level, the technology level, or the data level?

A design for an application or solution must be built with the following non-functional requirements as key considerations, as well as supporting, point by point, the defined functional requirements.

- **Performance:** This must be within the service level agreement, but have the capability for improvement through some easy-to-access focal points.
- **Completeness:** The design should be an end-to-end solution in being able to drive an architecture to a lower level of detail to satisfy all the defined requirements.
- **Flexibility:** The design must be flexible enough to accommodate future business requirements without requiring extensive rework. More on the meaning of this later in this chapter.
- **Modern:** The technology and techniques used in the design should be within the industry mainstream. Design that requires techniques or technology that is legacy or too bleeding edge results in very similar problems. This includes the difficulty of finding appropriate resources to build out the design and having to pay a premium for their services.

- **Extensible:** The design must be open and connectable to a range of technical solutions while also being flexible enough to support future expansion without requiring massive rewrites.
- **Scalable:** Growing load on the application should be supported by the design. This may still require additional technology or software upgrades to support the design.
- **Right-sized:** The design must solve a business problem and not try to be all things to all people.
- **Throughput:** Ability to handle increasing volumes of data by the application throughout a day and at peak points in time. The application should respond reasonably well under increasing loads (e.g., not result in an exponential impact). For example, say it takes 30 minutes to process one million records. Two million records should take 60 minutes or so. Bad design would start to see the curve rise much more rapidly with increasing throughput.
- **Operability:** This refers to how well the application works and is maintained, as well as how it operates within the entire environment.

Rating a Design

Good design is not always possible because of real-life resource constraints that restrict implementation of the solution that was defined. There are several evaluation criteria elements that can be applied to a given design to determine an objective rating for it. Figure 12.2 shows several other ratings that can be considered, with the desirable ones shown near the top of the list.

The design ratings on the left side of the figure lead toward *excellent* design. Increasing time and money can take an incomplete design and still move it forward on an iterative and manageable basis. Excellent design is a desirable project goal, but generally unattainable in the real world. *Bad* design cannot be improved by spending more time on it, nor by increasing the financial investment. It has too many inherent flaws to be iteratively improved. In fact, the only way to react to bad design may be to throw it out and start over, making sure that the same thing does not happen again.

Designs on the left side of Figure 12.2, below the *good* rating level, can be augmented by a set of conditions and clarity that describe when and where further investment should be made to adjust the design to the next level.

The ratings on the left side of Figure 12.2 are characterized by degree of completeness and the ability to anticipate future needs. The ratings at the bottom of the list are focused on supporting immediate requirements. Moving up the list introduces support for future anticipated needs. The following sections of this chapter describe each of the evaluation categories in the context of the design components and the criteria that should be applied to decide where a given design lies.

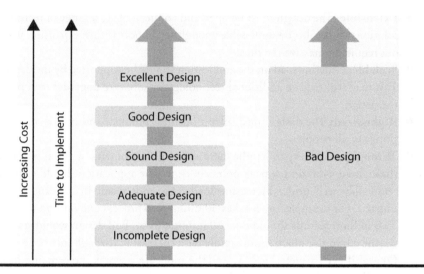

Figure 12.2   Design evaluation.

The ratings shown in Figure 12.2 are defined here. Subsequent sections expand on the attributes and their values in each of the rankings below.

- **Excellent Design:** As mentioned previously, this rating may be virtually unattainable due to internal contradictions. An excellent design will need to be immensely flexible and open, yet affordably priced. It must also be completed within a timeframe needed by an organization. Trying to build an excellent design can also be a trap. An excellent design may draw a lot of resources and energy in a futile attempt to complete it, or development time may run out and the effort may need to be abandoned part way. This may force the team to settle for something at a far lower rank.
- **Good Design:** This is arguably the desired level of design for modern projects. It balances the ability to scale a solution in the future and be flexible, but be achievable within realistic budgets and timelines. Good design focuses on the requirements at hand, but anticipates what will be required in the future as enhancements. Good design builds an infrastructure that can scale to this future view using a positive return-on-investment analysis.
- **Sound Design:** This is a step lower than good design because budget and timeline pressures may force a good design to be compromised. A sound design should be extendable into a good design at some point in the future.
- **Adequate Design:** This may be driven by timeline and budget pressures. Adequate design provides a solution to documented current business requirements, and does not necessarily address any future requirements.
- **Incomplete Design:** An incomplete design only solves a partial business problem. While an incomplete design might be used to implement a solu-

tion iteratively, it is also highly risky as future details might cause substantial reworking. This can be a result of bad planning or because of trying to do too much and then having to settle for a lot less in a worried hurry.

- **Bad Design:** A bad design means that one or more components do not adequately address the business requirements. This could involve building a batch solution for a real-time application or setting up a database to satisfy update/insert requests with no consideration for massive searches in a call center application.

The following subsections discuss what the design attributes and their values would need to be to fall within each of the rankings shown in Figure 12.2.

Excellent Design

An excellent design requires a thorough understanding of current requirements, but also requires an ability to forecast or anticipate the future—generally 2–5 years out—to build a design that requires minimal redevelopment or new code while being able to deal with the domain of known non-functional requirements and business/functional requirements. The design also needs to consider a range of potential technologies and techniques as well. A design that is ranked as excellent would also need to be adaptable to a range of future outcomes. This level of design is characterized by reaching an excellent rating in each of the following functional areas:

- **Performance:** Design should meet the current performance requirements as per a service level agreement, but be capable of scaling into the future with iterative design enhancements.
- **Completeness:** The design needs to cover end-to-end functionality, be fully reused and leveraged wherever possible without creating redundancy.
- **Flexibility:** Highly table driven, built on a sea of reusable components, and support future requirements at an environmentally configurable level.
- **Modern:** As technology moves into the legacy space, it becomes increasingly difficult to support, as fewer resources are knowledgeable and available in the marketplace. The technology itself also becomes unsupported over time. On the flip side, bleeding edge technology is often unproven and technical bottlenecks may not be clearly known. Bleeding edge design needs to be thoroughly tested. Resources may still be costly to acquire.
- **Extensible:** The degree to which a solution can be extended in the future without significant reinvestment or rework must be very broad at this rating level.
- **Scalable:** The design needs to scale to multiple scenarios inside the future timetable defined by the organization.

- **Right-sized:** This may not apply to an excellent design in a meaningful way because the scope is large and goes beyond known requirements. An excellent design, by definition, cannot be right-sized.
- **Throughput:** Needs to accommodate multiples of known and acceptable throughput going through the system.
- **Operability:** Can operate under any situation.

The problem with excellent design is that it tries to do too much. After the known business requirements, and some meaningful forecasting, the situation begins to get hazy—after, say, 2 years. At this point, design considerations become highly speculative and based on assumptions that may not come to pass.

Excellent design is expensive to define and build. It also requires a significantly long timeline. The need to support multiple years, multiple technologies, and multiple business scenarios requires a valiant amount of work and assumptions. Many projects cannot afford these. Even worse, once the process starts, valuable deliverables may not even be created, before management determines that there is not enough time to finish the design and to mandate a switch in strategy.

Good Design

As stated previously, a good design is a reasonable and achievable objective for most modern systems. It is built to support known functionality, but uses a forecasting approach to anticipate future business needs, possibly based on business forecasts, to build a set of likely scenarios. A good design also needs to consider reality in terms of the resources (money and people) available and the timeline that exists to be able to support the design. During aggressive timelines, a good design can be formulated but implemented in stages based on the resources available and the needs of the business. The following design considerations apply.

- **Performance:** Meet the known requirements, forecast for future requirements based on known business scenarios, and define an enhancement roadmap.
- **Completeness:** The design needs to support end-to-end functionality and still be reusable wherever possible across the solution base.
- **Flexibility:** Still needs to be table driven, not hard coded, and reusable wherever possible. Future demands should not require changes to the code base as a starting position.
- **Modern:** Technology should be mainstream with a wide support base. There should be other implementations of the design in the marketplace that can be referenced so that best practices can be employed in the design.
- **Extensible:** Should examine likely business scenarios for a period of 1–3 years. There can be assumptions and limitations in some areas.

- **Scalable:** Should support known requirements and likely business scenarios for a period of 1–3 years.
- **Right-sized:** The design should be appropriately sized for the application. This means reasonable and practicable in terms of what is trying to be achieved by the business.
- **Throughput:** Should support known requirements and likely scenarios for a period of 1–3 years.
- **Operability:** Can operate under the known business scenarios.

Sound Design

Sound design can be viewed as a scaled-down version of good design, one that needs to be filled out over a period of time. The principle behind a sound design is that it can support known requirements, but can be extended for future requirements as they emerge. Forecasting is kept to a minimum. A sound design should be used as a stepping stone to good design if there are time or resource limitations that keep a good design from being constructed. It is best to define a good design and implement at a sound design than to operate only at the sound design level. The following design considerations apply at the functional requirements level.

- **Performance:** Meet the known requirements but have a roadmap for satisfying future requirements.
- **Completeness:** Addresses all the functional needs of the application.
- **Flexibility:** Defines flexibility, but may have compromises to meet a timeline within a set of resources.
- **Modern:** Same as good design.
- **Extensible:** Should have a roadmap for the future, but details may be missing.
- **Scalable:** Roadmap for scaling the application.
- **Right-sized:** The design is suited to the implementation schedule.
- **Throughput:** Designed for the known throughput, with a roadmap for future likely scenarios.
- **Operability:** Can operate under the known business situations.

Adequate Design

Adequate design is a dramatic compromise to meet a current business need, but with an understanding that reworking will be required to improve the design at some point in the future. It is better to define at the good design level, but implement at the adequate design level, than to define at the adequate level and then try to move up. However, the former approach may not be possible given resources or budgets available to the initiative.

An adequate design needs to be clearly communicated to the project sponsors as such, because it is a compromise that will exhibit limitations much sooner than later. An adequate design will cost more in the long term, even though it may allow a short-term implementation.

Trying to define an excellent design often leads to this compromise when internal contradictions show up, too much time has already been spent on the design process, and a compromise must be reached to meet a business deadline.

Incomplete Design

An incomplete design is work in progress; time for the design activities has run out. This could be due to bad project management, or focusing on the wrong things, or some change requirements, or some combination of all of these and more. An incomplete design may show up during testing. It could be apparent in a couple of places in the overall design. An incomplete design needs to be moved up before an application can be deployed into a production environment.

Bad Design

The worst side of the design process is ending up with a bad design that does not and cannot meet the functional and non-functional requirements of the application. This can be the result of many factors, including the following functional areas.

- **Performance:** Insufficient to meet the business requirements.
- **Completeness:** Does not address all the business requirements.
- **Flexibility.** Not flexible—rigid for a set of requirements. Requires code modifications.
- **Modern:** Inappropriate use of tools for the resources available.
- **Extensible:** Not extensible at all.
- **Scalable:** Will not scale.
- **Right-sized:** Not sized for the business requirements.
- **Throughput:** Insufficient ability to meet the required throughput.
- **Operability:** Does not operate within the business service service level agreements.

Testing a Design

Testing a design requires a combination of inspection techniques and tool sets. Inspection techniques involve activities such as design reviews, expert reviews, expert analysis, and evaluation templates. One such form these can take is in the way of questions that can detect the soundness of a design through workshops involving business users, designers, architects, and other stakeholders on the project team.

Design testing requires a focus on the known requirements, likely scenarios, and anticipated requirements. Tools include simulation tools, measurement tools, regression tools, and automated test scripts.

Contributors to Bad Design

Bad design is not entirely the opposite of good design. Depending on the amount of time and money available to a project team, a given application may only be able to afford a less-than-ideal design. An incomplete design may sometimes be barely satisfactory for a limited number of scenarios. Here the implication is that enough work was not done to complete the design, which could mean that some money was left over for future enhancements in a just-in-time design philosophy.

Bad design is worse. It implies that both effort and money were spent. The result, however, is going down the wrong path. One of the implications shown in Figure 12.2 is that bad design does not get better with further investment—neither in terms of money nor time. Trying to fix a bad design is doomed to fail. A bad design should be abandoned as soon as it is detected.

Common elements of bad design include the following.

- Does not solve the business problem.
- Difficult to modify for changing conditions.
- Cannot be built within the constraints available.
- Too expensive.
- Does not have any standards.
- Solves the wrong business problem or one that will likely never materialize.
- Does not meet the functional requirements.
- Does not meet the non-functional requirements.

Project delivery risk greatly increases with a less-than-optimal design.

Common Impediments to Good Design

Achieving a good design solution faces many obstacles and impediments from a wide array of places. These risk factors need to be evaluated and addressed in order to have a fighting chance at avoiding bad design altogether. However, information technology (IT) is a combination of science and art that complicates the ultimate outcomes of every deliverable.

Confusing Architecture with Design

Design has a completely different set of deliverables from architecture, yet these deliverables are often confused with each other. Specifically, architecture is often described as design, when it clearly is not. This creates a false sense of security in project planning and budgeting because there may be a belief that more work has been completed than actually has been.

Design requires detailed analysis of all the information that is available, while also anticipating future changes, to drive out details of how the technical, data, and application components will work together. Architecture examines integration activities and channels between these components. Not having information at the design level leaves holes in the project plan and increases the project risk level.

Insufficient Time/Tight Timeframes

Architecture is often confused with design for expediency because there is not enough time in the project timeline to support a detailed design phase. The risk of doing this is no different than starting to build a solution without having clear business requirements signed off. This is a big risk factor, as design suffers due to an inattention to details, rushing at the last minute, and having to settle for an inferior deliverable. A last-minute rush to complete a design will generally leave it in nothing higher than the *inadequate* or *sound* design states.

Missing Design Skills on the Project Team

In addition to confusing architecture and design, relevant skills are sometimes lacking in the team members doing the design work. Most project managers have experienced this frustrating situation. Architecture is not design; neither is development. Yet, it is not uncommon to have either architects or developers act as designers. Design skills are required to drive out the design. While architects or developers may have these, this is not always the case, and experienced designers may have to be brought onto the project team to complete the design activities. The designers may be highly specialized, so they may not be able to fit at other places in the project.

Lack of Design Standards

A project generally fits into a wider corporate infrastructure or may be part of a project program that has many other initiatives. A clearly defined set of design standards need to be communicated to the designers on the different initiatives.

Compliance may need to be enforced so that a good design in a project perspective remains good when it is viewed and deployed to the rest of the organization.

Personal Design Preferences

Personal design preferences, or biases, are yet another source of potential problems in defining a good design. Strong existing preferences can reduce the overall selection domain to such a degree that a good answer may not be on the radar any longer. Existing preferences can also lead to prolonged discussions that are impossible to conclude because of the inherent biases of the participants. This will ultimately lead to some of the other impediments on this list, such as timeline problems.

Insufficient Information

A proper set of design activities require several sources of input information (as shown in Figure 12.3). The degree of completeness in these input deliverables will drive the rating on the design being defined. Gaps or lack of details in these areas lead to assumptions that result in ambiguity.

Constantly Changing Technology

Rapid technological evolution is a problem from several perspectives, but especially around skills shortages, timeline, and available best practices. There was a time when the pace of technology change in the IT industry was at the order of ten years or so when massive changes in available technology solutions would drive changes in the application design. The rate of technological change moved more rapidly beginning in the early 1990s. Now, at the start of the 21st century,

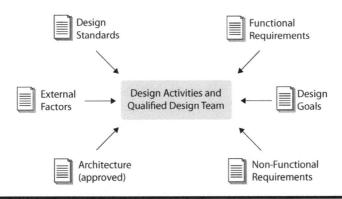

Figure 12.3 Design inputs.

the rate of technological change is very rapid—within five years. This means that design may only be valid for at most five years before new technologies bring new solution options.

Technology is evolving so rapidly that a two-year timeline can see dramatic changes in available tools. Keeping pace with this rapid change is difficult. Knowledgeable resources are difficult to find. References that show how the solutions should fit together, and their limitations, are not prevalent as an industrywide set of best practices. Bottlenecks may not be known until the testing activities begin.

Fad Designs

While rapidly changing technology poses problems in building good design from a time and skills perspective, fad designs are even worse. The IT industry has had many cycles in which a new technology or technique led to some rapid design decisions that did not pan out. Incorporating fad designs is a problem from several perspectives. The design may look reasonable under certain situations, but its implications may not be known until later in the lifecycle. When the fad passes, the design may need to be revised, at great expense.

Trying to Do Too Much

Overly optimistic designs that try to be all things to all people in an organization are also problematic. These can be attempted in the pretext of anticipating future needs and designing for them. However, assumptions have to be made as you move forward, and these become more of a guess the farther out you proceed. This can take up a lot of time and resources that may be invalidated along with the assumptions.

The 80/20 Rule

When building the design, the team needs to be careful to invest their resources in satisfying the most prevalent requirements. Many designs fail because the resources are spent on portions of the design that only affect a small portion of the outcome. This means that 80% of the business value could result from 20% of the design.

Minimalistic Viewpoint

Building a design for tactical reasons, which leads to an adequate or sound design, could in fact be considered bad design when a wider perspective is considered. Building only for the present opens up this risk.

Lack of Consensus

This can be caused by an inconsistent set of standards. Lack of consensus can exist around requirements, needs, and potential solutions. Team members may have individual ideas that are too strong to compromise. This makes design decisions difficult, and infighting or divergent opinions may make it impossible to determine and prove the correct designs.

Constantly Changing Requirements

Having to constantly modify a design to match changing requirements is a source of potential problems. Change control needs to be implemented as early as is reasonable to provide the stability to build a stable design. However, when aiming at an excellent design target, the resulting design might be able to absorb change more rapidly.

Bad Decisions/Incorrect Decisions

At a basic level, the design team can make bad decisions from time to time based on the information available to them. These will need to be fixed. However, given that the decisions were made, presumably without the design team knowing, their existence may remain hidden until the testing or a later phase.

Lack of Facts

Design is a combination of science and art. Decisions need to be based on facts. However, when these are not known, guesses or near guesses may be used to drive design decisions to meet a project schedule.

External Impacts

External impacts can either affect the design or the requirements. This can negatively impact a good design at the last minute. These are difficult to ignore, especially when they are of the legislative variety.

Insufficient Testing

Design deliverables on paper may look good; however, they still need to be validated as early in the project lifecycle as possible. Several types of testing can be considered, mostly in the non-functional variety. This includes stress and regression testing.

Lack of Design Tools

As systems become more complex, a lack of design tools can result in gaps that cannot be effectively filled in without prototyping or piloting.

Design Patterns Matter

Building designs from scratch can result in re-experiencing problems. These can vary by application, date, and technical design. Reusing designs from previous projects can mitigate risk. Design patterns are another source of reusability that can be considered.

Lack of Financial Resources

Insufficient resources have been named as a recurring design impediment. A lack of financial resources is one of these. Trying to spend too much on the design activities introduces a large risk to the project, while trying to accomplish too much with little investment will result in the same problems.

Design Principles

Is there a bad design inside every good one, trying to get out? Not exactly, although it might seem that way most of the time. There are certain things that a design team and project management should consider to improve the odds of building a good design, in the context of functional and non-functional requirements:

- **Reuse:** Try to leverage an existing successful design from the organization or from a set of best practices.
- **Test:** Always test and prove as you go.
- **Methodology:** Use design methodologies that describe and provide examples of design deliverables.
- **Metrics:** Building design to a set of measurable objectives will help to remove many of the obstacles, especially around incorrect preferences and incorrect assumptions.
- **Resources:** Ensure that there are experienced designers dedicated to the project during the design phase. Ensure that their skills are relevant for the project.
- **Realistic:** Manage to expectations that can be achieved with the resources and constraints that are available.
- **Budget:** Set aside a portion of the budget for the design activities and resources.
- **Time:** Build the design iteratively on top of the architecture.

- **Contradictions:** Look for and remove design contradictions as early as possible.
- **Communication:** Communicate design considerations, issues, and decisions to the project team and other stakeholders.

Summary

Design refers to the portion of the project lifecycle in which business or functional requirements, non-functional requirements, and architecture are brought together to map out how an application is going to be built and whether the end result is going to be successful.

Each of the initial phases of the standard development lifecycle are crucial to the outcome by definition. However, the design phase really acts as the glue that binds the creative, often abstract nature of functional and non-functional requirements with the development phase.

The first requirement of a good design is that it meet the known requirements. This includes satisfying the business or functional requirements of an application as they are currently defined. This must also extend to the support of non-functional requirements. The second requirement of a good design is to anticipate future needs and provide a roadmap for supporting these within a timeframe and cost model that is acceptable to the business.

References

Articles

Bacon, David F. 2007. Realtime Garbage Collection. *Queue* 5, (1) 40–49.

Heisenberg, Werner. 1927.Ueber die Grandprincipien der "Quantenmechanik". Forschungen und Fortschritte 3:83 1927.

Koenig, Andrew. "Patterns and Antipatterns." *Journal of Object-Oriented Programming*, 8 (April): 46–48.

MacMcLellan, J. 2003. Wrong Worry in Twins Versus Singles. *Flying Magazine.* (February)

Books

Gamma, Erich, Richard Helm, Ralph Johnson, and John Vlissides. *Design Patterns: Elements of Reusable Object-Oriented Software.* Boston: Addison-Wesley Professional, 1994.

Gladwell, Malcolm. *Blink: The Power of Thinking without Thinking,* New York: Little, Brown, 2005.

Knuth, Donald E. *The Art of Computer Programming.* 3 vols., 2d ed. Boston: Addison-Wesley Professional, 1998.

Singer, Jeremy. *JVM versus CLR: A Comparative Study.* ACM International Conference Proceeding Series 42. New York: Computer Science Press, 2003.

Web Sites

The Apache Logging Services Project log4j: http://logging.apache.org/log4j/docs

Ask Tom: http://asktom.oracle.com/

AspectJ: http://www.eclipse.org/aspectj/

Aspect-Oriented Programming at Wikipedia: http://en.wikipedia.org/wiki/Aspect_programming

Empirix e-Load: http://empirix.com/products/testing/e-Load.asp

Enterprise JavaBeans Technology: http://java.sun.com/products/ejb/

The "Ilities" at Wikipedia: http://en.wikipedia.org/wiki/Ilities

The ISO 9126 Standard: http://www.issco.unige.ch/projects/ewg96/node13.html

Mercury LoadRunner: http://www.mercury.com/us/products/performance-center/loadrunner/

Moore's Law at Wikipedia: http://en.wikipedia.org/wiki/Moore%27s_law

Oracle Real Application Clusters (RAC): http://www.oracle.com/database/rac_home.html

Simple Network Management Protocol (SNMP): http://www.cisco.com/univercd/cc/td/doc/cisintwk/ito_doc/snmp.htm

The Spring Framework: http://www.springframework.org/

Understanding WebLogic Server Clustering: http://edocs.bea.com/wls/docs90/cluster/overview.html

Index

A

ABEND, *see* Abnormal ending or termination codes
Abnormal ending or termination (ABEND) codes, 263
Aborting after errors, 86–87
Acceptance
    non-functional requirement documentation, 42
    non-functional requirements, 139
    performance, 173, *174,* 175–176
Access methods, 22
Accountability, 21
Accuracy
    capacity plan, 247
    extent of testing, 19–20
    non-functional *vs.* functional test environments, 21
    simulations, 5
Activities, test preparation and execution, 159–160
Adequate design rating, 285–286
Administration changes, 261
Aggregating results, 105–107
AIX, 184, 186
AJAX solutions, 136
Alerts
    detailed, 228
    operability testing, 24
Algorithms, 119–120
Alternative flows, 64
Antipatterns, performance design
    overdesign, 114
    overserialization, 114–117
    oversynchronization, 117–119
    user session memory consumption, 118–119

AOP, *see* Aspect-oriented programming
Apache Software Foundation, 148
API, *see* Application programming interfaces
Apparatus, test planning, 149–150
Application architect, 218
Application availability, *see* Availability
Application code, 31
Application exception handling, *see* Exceptions
Application logging, 80–83, *see also* Logging
Application programming interfaces (APIs), 236
Applications
    availability and health, 14
    behavior testing, scope determination, 25
    monitoring, 229, 238–239
    operability patterns, 11–14
    pitfalls, 8
    profiling, 81
    resilient, 6
    shutdown, failover testing, 34
Application servers, 129, *130–131*
Application stack, 36
Architects
    recoverability, 100
    roles and responsibilities, 218
    securability, 98
Architectural hotspots, 24
Architecture
    common design impediments, 288
    operability scope, 144–145
    performance design, 101–102
    project framework extension, 219
    securability, 98
    simplicity, 101
Archives
    documentation, 43
    non-functional requirements, 65, *66*

T - #0098 - 101024 - C0 - 234/156/19 [21] - CB - 9781420053340 - Gloss Lamination